Praise for
The Eagle and the Condor

"I love authentic stories of spirituality, and this one is wrapped in incredible beauty in one of the most mystical settings on earth. It has a powerful message that will leave your heart changed forever."

Glenda Green, author *Love without End*

"The commitment to serving human kind and all that we are connected to, at the risk of losing all things dear, including ones reputation, is clearly at the core of this woman's soul. Living from that place has made her life an adventure from which we can all take inspiration."

Lindsay Wagner, actress

"Just like the *Celestine Prophecy* and *Conversations with God* brought truths to spiritual seekers, this book will open many doors on many more levels while reading the incredible mystical journey of Jonette. Her pure heart and soul will touch and open the hearts of many. Thank you!"

Henriette Reineke, The Netherlands

"A fascinating book on the enduring mysteries of South America and the past. This is a book that will enthrall the traveler and reseacher alike."

David Hatcher Childress, author
Lost Cities & Ancient Mysteries of South America

"I love it! It is mystical, beautiful, wonderful, emotional, true, and complete, and it engages the reader. You have done some magnificent work."

Nancy Mitchell, California

"I have been reading it and can't put it down. It has been transforming for me. I am absolutely drawn spiritually and energetically to your words and works. To say it is fascinating would truly be inaccurate, because it goes so much deeper than that. This is a great book, so well written, entertaining and enlightening! You are doing a great work for consciousness. Thank you!"

Linda Hansen, Colorado

"We are far greater than we allow ourselves to be! A masterpiece that bravely leads by example and acts as a perfect mirror for those who dare to look at themselves in that light…"

Asena Gurs, Turkey

"*The Eagle and the Condor* is fascinating, exciting, full of unexpected twists and turns. It's funny yet filled with wise messages."

Shahid Khatai, India

"Jonette is a great writer. The book encourages me to listen and trust my inner voices and to follow my heart. I was extremely touched. I could laugh and I could cry."

Gabriela Contreras, Mexico

"An amazing book! It invites you to awaken your heart and illuminate your soul. You feel compelled to follow the author on her quest to mystical places where physical reality intersects with spirit."

Nancy Prins Bush, Colorado

"Thank you for sharing your personal life story with all of us. I just love reading it and learning. This book will be a real hit because you write as though you are talking to a friend; you invite me in as though we are sharing a cup of tea or coffee together."

Deb Moe, Minnesota

"I devoured the book. I could have read and read and read… I'm fascinated! It's incredible how it felt like I could have lived this experience. You cannot imagine what this text means to me, it shines the way I have to walk. My thanks to you is bottomless for having shared this. I love your honesty, your messages and your laughter."

Anita Muetterken, Argentina

"Your experiences are truly very inspiring. The thread throughout is that we are all so much more than we think we are, and our growth depends on our willingness to accept the expansion and greatness of ourselves."

Toril Storoe, Norway

"I really enjoyed reading your magical, inspiring adventures... I find them exciting, impossible, and very real all at the same time. I appreciate how well you share the altered state experiences, mixed with the mundane. You write beautifully, and what you have to share is deeply moving and confirms the magic and mystery that is a part of all life. Thank you for your courage."

Nancy Mayans, New York

"Congratulations!! Your book is beautiful. I couldn't stop reading until I finished it. There were many passages that tears filled my eyes, I felt so connected ... just beautiful. I was especially touched by the passages concerning your relationship with your twin soul, Mallku. Your description is so real, so alive. I could be with you. When you commanded the mountain, it echoed inside me. Thank you so much for this beautiful book and for all you are."

Meggi Erman, Israel

"I can't believe you haven't been writing books all your life! It flows so beautifully that I was just mesmerized while I read. You have such an amazing ability to weave yourself so naturally into words. The book captures the mystical and funny, godlike and oh so human in such a way that the reader is actually along on every step. It felt like I was sitting with my best friends, laughing and sharing our hearts. I was able to walk your journey with you in another reality."

Susan Nakhleh, Louisiana

"I feel very strong for the energies in the book and especially for the power of the 'Spirit of the Water.' It gives me help in finding my own flow rather than focusing on events."

Ralph Johnson, Sweden

"What an amazing story and experience. I felt as if I was there experiencing it with you. Once I started reading it, I couldn't stop. This is highly unusual for me. Much of what you said, I could relate to in one way or another. I shared your story with a group of my spiritual family here in Chicago. Thank you so much for helping us to see even more possibilities."

Janelle Brittain, Illinois

The Eagle and the Condor

Love & light,
Janette

The Eagle and the Condor

A True Story of an
Unexpected Mystical Journey

The Eagle and the Condor

The Eagle and the Condor

A True Story of an
Unexpected Mystical Journey

Jonette Crowley

**Stone Tree
Publishing**

Published by StoneTree Publishing
5380 S. Monaco St., Suite 110
Greenwood Village, Colorado 80111

www.StoneTreePublishing.com
www.TheEagleandtheCondor.com
Voice: (303) 689-9318
Fax: (303) 689-7666

Second Printing 2008
Printed in the United States of America
ISBN-13 978-0-9785384-4-6
ISBN-10 0-9785384-4-7
Library of Congress Control Number: 2006930597
Crowley, Jonette
The eagle and the condor/by Jonette Crowley
Includes bibliographical references and index
First Edition

Publisher's Cataloging-in-Publication
(Provided by Quality Books, Inc.)

Crowley, Jonette.
     The eagle and the condor : a true story of an unexpected mystical journey / Jonette Crowley.
     p. cm.
     Includes bibliographical references and index.
     ISBN-13 978-0-9785384-4-6
     ISBN-10 0-9785384-4-7
     1. Crowley, Jonette. 2. Spiritualists—Biography.
3. Channeling (Spiritualism) 4. Self-realization.
5. Spiritual life—New Age movement. 6. Spiritual biography. I. Title.
BF1283.C88A3 2006   133.9'092
                        QBI06-600258

Cover photo Machu Picchu by Marlene Tuttle
Condor by Image@www.roughwood.net used by permission
Back cover photo Mallku Arévelo by Erin Crowley
Cover design by Corey Fowler, Daniel Yaeger, and Jim Bisakowski
Book design & layout by Desktop Publishing Ltd.
Edited by Michael Cowger and Helenita Ziegler

Dedicated to the memory of:

H. Louette Crowley

John R. Crowley

Suzanne L. Burch

For their love and wisdom

*"In your longing for your giant self lies your goodness,
and that longing is in all of you."*

Kahlil Gibran, The Prophet

*"Incremental learning, knowledge that merely expands on
what you've always believed, is nothing compared to knowledge whose very presence renders meaningless all previous
ideas."*

Jonette Crowley

Contents

PART IV
So Much to Understand

PART V
The Prophecy Today

Acknowledgments

Writing a book is a team sport. For me, an extreme extrovert, it had to be. First, my gratitude goes to family and friends who supported me in my explorations of—everything. There would be no adventure in this story without my fellow travelers and trekkers, first in Australia, then the Himalayas, and finally in the Peruvian Andes. Thank you for going with me to the ends of the Earth.

From the very beginning of this writing project, I dragged various girlfriends to our condo in the Colorado Rockies to help me edit, and—when my wrists hurt from the keyboard—to type. My deepest thanks go out to Becca Oldt, Deborah Bergman, Gloria Barschdorf, Marlene Tuttle, and Amara Whitney for your hard work, insightful suggestions, and most of all for your friendship. Family helped too. My beloved husband, Ed Oakley, who is also an author, supported, proofread and was a great help in all the publishing decisions. My sister, Erin Crowley, was a thorough and thoughtful editor, and sister Maureen Rodwin helped with her comment, "Jonette that section is just too weird for normal readers." My niece, Kelly Crowley, typed and edited without slipping any smart aleck comments into the manuscript. Amy MacDonald was great at making out my scribbles. Dear friends read the manuscript at different stages, always improving it significantly: Jarla Ahlers, Nancy Mitchell, Brad Johnson, Berdine and Muriel de Visser, Yolanda Groeneveld, Vicki Staudte and so many more. Countless others from all over the world read it and sent me encouragement and endorsements. I am grateful for the advice of best-selling author James Redfield, "Take your time, and don't send it out until it's perfect."

For professional editing, I relied on the expertise of Michael Cowger and Helenita Ziegler. Reya Ingle helped with final proofreading. For help in so many details, I am grateful to Dave Gordon in my office, a man of many talents. An especially huge hug goes to Ginny Hill, who worked tirelessly the last few months to edit, type, coordinate, make decisions and pull together the hundreds of details that go into getting a book out.

My greatest gratitude goes to all of you who read this book and allow it into your hearts. By reading, by learning, by growing, and by loving more fully we make this wonderful world an even better place. Thank you.

Introduction

If I had known I was supposed to write a book, I would have taken some notes.

So went the dialogue with my inner voice that insisted I write a book about my spiritual adventures in the Andes. I was back home from South America for just two days, and writing a book was nowhere on my 'to do' list. What you're reading is proof that the inner voice prevailed.

I'm an accidental mystic, a normal person with extraordinary curiosity. I'm a wife, a sister, a businesswoman who has stumbled along a path of spiritual awakening, discovering truths that are clamoring to be released from the mostly inaccessible vaults of ancient mysticism.

While this is a very personal story, every paragraph urges you to consider, what is *your* story? Trust *your* truth. Your story, your destiny is unfolding in the subtle play and patterns of synchronicity, of insights discounted then discarded, and of little scraps of truth that whisper just below the surface of what you think is your ordinary life. There is no ordinary life. *You* aren't ordinary! You may discover that there is a bigger pattern and a purpose in your life if you look closely.

When I wanted to back off from some aspect of this story for fear of what others would think of me, I remembered my commitment to being a leader. As far as I can tell, there is no other way to lead than by example. I hope this story entertains you, makes you laugh and cry, challenges you, and awakens you. The meditations, ceremonies, and spiritual initiations included here can carry you along into the energies and wisdom of ancient mysteries. They are a gift of light to you.

Jonette Crowley
Denver, Colorado

If you wish to order the *Eagle and the Condor Companion Meditations and Spiritual Initiations Audio Set*, which contains the meditations and ceremonies as they were recorded live in Nepal and Peru, go to www.JonetteCrowley.com or www.TheEagleandtheCondor.com or phone (303) 689-9318. The set is available on CD, audio tape, or as digital downloads.

PART 1

Spirits on My Path

*"Imagine having a tremendous, mystical experience…
when you come back from that you are not the same
person and cannot be."*

White Eagle

The Eagle and the Condor

1

An Incan Prophecy

n ancient prophecy, shared by indigenous people throughout the Americas, says when the Eagle of North America and the Condor of South America unite, the spirit of peace will awaken on Earth. After waiting for millennia, many native peoples believe the time is now.

It's the morning of December 21, 2004, and I sit in the front car of the tourist train passing through Peru's Sacred Valley to Machu Picchu. The train's horn sounds a warning to a dozen hard-hatted men laboring to clear fallen boulders from the right-of-way. Gashes from too much rain punctuate steep hills of cactus, bougainvillea, and a place where someone has planted calla lilies. From the window, I gaze across the Urubamba River. The Inca Trail, which I had hiked just four months earlier, cuts into the hills that are beginning to turn green from seasonal rains. Stone terraces built long ago, still in use by native farmers, ascend from remnants of an Incan bridge. As we approach the jungle near Machu Picchu, the eucalyptus forests—leaves dripping muted green—give way to rich, native cascades of vegetation.

I just left Mallku and now travel alone, one of many day-packed tourists on the train to Aguas Calientes, the town at the foot of Machu Picchu. Is it only four months ago since I was here? This time is different. I am not leading a group, and today is the summer solstice in the southern hemisphere—the second most important day of the Incan calendar.

What does the prophecy of the Eagle and the Condor really mean? Is it only a myth? If the time is now, how will we know? What about the legend of the golden Sun Disc of the Incas—did it originally come from the lost continent of Lemuria? Is it hidden in Peru's Lake Titicaca as some believe? What does this all mean for us today? Moreover, what can these ancient legends possibly have to do with *me*?

Now I know that we are deeply woven into ancient myths—an intrinsic part of prophecies and their fulfillment. Yet we hurtle through life, oblivious to the greater vision we are creating, until the pieces finally come together. The journey that today ends at Machu Picchu has taken me more than twenty years of traveling across Australia, Africa, Nepal and finally South America. In hindsight, I can see the pieces, like shards of stained glass form into an incredible picture, the Eagle and the Condor prophecy only a part of it.

2

An Otherwise Normal Life

or the first thirty years of my life, voices didn't pop into my head and I had no unusual visions. At the age of twelve, my second sight consisted of my dressing up like a gypsy and pretending to tell fortunes to neighborhood kids using a pack of playing cards.

Growing up in suburban Denver, the eldest of a large, Catholic family, I went through all the phases typical of a young girl deciding her destiny. In second grade I wanted to be a nun; in fourth grade a missionary; by sixth grade a teacher. Excelling in school and altruistic by nature, I settled on being a pediatrician. Of course, I would become none of these.

During those years at home, we went to Mass every Sunday and Confession after Mom reminded us how mean we were to our siblings. Like all good Catholic children, we had contests to see who could recite ten Hail Marys the fastest. Then, in eighth grade, I took a radical turn from the church's teachings. Virginia Tighe, a mother of one of the students in my junior high class, came to our school to tell us about her past life experience. Several years before, during clinical hypnosis, Mrs. Tighe began speaking in an authentic Irish brogue, providing verifiable facts about the life she had lived in Ireland as a girl named Bridey Murphy. The book, *The Search for Bridey Murphy*,[1] written about her case, became one of the first popular works that provided evidence that we have lived other lives in the past.

Once I heard this fantastic story, it was easy to become a

believer in past lives. I began to doubt much of what I had learned in Catechism. I questioned, "Why don't Catholics believe in past lives? Why do you have to be Catholic to go to heaven?" Mom prayed for me and asked me to talk with a priest about my many doubts. I did, but his answers didn't sway me. When I went to college and was away from home, I stopped going to church. What could be better? I attended the University of Colorado in Boulder in the 1970s—hippies, drugs, campus streaking, Transcendental Meditation. Yet as a straight arrow, I steered clear of the first three and couldn't afford the fee to learn TM. There were always philosophy courses, classes in comparative religion and thought-provoking books to quench my growing curiosity about the spiritual world.

Mostly, I spent my college days in the library, organizing sorority parties and campus events, or getting involved in national politics. When my plan to be a doctor was dashed by my inability to learn calculus, I picked Environmental Conservation as a major. It allowed me to take all the science and economics courses I enjoyed, while still believing I could save the world. After graduation, my dream of making a difference began with a move to Washington D.C. to work as an intern in the U.S. House of Representatives.

Even in the idealistic seventies, an environmental major wasn't the meal ticket I had hoped it would be. So after a summer of politics, I enrolled at the University of Missouri to get an MBA. From there, everything progressed quite logically on a fast track. My first job was with Andersen Consulting. My next job—I was twenty-five—was as the national Executive Director of the sorority I had pledged in college. I loved every day of it—the work and the women. I enjoyed the challenge of running a multi-million dollar organization—that is, until the day the board of directors fired me. My youthful idealism, not yet tempered by business experience or organizational savvy caused me to push for change too quickly. "Jonette, you are much more suited for the business world, not a non-profit," was the summation of the president at my dismissal.

Heartbroken from my first career failure, I plotted an

escape. "Let's hitchhike around New Zealand and Australia," I excitedly suggested to Mary Fran, my traveling buddy from college. Waving goodbye to worried parents, we donned our overstuffed backpacks, and within days were standing on the side of a road north of Auckland, our thumbs out to catch a ride. For over six months, we camped, hiked, slept in train stations and youth hostels, and discovered the joys of young sojourners in friendly, English-speaking lands.

Sydney, with its breathtaking harbor and waterways, famed Opera House and sparkling weather was a jewel we saved for the end of our journey. Standing in the summer sun on the main plaza, my heart was filled with the city's gleaming beauty. "I could live here!"

"Be careful what you ask for," says the old adage. How could I have known that the Universe had heard my off-hand request?

After picking up our mail at the general post office, we found a trendy pub for a Friday evening brew and to meet a friend-of-a-friend—a businessman. This was our last night in Australia so Mary Fran and I celebrated. David, the businessman, asked me, "What do you do for a living?"

Since hitchhiking couldn't possibly be the correct answer, I puffed myself up to reply, "I have an MBA and was a management consultant."

"Hmm," he considered, "I need someone to help run my companies."

Another beer, some in-depth discussion—as in-depth as you can get in a popular pub on a Friday after work, and I had myself a job interview. The only trouble was that the interview would have to be in the U.S. since I was flying home the next day. I must have made a good impression because I was back in Colorado only a week when David called to arrange an interview in Los Angeles. Have you ever noticed that when the Universe is serious about granting your wish, nothing can stop it?

Within a month, job contract and work visa in hand, I returned to Australia to live. Slowly, I made friends in the world Down Under. I worked for David for a year, obtained permanent residency and then moved into the field of software consulting. I was single, a yuppie in one of the world's most magnificent cities, sharing a flat on Sydney Harbor. It seemed that I had found my niche.

Your Path Is Made by Walking

With the freedom of the outdoors singing in my blood, I got away whenever possible with friends to backpack and camp in the New South Wales wilderness. Once, we were lucky to spot a koala. Another time we saw a herd of wild horses, "brumbies" as the Australians call them, grazing near our tent. I never would have imagined that the end to my otherwise normal life would have occurred on one of those camping trips. Something so strange and otherworldly happened that its significance only became clear twenty years later when I hiked the Inca Trail.

Our trek that Easter weekend was to the Blue Gum Forest in the mountains west of Sydney. Here, vast stands of eucalyptus, or gum trees, grew so straight and tall that the earliest settlers logged most of them to become masts for sailing ships. However, this particular forest was too far inland for the ship builders of 200 years ago, so the trees stood elegant and sacred. They are called blue gums because their papery bark is so bright white as to actually shine with a blue tint.

The midday sun dappled through the dancing, fragrant leaves, down onto tall grasses on the open forest floor. I was in a reverie hiking in front of a group of my friends. As I tramped peacefully along the trail, another, more ethereal world appeared beside me, much like a split screen television. I found myself simultaneously inhabiting my ordinary reality and a mystical, nonphysical realm. It was as if there were two of me—a physical Jonette and an etheric replica. In that other dimension, an apparition of a beautiful woman with long, straight hair, dressed in white, sat on a rock in a clearing. Her hair was white but her face was not of an old woman. Everything about her was magnificently luminous. Telepathically, she beckoned my etheric self to walk toward her and set my pack down so I could rest. Her angelic gaze lovingly filled me.

After several minutes of soul connection, the Spirit Woman indicated that it was time for my ethereal double to continue. I understood that I was to keep on walking through the other-worldly forest. With her thoughts, she communicated that my non-physical self was to leave my backpack—also etheric—with her.

Spirit world or not, I was miffed at the idea of leaving my pack behind. "After all," I thought, "I'm already traveling light. My tent, my stove, my food are pared down to the very basics." It was clear I couldn't win a telepathic argument with the Spirit Woman in white, so I reluctantly agreed in the invisible world to walk on with nothing. Yet, I tried to negotiate with her, "Since you won't let me take my backpack with me, can you at least tell me which way I should go?" I could see no paths or markers in this other-dimensional forest.

In her gentle way she indicated, *No deal.* She would not tell me which way to start out; only that it was time for me to leave. She spoke into my mind, *Your path is made by walking.*

I wasn't pleased to be told by a spirit being that I could take nothing with me and that I would have no one or no path to follow. Yet in that other, simultaneous dimension, I followed the Spirit Woman's bidding. My spirit self left my etheric possessions with her in the mystical meadow, striking off into the woods without a path, in a direction of my choosing. Even today, my main complaint, as a spiritual explorer, is that most of my knowledge comes from inner guidance. Sometimes it would be easier to follow a guru or teacher; to have someone else tell me what to do. Maybe the woman in white was showing me that each of us must discover our own way and walk our path with confidence. On the other hand, perhaps this was a personal spiritual test and that my agreement to continue unencumbered and follow no known path has made all the difference in my life.

After a few minutes, the luminous Spirit Woman and her ethereal world disappeared. I continued hiking in the normal physical reality, still carrying my physical backpack. Since then, I've often wondered, "Who was she?" She was certainly angelic, but she wasn't an angel. The answer to my persistent question would have to wait until I arrived in the Andes, more than two decades later. This was the first time, but it wouldn't be the last that I had Spirit enter my otherwise normal life. For the time being, I kept the incident to myself. My hiking friends were mostly business associates who probably wouldn't understand that while I trekked in front of them, I was participating in mystical communications with an invisible woman.

3

White Eagle

ike most of us, I've come a long way to understand the things I now believe. When the incident in the Blue Gum Forest occurred, my spiritual explorations had consisted of a couple of visits to psychics and reading Carlos Castaneda's early books. I had always wanted to meditate, but never took the time to learn. In the 1980s there was a popular, personal growth course in Sydney called "Self Transformation," which included a segment on meditation. Since my friends were all going, I signed up too.

At the introduction, the facilitator told us we would be learning the fundamentals of an easy mantra technique for meditating. She explained, "By the end of the class you will learn to meditate with a crystal on your forehead or third- eye."

I didn't hear anything else she said because my mind catapulted to this crystal-on-my-forehead idea. "Crystal? Does that mean Waterford?" In my naiveté, I pictured myself holding a wine goblet or a glass vase to my head. This was all going to be *very* interesting. I glanced around at the hundred or so people in the audience. *They* didn't seem to be struggling with the notion of holding a glass to their foreheads to meditate. They all looked normal. Besides, it was too late to get my money back.

Learning to meditate was the single greatest gift I have ever given myself. Much as reading is the basic skill that allows us to know our world, meditation is the tool that enables access to so much more. Meditation helps you become more of who you already are. By the end of the course, I had purchased a clear, quartz crystal to hold when I meditated. I *had* come a long way already!

Twenty years later, I can casually discuss other dimensions, parallel realities, the lost continent of Lemuria, and twin flames —ideas that I might have condemned as crazy back when I lived in Australia. While my beliefs might now be somewhat out of the mainstream, each step I've taken has been fully supported by the previous one. My own experiences have stretched my belief systems, yet no single step seemed flawed.

I committed myself to the practice of meditation with the words of our instructor ringing through my ears. "Meditation is the practice of sitting quietly; it's not about what you get. Only meditating teaches meditation." My favorite explanation was, "Prayer is talking to God. Meditation is listening to the answer." I wasn't very good at it; usually I spent the allotted twenty minutes thinking about my shopping list, planning work projects or nodding off.

Because I found it was easier to stay awake if I meditated in a group, a friend suggested I attend a weekly class at a Spiritualist Church in a Sydney suburb. The basis of the Spiritualist movement is the belief that spirits can communicate with us. To me, it was a whole new world. Yet, growing up in a Catholic family, we *did* pray to saints; and in college, I *did* believe the ghost stories friends shared in front of the fireplace at the Chi Psi fraternity. By expanding my normal frame of reference, I could entertain the idea of mediums, or channels as they are called.

Thirty people came to the orientation for classes at the Spiritualist Church in Enmore, a working class suburb of Sydney. It was 1985. As we sat in a circle of chairs with our eyes closed, the instructors used their intuitive abilities to choose which students should be in the beginning classes and which could join the on-going, advanced group. Since my purpose for being there was remedial meditation only, I was astonished to be one of the four people to be tapped for the advanced class! The psychic instructors apparently saw something hidden in me that indicated I was ready for advanced spiritual work. That weekly group had met together for more than a year, learning skills in psychic readings, clairvoyance and channeling spirit guides. I felt out of my league in every way.

During the second class, I was so surprised by what happened that I later admitted to a friend, "This meditation thing is *really* powerful!" I was sitting in silence with my eyes closed as Marcia, the instructor, led an opening prayer. I barely followed Marcia's invocation because an inner vision of a pretty, Asian woman was impressed sharply on my mind's eye. I was frustrated because I couldn't get her out of my vision and couldn't figure out who she was. This was just the kind of distraction that made me such a poor meditator in the first place. As I struggled to get my thoughts clear, I heard the classroom door open and Marcia say, "Hi, glad you made it. We've already started." The newcomer apologized for being late. It was her first time to join our class. When I opened my eyes to see who had just arrived, I was amazed to see that it was the woman whose face I had envisioned so prominently just minutes before!

In another class at the Spiritualist Church, Marcia came up to me while I strived to meditate. "Hello friend," she said, speaking to a spirit that she could 'see' with me. I felt nothing. Marcia continued to address the being, "Welcome. What is your name?"

I still felt nothing. However, in the spirit of 'nothing ventured, nothing gained,' I opened my mouth to see what would come out.

My name is Melissa. I've come to bring you flowers, I answered in a childlike voice.

That was it. Two emotions swept through me. One was excitement that I had successfully channeled, and the second was disappointment that I channeled some little girl and not great wisdom and deep truth. I didn't allow myself to channel in class again and for the most part forgot about it.

Several months later while meditating in that same group, I saw in my inner vision a Native American Indian chief dressed in white, ceremonial regalia. Marcia's spirit guide was an

Indian so I hoped this fellow was my guide. I began to try to guess his name, "White Cloud? White Feather?" I must have been off base, so he made it easy for me. The inner vision of the Indian transformed into a huge, white bird—an eagle. I knew he was telling me his name was "White Eagle." As quickly as it came, the vision dissolved. Thinking it unimportant, I didn't mention the experience to anyone.

A month or so after the episode with White Eagle, one of my friends in the meditation group presented me with a small book. Unwrapping it, I was shocked by the title and the hair stood up on the back of my neck: *The Quiet Mind: Sayings of White Eagle.*[2]

"How can this be?" I thought to myself. I had never heard of White Eagle. No one knew about my vision of the Native American. This was too much for my analytical mind to accept. Frankly, I thought it was creepy! Quickly I perused the little book, long enough to discover that White Eagle was an evolved being who had been a Native American. From the 'other side,' he was a spirit guide channeled by Grace Cooke, an English woman.[3] It was too weird, too much of a coincidence. I packed the book away and didn't pick it up again for a year. I wasn't prepared to ask the bigger question, "Why did White Eagle come to me?" It seemed that I was stumbling onto a spiritual path. Or was I being pushed, in spite of myself?

Despite my ignorance, the die had been cast. Now I knew who White Eagle was, and although invisible, he was very real to me. After his first appearance in my mind, I never again saw White Eagle as an Indian or an eagle—but experience him only as an essence of golden light. In the two decades since we've met, I've learned that White Eagle has been a spirit guide to hundreds of people around the world. Spirit guides are often North American Indians—which seemed strange to me since he first came to me in Australia.

Sojourn Through Africa

After living in Sydney from 1981 to 1986, my traveling feet got itchy again. An Aussie friend, Jan Roberts, and I quit our

high-tech jobs to take a year off from work. We joined an over-
land camping expedition traveling for six months through fifteen countries in Africa. To entertain myself in the evenings
around the campfire, I brought along a deck of Tarot cards and
a how-to book for understanding the symbols. Practicing on
my fellow travelers, I soon found my words were more accurate when I ignored the book and just used the Tarot cards to
trigger thoughts. As we floated on a banged-up barge down
the Congo River for three days, I read Tarot cards for the
African traders and the ship's captain and his wife. Raymond,
one of our fellow overlanders, translated my words into
French, the main language of commerce in central and western
Africa. The cards became a conversation starter that enabled
me to connect with the local people. In Algeria, I was invited
into a home to do a reading for a traditional Moslem mother
and wife. Never once did I consider my ability to sense things
about people as anything more than coincidence.

We traveled slowly in a canvas-covered truck from Nairobi,
Kenya to London, England. Throughout the months on the
road, I did my best to meditate. I assumed White Eagle was my
personal spirit guide because I often experienced warm, loving
feelings that I associated with his presence.

A Very Short Marriage

After so many months living out of a backpack, at age
thirty-three, I returned to Mom and Dad in Colorado. I was
ready for a home of my own and a permanent relationship…
and I needed a job.

John was a friend from my college days. We dated briefly
when he vacationed in Sydney in 1981, but with an ocean
between us, the relationship languished. Once I was back in the
States, our romance blossomed. In August 1988, a year after I
left Africa, John and I were married. I moved to his home in
southern California and landed a great job as a consulting manager for a prestigious software company. It all should have
been wonderful. Wrong.

My first night as a wife in my new home I slept on the couch.

When we couldn't agree on household decisions, John told me, "I'm the boss. I need to make all our decisions… with your input of course." I lay in bed for a day, not knowing how to move if I couldn't make my own choices. Within two weeks of our honeymoon, we were in counseling. The person I had always been rapidly crumbled as I tried to keep the marriage together. I had waited so long to get married and now I was failing miserably. "Why did he marry me, of all people, if he needed a subservient wife?" I asked myself endlessly.

The therapist helped me see that the better question was, "Why did I think I needed to marry him?" I was ashamed of the answer. In my eagerness to be married, I was blind to the warning signals of unwinnable personality conflicts.

Defeated in every way, I moved out in January. My heart and soul were bruised and battered. I was always petite, but now I didn't feel like eating. My weight dropped to 100 pounds. I cried constantly. A health condition that lingered from my African travels worsened, causing my short-term memory to fail. I was constantly tired. I couldn't grasp concepts or think as quickly as before. Divorced before the thank-you cards for the wedding gifts had been written, I was now too sick to hold my new job. I needed a sabbatical from life.

I was in the void, that place in which the old way of life has crumbled and the new is waiting to be born. For many, the void, or emptying out of life's previous structures, happens as a *result* of major spiritual epiphanies. For me, the void *preceded* my rapid spiritual awakening and it paved the way for new ways of thinking and being.

White Eagle Speaks

There is a Zen saying, "When the student is ready, the teacher appears." That was what happened to me after my marriage fell apart. Synchronistically, a flyer came in the mail from Sanaya Roman and Duane Packer, successful authors who offered a weekend workshop called "Being a Writer."[4] The thought came, "A writer? Yes! I can turn my African journal into a novel!" I quit my job and hopped on a plane to San

Francisco for the seminar, eager to begin my new life as a writer.

In the workshop, we were asked to visualize a symbol for our writing project, something we could use to empower our work. Because my book was to be based on my camping expedition through Africa, I expected to envision a pygmy or an elephant. Instead, a gigantic crystal that emanated light appeared in my mind. It felt grand, lofty… metaphysical. "How can a towering, radiant crystal have anything to do with me?" I asked myself, bewildered.

The next surprise of the seminar came when we were to connect with our inner writer. I expected words to flow forth on how to organize the Africa book. Instead, I said these words aloud: *This is White Eagle. The book you will write is a gift of light.*

"Who invited him?!" I asked myself. He had never popped in unexpectedly before, and I hadn't channeled since that day in our meditation group in Sydney four years earlier. "He must have the wrong person," I thought. After all, it was the darkest time of my life. Nothing was going right, and I certainly didn't feel the least bit light! Yet, somewhere in that vision of the crystal and the words of White Eagle, I felt the truth behind his message.

Shortly after the writer's workshop, I relocated to Vail, Colorado, to live with my sister Erin who was managing a ski lodge. It was an enchanting place to heal, both physically and emotionally.

On a gloriously clear autumn day, for which the Rockies are famous, I started to hike up the mountain behind the Vail high school. Evergreens and the spicy fragrance of fallen aspen leaves scented the cool, high altitude air. The trailhead, rutted and muddy in spots from the previous night's thundershower, required careful navigation. I saw the outline of boot prints made by a hiker in the past few days. Then some fresh paw prints caught my attention. "A big animal," I thought. Immediately that part of my mind that always knows the truth sent out the single message: *Bear.* However, my logical mind refused to consider the possibility of a bear and countered with its own thought: "This is the print of a very big dog." Without a second thought, I chose to believe the big dog theory and continued on the gently climbing path. For another half hour I hiked in an exalted, safe reality, breathing in the aroma of the mountains.

My comfortable world, where only friendly dogs make large paw prints, consoled me. Until, on the trail ahead of me, standing on hind legs, looming ominously was: *The Bear!* How could I dare to be shocked? The bear left a clear print to announce his presence on the trail. How could I choose to believe my mind's invention over what the intuitive part of me knew to be true? It wasn't the first or the last time I had convinced myself that some sign on the path couldn't possibly be what I knew it to be. I constructed logical but erroneous explanations to avoid considering the implications of one truth or another. Since that morning, the sign on the path has never again been a bear, but it has often been some other, larger truth that I was not yet ready to see.

On the trail, I made a loud racket so I wouldn't surprise the bear and quickly turned back downhill. Suddenly, a latté seemed more desirable than a hike.

A few weeks later, as I sat alone in my sister's living room, a surge of energy swept through me: White Eagle. Excited, I found myself standing and speaking as if I was addressing hundreds of people. I grabbed a tape recorder and began to channel:

This is White Eagle. You on Earth are standing on the threshold of a great and beautiful emergence. It will eclipse anything that has occurred before. The Renaissance and the Period of Enlightenment in your history are nothing compared to the power that is waiting to be born in your lifetime.

So much is happening and it is at your feet. You who are listening are the activators. You are the people whose minds are open to a new dawn. I bow to you. More than at any time before, the future is in your hands. I am here to tell you that your hands are capable. Each of you has a unique set of talents, skills and experiences so that you are the perfect holder of these dreams. You will take the essence of dreams and mold them into form. My friends, you are not just doing the groundwork, because the seeds have already been planted. The sense of immediacy is so strong. Great things are happening. Listen to your hearts. Each of you has a different part to play and your message is sounding in your soul.

The light is so powerful. I honor you deeply as spiritual brothers and sisters. You are more than caretakers on this Earth. You are life givers. Go now, listen to your hearts, and give back life. Thank you.

I felt unsettled by the fact that White Eagle had so much to say and seemed to be speaking to so many people. Nevertheless, I quickly began to understand; I was supposed to take White Eagle public! My first spiritual partnership was born. In the beginning, I practiced by doing channeled readings for friends. They asked questions and White Eagle astounded us with clear and accurate answers. Later, I experimented and found that the readings worked as well on the phone as in person.

One day in 1989, I received an invitation from Sanaya Roman and Duane Packer to participate in their first series of classes: Awakening Your Light Body. It sounded intriguing — get yourself to a higher vibration, make breakthroughs in your emotional and mental bodies, become more connected to your soul… All of those things I certainly needed right then. I was stuck in a deep, black hole.

However, my rational self argued, "Don't be silly, Jonette. Why awaken something that you didn't even know was asleep? Besides, how can you possibly afford to fly to California for three weekends, stay in hotels, and pay for the seminar series?" I couldn't. The rational side had won — for now.

The idea just wouldn't let go of me. In a fit of exasperation, I reread the invitation packet and asked White Eagle if it was something that I should attend. *It is one of the most important things that you can possibly do,* came his answer.

"Then how will I pay for it?" My rational side was in an argumentative mood.

With your engagement ring, was White Eagle's reply. So I sold my diamond and signed up for the course that would change my life. My brother bought the diamond and thoughtfully replaced the stone with a cubic zirconium so no one would know the difference.

The series for Awakening Your Light Body was three, four-day weekends of meditation and energy processes. After about 80% of them, I could remember nothing. People talked about incredible journeys—I fell asleep.

Still, something seemed to have shifted, or opened up. The hurt and pain in my life began to dissolve. The dark hole got lighter. I felt more content. I worked with the tapes of the class between workshops, again, sleeping through most of them. Yet strangers commented on the calmness around me. Acquaintances told me that I looked radiant. Something magical was clearly happening.

Looking back at that period, I'm amazed at my blind faith. I was fortunate to have friends, David and Carol Shouldice, who were much more knowledgeable than I was about the world of spirit guides and channeling. They supported me in every way. Carol and I organized my first public event with White Eagle. We rented a meeting room, posted fliers, and I began the transition to my calling as a channel. The entire time part of me thought I must be crazy. Here I was—an MBA, a Phi Beta Kappa, a consulting manager, previously a Catholic, and now I presumed to speak on behalf of a wise, dead Indian. "How can I explain this to my family, not to mention my sorority sisters?!"

My Mother wasn't so sure about this shift in my career pursuits, since all of this was outside her normal paradigm. One day while she sat in the family room at her sewing machine, I explained to her my interest in channeling. She asked the question that I've been asked many times since, "How do you know this isn't from the devil?"

"Let me read you something from White Eagle," I answered. After reading to her the graceful, beautiful, channeled words that I had recorded and transcribed, I asked Mom "Does this sound like words of the devil? Have I *ever* said anything that sounded so sweet or holy? Does it sound like me?"

"No," she admitted readily.

I paraphrased a quote from the Bible, "You shall know it by its fruit." We both agreed that the words and ideas I was bringing through were good and kind, not devilish. Mom, out of her incredible love and open-mindedness expanded her traditional religious beliefs to accept, respect and eventually support my foray into the spiritual world. That day, I made a deal with her: "I will stop channeling immediately if anything ever comes out of my mouth that isn't uplifting, high and holy." Laughingly I added, "And you can disown me if I change my name or start a religion."

4

Mark

I've always been a practical person. I was filled with questions about how channeling and the belief in an unseen world fit into modern physics. After reading every book I could find to decipher the relationship between the worlds of spirit and matter, I wasn't any closer to understanding. Therefore, I peppered White Eagle with questions about the nature of reality. Evidently, he didn't think he was the best guide for the job, so he brought in Mark.

On a Colorado midsummer's evening in 1989, I sat with my friends Carol and David practicing my new skill of channeling. Unexpectedly, I found myself slipping through a tiny tear in the fabric of consciousness. Little did I realize that this crack would open to create a path that many would explore in the following decades.

Suddenly a vast and overpowering presence engulfed me. "This is not White Eagle," I thought, as I tried to hold onto my equilibrium. My heart raced. I was on fire with an inner heat. I felt weak, shaky and scared. With great difficulty, I opened my mouth. A new and powerful entity spoke:

I am Mark. I have traveled a great distance in terms of energy. I come to bridge a gap between dimensions unknown. My world is on the other side of time, the other side of matter as you know it. I have come to birth new ideas. I have come in response to the thought requests of the world. I am a teacher and a student of the cosmos.

That was it. The entity who called himself Mark was gone. I

could no longer hold on to the immense force field of energy. White Eagle returned to pull me together and share his insights on what had just happened. I channeled this explanation:

You must begin awakening to different realities in order to activate the expansion of consciousness that will allow you to know God. The ultimate goal of Mark's work with you is to help mankind evolve to states of harmony, oneness, and the creative, infinite energy that you call God.

White Eagle went on to explain that this work would not merely be an intellectual endeavor but experiential:

The experiences will be powerful. Imagine having a tremendous, mystical encounter in which you feel joy, bliss, oneness and harmony beyond description. When you come back from that, you will know that a supreme change has taken place. Though you may discount the experience with your words and logic, you are not the same person and cannot be.

This all sounded as if I had volunteered for some cutting-edge consciousness work, and although I felt apprehensive, I was ready to pursue it. I later asked Mark, "Why me?"

Two reasons, he said into my mind. *First, because you are naïve; you don't have rigid belief systems, dogma, or a lot of preconceived notions on how the world should work. Second, you are willing to teach what you don't know.*

That second part, teaching what I don't know was *very* difficult for me. It was uncomfortable to allow myself to channel about things I didn't fully understand, yet I chose to trust what was coming through. I was, and continue to be, a conscious channel, which means I am fully aware and actively partner with Mark and White Eagle to find the right words to speak.

Mark asked me to channel him every Tuesday evening with David and Carol assisting me to hold the tremendous spiritual energies. I hated Tuesdays. I've always been proud of my ability to articulate my thoughts, and I've *always* agreed with what came out of my mouth. Suddenly I was speaking of complicated states of consciousness that I didn't know anything about. My desire to control, edit, or at least to understand what I was saying must have been slowing Mark down. He came up with a very creative solution. He requested that on Tuesdays I spend the night at Carol and David's home. We were told to set our alarm for 2 a.m. so that I could channel Mark when I was too sleepy to try to control what he wanted to say. I still didn't like Tuesdays!

Once we graduated from the middle of the night routine, a small group of friends met weekly for our learning sessions with Mark. The greeting, 'Welcome students,' which issued sternly out of my mouth, was the signal that Mark was ready to lead us on magical meditations or explain the intricate physics of the universe. Through Mark, we experienced the nature of reality beyond our senses. We traveled in consciousness to dimensions similar to those that Jane Roberts wrote about in her groundbreaking books channeled from Seth.[5] As my confidence and my ability with these new energies grew, Mark requested that we expand the number of students in our group. When he said we needed fourteen people, fourteen eager spiritual pioneers were there.

Being a channel for Mark is an extremely difficult experience to explain. His energy is so vast that, for the first many years, I could only channel him when a group was present to help me hold his immense vibration. It's strange to refer to Mark with a human pronoun like he or him, because he is more of an energy field than a spirit guide or being. In fact, Mark has never existed in a physical reality.

Since that first evening, I've channeled Mark for groups in the United States and Europe, helping individuals break through the limits of linear thinking and lift the veils to their own power and understanding. Mark doesn't just *talk* about possibilities; he partners with me to *transport* people to levels of awareness so that we can experience insights far beyond words. Because this kind of experiential, energetic teaching links directly to personal experience, the truths discovered are uniquely our own. Mark provides tools of awakening to encourage us to travel beyond the limits that have held us in the past. With Mark's guidance, we experience our minds as limitless, fluid, and vast.

I consider myself an explorer of the outer edges of human consciousness. Those edges grow to the extent we can stretch our abilities. On a few occasions, I've probably gone further than I should have. Once, during an amazingly high meditation, I heard an inner voice that seemed to be coming to me from a vast distance, *Jonette, this time you've gone too far.* I managed to pull myself together to re-emerge unscathed back into my normal state. However, in the future I was more careful not to push too hard for growth.

Two years later, I could easily go to that same expanded state of consciousness and bring others along to what Mark called the 'sixth dimension' or 'the place of miracles.' The abilities of the collective human consciousness are developing so quickly that a state I could attain only in a mystical experience, could now be accessed by many people within a couple of years, or sometimes only a couple of months.

Nothing, and Everything

One example of how Mark created a space, or an energy field for me to move beyond my past limits, came in the mid-1990s. I was channeling Mark for a spiritual growth seminar when an extraordinary yet simple event took place. I had a direct experience of what I called 'God-consciousness.' It was a spiritual experience unlike anything I had known in previous meditations. The workshop title "A Weekend of Transcendence," should have given me an inkling that breakthroughs were in store.

Mark and I began the meditation process by leading our group of twenty-five people into high states of enlightened human consciousness. He then asked us to expand our awareness to the level of the Creator/Creation. I had never before experienced such a profound state of infinite beingness. I sat spellbound. I had thoughts, but they were nothing; emotions, but they were nothing. Indeed, there was nothing to see, nothing to learn, nothing to do, nothing to remember. This place was *no*-thing, yet *every*-thing.

What I remembered most was the lack of meaning in this space. When I tried to understand what really mattered, *nothing* mattered. My experience was infinitely small and gigantic all at once. It went beyond words, beyond describing or understanding. I didn't sense a being, a light, a force, or even a power. I simply *was*.

When the meditation ended, I sat with my head in my hands. I could find no thoughts, no voice, and no explanation for what had just happened. I struggled to find meaning. Why did I feel I needed to *understand* something in order to *accept* the experience of it? Did understanding something make it real or true? What then was I to do with an experience that was so far above understanding that it had no meaning that was applicable to my ordinary world?

I became filled with emotions: gratitude, fear, fearlessness and guilt. First, I sobbed in gratitude. I was humbled and deified at the same moment: "Did I really touch the Creator/Creation? Did I really touch God?" Even while my soul communed with the consciousness of Masters, my human emotions had been petty. Early in the meditation, I heard someone making noise in the kitchen and I felt angry. I prayed that I could get where I needed to go in spite of my negative thoughts. By the grace of God, I did.

"Is there a lesson here?" You see, as a teacher, nothing had real meaning to me unless there was a lesson to share. What did it mean if I could gain access to such a holy state, even if I was angry? It may have meant the part of me that gets angry was not big or important enough to impede my progress to the Divine. I didn't have to fix my emotions or have a perfect personality to know God. My rational self questioned, "Did I really experience God?" My answer was, "Yes!" I experienced God as much as I was capable of at that time. How did I know? Because, just because.

Emotions other than gratitude came bubbling out: Fear. Did this mean I would have to live differently? If so, could I? Moreover, if my life didn't change, of what value was the experience? I knew *that* answer. The experience was so whole, complete and profound unto itself that *it didn't matter if I*

The Eagle and the Condor

changed or not. It was nothing. It wasn't about learning something or changing anything. It didn't matter.

Another emotion was present too: Fearlessness. I felt that I no longer needed to worry whether I was doing the right thing. "Am I doing the right work? Am I doing it well enough? Fast enough?" It didn't matter. The only one it mattered to was me, and I don't really matter, for that matter.

I experienced guilt also. How could I achieve this state even though I ate meat, even though I didn't meditate daily, even though I was just angry? Right and wrong, I realized, are inventions of the human mind that keep us from God.

I was both amused and annoyed when one of the students asked me later, "What is the difference between the Higher Self and Soul?"

I wanted to shout, "It doesn't matter! Who cares? Who cares!?!" The part of us that needs to analyze will never get it! There will *never* be enough information or right answers for that part of us! Our constant human need to understand and evaluate the mystical may be the *very thing* that keeps us from it.

At dinner that evening, a friend asked me, "What were the two or three things you learned from your experience?"

I had to say, "Nothing." I appreciated why people who had near death experiences often kept them to themselves. There was really nothing to say that was in the same realm as the experience. I learned nothing. There was nothing more to say than this: *It is.*

Despite those thoughts, I realized I created all the meaning, conclusions, lessons and insights *after* the fact. The experience itself needed no explanation. This was how Mark fulfilled the first words that were spoken when he came five years before. *Imagine having a tremendous, mystical experience... When you come back from that, you will know that a supreme change has taken place. Though you may discount the experience with your words and logic, you are not the same person and cannot be.*

Mark teaches by taking us to the threshold of our own wisdom. Sometimes, we're dropped there without explanation, or without need of any.

While I channel Mark for regular classes, White Eagle has always been my primary spirit guide. It is White Eagle who gives me personal advice when I ask, and White Eagle I channel in private readings for clients. Although Mark and White Eagle are always there when I call, they never come except in response to specific requests for assistance. With such wise and wonderful spirit helpers, you might think that I rely heavily on them in my day-to-day life. Call me stubborn, but I most often hang onto the childhood philosophy, "I want to do it myself!" When my way hasn't worked, I call on White Eagle for a higher perspective.

Initiation into the White Brotherhood

White Eagle and Mark both identified themselves as coming from the "Great White Brotherhood," or "Brotherhood of Light." This group of highly evolved souls is comprised of Masters whose focus is to assist humankind's spiritual awakening. Their symbol through the ages has been a gold, six-pointed star in a circle. Some say that the beings of the Great White Brotherhood were the spiritual leaders of Lemuria, the lost continent in the Pacific. After Lemuria's submergence, the Masters brought their wisdom to what is now Tibet, where they established libraries and Mystery Schools. I learned later that the White Brotherhood had mystical connections in the Andes and to the Incas as well.

Naturally, I assumed that being dead was the first prerequisite for admission to such a rarefied fraternity. You can imagine my surprise when in a particularly deep meditation in 1989—I had only recently met White Eagle and Mark—I was told by White Eagle that I was a *human* member of the White Brotherhood. Sitting on my bed at my parents' house, I experienced a golden six-pointed star in a circle on the center of my forehead, on my third-eye chakra.[6] From that moment on, I confidently saw myself as a spiritual teacher and healer.

White Eagle told me that I would recognize other initiates by sensing the same gold stars on their foreheads. If I saw only the outline of the star, it meant that they had the potential, but had not yet fully awakened to their spiritual knowledge. For the time being, I was not to tell anyone about my initiation into the White Brotherhood. That wasn't a hard commitment to keep. Who would care?

Meditating two years later, I was again given a spiritual promotion. In place of the golden six-pointed star placed ethereally on my forehead, I was granted an eleven-pointed star. It signified the blending of the six-pointed star and the five-pointed star—an ancient symbol for Venus. I understood that this merging of the two stars indicated that I was graduating from being a teacher and a healer to being a leader. I graciously accepted the inner appointment and the responsibility it carried. According to Alice A. Bailey, in her 1922 book, *Initiations: Human and Solar*, "An initiation is an expansion of consciousness—a means of opening the mind and heart to a recognition of what already exists in reality."[7] The eleven-pointed star of leadership was a higher initiation for me within the White Brotherhood.

The gifts from this initiation have enabled me to call forth, orchestrate and transmit complex, multidimensional energies. As a result, I can assist people to expand their consciousness. Together we navigate through time and space, allowing us to know things outside our personal experiences. My goal has always been to move toward Enlightenment and serve others by inspiring them to keep moving along their own personal paths.

In 1998, nine years after my first secret initiation into the White Brotherhood, White Eagle asked me to initiate an entire group that I was teaching with the six-pointed star insignia of the White Brotherhood. The significance of this larger scale initiation was that the doors to the inner sanctum of mystical wisdom were being pushed open by all of us who seek knowledge beyond this material reality. I welcomed the inclusion of so many others into the Brotherhood of Light.

Only four years later, as I was channeling Mark at a workshop in the Yucatan, the eleven-pointed star "Initiation into Leadership" was given to the participants. Again, this indicated to me the rapidity of humanity's current spiritual growth and was a sign that so many were becoming leaders of this awakening.

5

My Blue Star Man

hile my spiritual life blossomed, I was also embarking on a new consulting career. Since working as a manager for a large software company didn't allow the time and flexibility I needed, my friend Jarla Ahlers and I formed a partnership to teach leadership training classes. Fifteen years later, I still provide consulting and leadership training to assist major organizations.

Even with all these positive changes, my personal life had a big hole in it. I was tired of dating the wrong men. I told the Universe not to bother sending me anyone who did not have both real world grounding and spirituality. Of course I had a much longer list: he had to live in Colorado, be active, intelligent, successful, not smoke, handsome... you know the list.

Every day I did what I called "my soulmate meditation." I went to the highest place possible in my consciousness, visualizing it as a mountaintop. From that place I sent out a 'spiritual personal ad,' reasoning that any man who could sense my high energetic request would have to be evolved spiritually. I pictured the request as a pink flag on top of the mountain. Faithfully, I visualized the pink flag waving on that peak in my daily meditation for a couple of weeks. At first, there were no results. So, I became more adamant with Spirit: "I want a definite clue about how to find my soulmate." That morning I received a hint. It wasn't exactly clear, but I had the knowing that it was important. "Blue Star" was the phrase that stuck, though I was hoping for a name and phone number.

Now I was on a search for my Blue Star! I belonged to a networking group that attracted interesting people. One morning, a nice-looking, well-dressed man attended the meeting for the first time. At the registration table, new people were given metallic stars to stick on their nametags. You guessed it; right there, next to his name was not a gold, silver, or red star… but a blue star! I thanked White Eagle for the clue as I circled in toward the group (of women mostly) who were gathering around the handsome newcomer.

As a single woman, my well-trained eye went immediately to his left hand. "Oh no, it can't be! There is a gold band! Why does the clue lead me to a married man? Maybe he has a friend," I thought, striking up a conversation with him.

"What do you do?" He asked.

"I'm a trainer and speak on leadership and corporate change management," I responded.

"Why don't you attend the next monthly meeting of the National Speakers Association in Denver?" he queried.

"Okay, it must be something of a treasure hunt. The Blue Star symbol is my first clue to lead me to the right man," I thought to myself. Therefore, to the NSA meeting I went, zeroing in on several 'un-ringed' males. No results. Then, I saw him. He was sitting in the front row next to a stack of new books. He was evidently the author. He was handsome. No gold glinted from his ring finger. The title of the book he had written spoke volumes: *Enlightened Leadership: Getting to the Heart of Change.*[8] "Hmmm," I thought, "he might have some potential." Introducing myself, I perused his book and went out on a limb to invite him to a major channeling event I was leading the next week.

I followed the clues to find Ed Oakley, the love of my life, my Blue Star, my husband. After three dates we were committed to each other, though it took me five full years to convince him that marriage was different from living together. I joined him and still work at the consulting company he founded.

The Eagle and the Condor

PART II

Wisdom of the
Grandmothers

"The more dangerous side of ego is pretending to be less than the greatness we are."

The Eagle and the Condor

6

Communicating with Nature

I n 1992, the year in which I met Ed Oakley, I met another very special friend, Sue Burch. She came to my house for a White Eagle channeled reading. Sixty-something with short gray hair and a medium build, Sue was a feisty lady who drove around in an old, gold Mazda RX7 sports car. White Eagle answered her questions—her finances, her failed marriage, her family—the usual. The session was nearly over when White Eagle said to her, *You talk to rocks don't you?*

"Why yes," she stammered, clearly surprised at my guide's directness. "I used to own a rock yard. I'm a landscaper and I love creating rock features." She paused and White Eagle waited, "And there is a special rock—in Wyoming. I sometimes drive up there just to sit on it, reflect, and listen. It helps me think."

Do you know what crop circles are? White Eagle's questioning turned a corner that only he understood.

Sue, a Colorado grandmother, responded in the only way you could have imagined. "Crop what?"

Go to the Tattered Cover Bookstore and find a book with photos of crop circles. Put your hands on the pictures, White Eagle directed.

A few days later I received a phone call from Sue. "What's this about?" she demanded. "I put my hands on the photographs right there in the bookstore and electricity shot through me. What's this about?" she repeated. "I need to talk to you and White Eagle again."

She began attending our Monday night classes channeled

from my spirit guide Mark. When she closed her eyes to follow Mark's consciousness journeys, she always went further than everyone else did. When others felt joy and peace, Sue would go to a blue universe or somewhere else equally esoteric and indefinable. She railed at God. "I don't like where I went. I don't understand what you're trying to show me! Where's the peace and joy?" Even Sue's spirit guide was different from everyone else's; hers was Ra, the Egyptian Sun God symbolized by a golden Solar Disc.

She came to be a friend and spiritual colleague. I loved her. Mark once described our spiritual relationship in terms of technical rock climbing. *Jonette is the belayer who holds the rope and protection from below for Sue, who is the lead climber.* Sue couldn't get to these high dimensions without me and I wasn't meant to go first.

Sue felt drawn to join a crop circle tour to England. She felt the vibrations in the center of the gigantic and unusual patterns in the fields. Sue 'saw' the crop circle energies go through the Earth to a portal under the Himalayan Mountains. She dreamed of a five-pointed star formation the day before it appeared in a field of grain. She was full of the mysteries of the Universe.

Meanwhile, Ed and I moved into a big, new house outside Denver. We asked Sue to design a rock and water feature for us. Her plan required massive rocks—not just ordinary rocks that you could get easily from a local landscape yard. These boulders were special, they had to speak to her. Wyoming. Her heart said that they must be red, Wyoming granite.

As Sue jumped in her old sports car to drive north, the voice of her intuition told her to take toilet paper. Her connection to nature and to the boulders she envisioned told her where to turn onto the dirt roads of Wyoming's windswept ranch lands. The dusty road forked right. A pinkish rock outcropping jutted up from the tumbleweeds near the horizon. A shed was nearby, and an outhouse—which she needed just then. Sue smiled as she grabbed the toilet paper roll and stepped over downed barbed wire, "I must be in the right place. Thanks," she said to the Universe.

Walter, an eighty-five year old rancher, owned the land from which our rocks were to be extracted. He must have thought it strange when he opened the door to face Sue's fiercely blue eyes and brisk manner. "I've come to buy some of your rocks," she informed him. He put on his well-worn cowboy hat to walk outside. She explained what she would pay him and that a crane and several flat bed trucks would arrive in two weeks. Sue wanted tons of rocks.

Sue knew exactly which boulders were meant for our yard and which needed to stay on the ranch. Unfortunately, to a crane operator and a truck driver, one red granite boulder looks pretty much like another. The men had busily loaded a few ten-ton boulders onto the truck before she arrived. Ever connected to nature and especially to her beloved rocks, Sue walked around the flat bed to hear a gigantic boulder already on the truck telepathically and unequivocally state, *I'm to stay here.* The rock-hauling men probably still relate over a beer about the time that bossy old lady made them remove a boulder that had taken them over an hour to extract and load, only to replace it with another that, to them, looked just the same.

With pond and waterfalls, ponderosas and red granite boulders she created a magical place that even the workers called "White Eagle's Garden." In the front yard is "Walter's Rock," the one the wizened rancher told Sue was his favorite. The garden, planted with gloriously bright flowers, was the site of our September wedding in 1996.

Because I Love You

By her example and her passion for nature, Sue demonstrated our oneness with the Universe. She could connect to rocks and trees, but could I? One day it happened unexpectedly as I crossed a busy street in downtown Seattle. When I stopped at a median to wait for the light to change, I noticed a colossal fir proudly towering over the intersection. Colorado trees are scrawny in comparison, so I was appreciative of its tremendous size and fullness. Without thinking, I looked up at its magnificent boughs and said aloud, "Wow! You are beautiful!"

Immediately I felt a physical shock opening at my heart! In that moment, I *knew* that the tree had heard me and was acknowledging my compliment! Never had I felt such a direct and clear sensory communication from nature. However, that was just the beginning of my relationship with that tree.

The next week, as I flew from Denver to Austin, to teach a leadership program, I read a passage in a book about connecting to devas, or nature spirits of specific plants. The book instructed the reader to sit in front of a plant and tune in. Flying in an airplane at 30,000 feet, I wasn't anywhere near a plant, but I figured I would try to connect with the tree in Seattle, since evidently we were friends.

Whoosh! As soon as I thought about the tree, I felt him—he was definitely a male. The spirit of that fir tree in Seattle was a strong presence in my head. Shocked, I asked telepathically, "How did you find me?"

Because I love you, was the instant thought reply. For a split second I marveled at the simplicity of that idea—that it is the power of love that connects everything through time and space. Love is the unifying field. The tree sensed my pause and asked, *Do you doubt that?* Well, how could I doubt that love? I knew the spirit of that tree because he touched my heart so palpably when I remarked that day about his beauty.

In my human insecurity, my next thought question was, "Why do you love me?" The tree spirit didn't respond directly to that question; but I understood that love is simply the essence of things. When we love something, our consciousness is connected to it. I had the feeling that the spirit of the tree could answer many things far beyond the tree kingdom. As I pondered why a tree would know or even care about other topics, I realized that there is no such thing as tree-consciousness or rock-consciousness or even me-consciousness; there is just one consciousness. I have believed intellectually and spiritually in the oneness of all, but until the spirit of the tree communicated to me, I had never actually felt it.

As it turned out, this connection was a prelude to an even greater personal connection to nature that I would experience on the Inca Trail in the Andes.

7

Encoding the Knowledge of the Incas

ver the years, Sue and I got together on solstices and equinoxes to meditate with Mark as our guide. We opened extraordinary spaces at the very edges of human consciousness. Sue had always known that she had special spiritual work to do in Peru, ironically a place she had never been. At seventy-one years of age, she was diagnosed with colon cancer, which had spread. She was dying. Both of us knew that her sojourn to the Andes would have to be a mystical, shamanic voyage, not a physical trip.

Therefore, on June 21, 2002, the solstice, we sat in my living room in Colorado to do whatever spiritual work she needed to do, virtually. Later, I learned that the June solstice, winter in the southern hemisphere, is the most powerful day to the Incan priesthood. Sue was clear that the place she was drawn to was not Machu Picchu or Cuzco, but beside Lake Titicaca, a massive, high altitude lake in the Andes.

Mark led the two of us on a shared inner journey to an Incan past life. In that life Sue was a high priest and astronomer with the powers of prophecy. She foresaw the coming of the people who would bring the end of the reign of the Golden Sun and their religion as it had been practiced in the Andes for millennia. The invaders were unconscious of the mystical wisdom of the ancients. As a priest, Sue in that past life knew that the Incas needed to protect the sacred knowledge that had been given to their initiated ones. If these secrets were not hidden, the esoteric energies and practices would fall into the wrong hands. Therefore, at all costs, the mysteries and the powers needed to be protected.

We experienced this mystical journey together—with Sue narrating what she saw and felt as I channeled Mark for clarification. In my mind's eye, I could see everything Sue described. It was as if I too, was part of a past life remembrance in which Sue was a priest and I a witness to what happened next. I tape-recorded the session.

Sue closed her eyes and began to speak. "I see myself on top of a mountain. My arms are up, reaching out and I feel great, great despair. I feel as if I am praying for some kind of Knowing to help me. I feel as if I am being touched by Light. I can feel star energy and the Sun enter my fingertips. It is as if I am entering a kingdom of Light—it's a Knowing. Yes, I can experience that again!"

I channeled Mark who added:

That Knowing was too strong for your human vessel in that life. You knew that calling forth this gift of Knowing would kill you but you knew you must do it. So you stood there and called forth the Spirit of Earth and Fire. The magnificent rock upon which you stood began to vibrate with the Wisdom that entered it through your feet. This incredible encoding of the Knowledge of the Universe all came whirling, twirling through your body. It passed through you—into what was a willing stone receptacle, then into the fires at the center of the Earth. This represented incredible Knowledge and Wisdom beyond any dimension we have held.

"All kinds of colorful light rays transferred from me to the rock," Sue continued, still experiencing her Andean life. "Light is shooting up from the center of the Earth as if all this Knowledge has been received. I feel as if it's over. I am turning now and leaving, going down the mountain. I feel totally drained, exhausted. Did I die?"

I channeled the answer we could both feel:

You went and found a place in nature, for your body was done. Your Spirit was lifted to a place of Knowing with the understanding that you would gain in consciousness through all your future lives until it was time again to come and bring the energy back out from the center of the Earth, through that rock to the world, almost a reverse of what you did in ancient times. You would know in the future when the world would again be ready for this Knowledge to be exploded back into humankind and not just held in a sacred way in the center of the Earth. You knew that you would come again for the second part of your agreement. So we ask you—are you ready to receive once again the encoding? This time it will be out from the Earth, through you to humanity and to nature.

She answered, "Mark, as I walked from the rock into nature, I was no longer physical. My body was filled, not with blood and muscle and bone... it was filled with Light. My skin held it in. I remember lying down and leaving. I also feel now, at this moment, that my body is filled with that very same Light or energy, and I feel I am ready to receive it."

Mark spoke through me:

This time Jonette will help you. In that life you did it alone; there was no one who dreamed what you dreamed and knew what you needed to know. Jonette is an apprentice to you. She is here to be with you and to help hold the power of this Wisdom, this Light, this encoding, that is now to be released. It comes through you and is gifted to nature and to all human hearts that are ready to receive it. Take yourself now to a higher dimension.

Sue was excited as she spoke, "There is a difference this time. Before my body contained the Light and it was very, very painful. Now the energies that are coming through me cannot be contained. It's as if the Knowledge is dispersing into eternity. It's flowing into all dimensions. It's such a soft and beautiful feeling! This isn't all the Knowing. This is only the part that is appropriate for us now. Am I correct Mark?"

Yes. It is only what can now be received by plants, minerals and most importantly by humanity. With this encoding, the true brotherhood of man and nature and stars will begin to be realized. The veils will be dropped. In many ways this is the remembering of the unified field; of the field in which everything is One. There is no longer separation and therefore amnesia between the human race and all the other parts of Oneness. It is an acknowledgment of the higher dimensions of non-separation. The world was not ready for more energy before. Now there are enough humans awake who can understand the higher purpose and can work with the Earth so that this rock alone does not have to hold all this Wisdom. There will be phases of activation in partnership with the Earth and stars, for this is a huge interdimensional opening.

"If I keep my eyes closed my body feels totally dissolved," Sue concluded. "I feel great, beautiful peace in my heart. It's strange. Everything seems so peaceful. It's as if I'm standing on this beautiful rock outcropping in the middle of the night with the moon shining down on me. The Earth is asleep and everything is at peace, but it's a peace beyond any I've experienced before. This I would love to share with the world."

You have, my guide answered.

Back in my living room, it took us a long while to speak. We had immersed ourselves into a past life event for which there could be no explanation. In recounting her experience, Sue related that the Light and energy she transferred through that portal into the Earth at Lake Titicaca couldn't be held by that place alone, but was somehow moving through the Earth's core to a mountain in the Himalayas.

I had no plans to physically travel to Peru. I thought I was only assisting a dear friend to die in peace by helping her complete her spiritual mission, one that even she didn't understand. Neither of us realized how prophetic this channeled session was.

8

Trekking the Himalayas

In the real world, as well as the spiritual planes, I'm an adventurer. I've ridden camels in the desert of India and in the Sahara near Timbuktu. I've been lost overnight in the wilderness of Australia, been hospitalized in Cairo, and have enjoyed visiting over 50 countries—so far. For the past fifteen years, I have been working with White Eagle and Mark to teach classes and do channeled readings for people. My favorite part of this work is combining my calling as a spiritual teacher and my love of adventure in order to lead groups to sacred sites around the world.

In 2003, a year before my trips to the Andes, I led a group on a spiritual journey to the Himalayas. My husband Ed, my seventeen year-old nephew John, five American friends, four Dutch women and a Swedish man set off to Nepal. Our goals were spiritual growth, planetary service, and the personal achievement of trekking for fourteen days to the Kalapathar summit. This 18,200-foot high, rocky peak provides clear vistas of Mount Everest and neighboring mountains and looks down on the Everest Base Camp.

A Blackbird Will Fly Above You

Before we left on our journey to Nepal, I met with my beloved Sue Burch at her small apartment. Even though she was quite weak from cancer and chemotherapy, Sue was eager to assist me in figuring out the higher spiritual purpose of our upcoming trip. She was convinced that the Himalayas were strongly connected to the Andes and especially to the inner work she had done nine months earlier, encoding energy into a megalith near Lake Titicaca. According to some, Lake Titicaca, high in the Andes between Peru and Bolivia is the female pole of the planet, and the area around Mount Everest in the Himalayas is the male pole. Sue also felt that the energies she experienced several years earlier in the center of a crop circle in England were directly connected to a mountain in the Himalayas. She asked questions and took notes as I channeled Mark. Most of the time she and I had similar visions and feelings, from which we pieced together a more complete understanding.

As soon as we asked what spiritual work our group was to do in Nepal, Sue and I were shown in meditation a monstrous cauldron of seething fire. It was as if we were gazing into the furnaced bowels of the Earth. The fiery, gaping entrance was guarded by a pair of gigantic, cosmic beings. At first, I couldn't tell if these guardians were Angels of the Light or dark spirits. Then I was told that this opening represented "The Gates of Hell." That disturbed me. Number one, I don't believe in hell, and two, I had no desire to hang around the doorway of the doomed. The vision was similar to the fire and brimstone stuff that I disagreed with in traditional Christianity.

Mark explained that all energy is created, both positive and negative, and persists into eternity unless it is consciously transformed. Humankind has forever been creating negative energy with thoughts, fears, hatred and struggles. Such energy is toxic and would have arrested spiritual evolution, except that the Earth, in order to protect us, stored it safely away at the root of the Himalayan Mountains. This hell that Sue and I were being shown was not a place to which humans would be condemned for their sins, but a place where the energetic result of humanity's negative thoughts and actions was stored until we humans had enough spiritual ability to transmute it. This would release planet Earth from the burden of having to hold this darkness protectively for humankind. The two cosmic beings we saw in our inner vision were good guys and their job was to keep the doors sealed from any beings who might release the negativity with the intent to do harm.

Our group's mission, which evidently we had accepted, was to go to this gate or portal and use the Light and the power of good to begin to release the darkness stored there. Mark told us that there was enough goodness to transmute the toxic negativity into higher, lighter frequencies. Knowing that I was in way over my head spiritually, I asked Mark meekly, "How will we know if we are successful in releasing the darkness stored under the Himalayan Mountains?"

A black bird will fly above you when your task is complete, came Mark's channeled reply. I hoped like heck that the Himalayas had plenty of black birds. Messing around with the Gates of Hell and failing didn't appeal to me.

Sue's Mountain: Ama Dablam

From the very beginning, our spiritual adventure to Nepal in April 2003 held unanticipated surprises. A rather frayed 18-seater plane from Ghorka Air ferried us out of Kathmandu to the airstrip at Lukla, in the Everest region. The runway, which is over 9,000 feet above sea level, is carved precariously out of the mountain itself. It is only 1,700 feet long, so short that it was more like landing on an aircraft carrier.

Pema,[9] our Sherpa guide, whom Ed and I had met the summer before on the summit of Colorado's highest peak, had our expedition team waiting for us in Lukla. We had two cooks, flown in from Kathmandu, three Sherpa guides and four cook-boys. Ten porters carried all the gear in baskets on their backs suspended by straps around their foreheads. Once we got to a higher altitude, we used yaks to carry some of the equipment.

In U.S. vernacular, "sherpa" has come to mean a trekking porter. In fact, Sherpa is a racial and cultural group made up of ethnic Tibetans, who, over 300 years ago migrated from Tibet to what is now the Everest region of Nepal. They practice a very traditional branch of Buddhism, incorporating the belief in a multitude of nature spirits. What I found fascinating is that every Sherpa's last name is Sherpa. For instance, our guide Pema's full name is Pema Dorji Sherpa. To make matters even more confusing to foreigners, a Sherpa child, no matter the gender, is given the first name depending on the day of the week of his or her birth.

After two days of a grueling, uphill hike, we camped at a site above Namche Bazaar, the biggest town in the Khumbu or Everest region and the Sherpa capital. For our first group meditation, twelve of us gathered in the dining tent before dinner. The thirteenth member of our group, my teenaged nephew John, had collapsed in our tent. He was so sick with stomach problems that he would have gladly taken a helicopter out of there and abandoned the entire climb. The rest of us perched on our campstools; our plastic mugs of steaming tea sat on the folding table in front of us.

I began channeling Mark who guided us in a meditation to connect with the mountains, nature, the local people, and each other. Halfway through, our peaceful state was shattered by an eruption of loud, obnoxious snoring! It seemed to come from the direction of one of our fellows, Larry Cooper. With my eyes closed, I tried to focus on bringing in Mark's words, ignoring the continued disruption. "How can a person even make that much noise?" I thought. Still convinced that it was Larry, I wondered, "Why doesn't someone hit him and wake him up?" We all tried valiantly to meditate in spite of the racket. The moment I finished channeling I popped open my eyes, staring in the direction of the sound. Larry was wide-awake, a grin across his face. In fact, everyone was awake—but the snoring continued! We opened up the tent flap to the dusky air. A shaggy head and big, brown eyes greeted us right outside the door; our culprit—a yak! His sonorous contribution to our meditation provided fodder for giggles every time we sat down in the dining tent.

Because of the need to acclimatize to the altitude, we hiked one or two days and then rested a day. One of those rest days was at Thengboche Monastery, said to be the highest monastery in Nepal. The repeated hiking up and down, at altitudes

Yak grazing

Ama Dablam mountain

over 13,000 feet made the day we arrived at the monastery an exhausting one. I had an altitude headache caused by cerebral edema that threatened to split my skull in two. We stopped to catch our breath at the outer gate of this Buddhist monastery. This gave us the opportunity to take in the unbelievably stunning Himalayan peaks instead of carefully watching our feet on the rocky trail. We gazed at the most majestic mountain I had ever seen, which stood regal and solitary above the valley. Ralph Johnson, a fellow trekker with scores of pockets everywhere, a map, compass, or GPS instrument in each one, knew the mountain's name as I pointed to it. "That is Ama Dablam, a very nice mountain," Ralph told me in his Swedish accent.

"A nice mountain. That is the understatement of the century!" I thought. In fact, Ama Dablam is said to be one of the five most magnificent peaks in the world. At just under 22,500 feet, this mountain reigned unparalled in her beauty, in a cohort of otherwise extraordinary mountains. She was robed in the pure snows that fall year-round on her shoulders. She was the crown, with two smaller peaks flanking her like courtiers. Ama means Mother, Dablam means necklace. To me it meant the bosom of the Mother Earth. She stood as a Himalayan Goddess; Mount Everest by comparison was merely the tallest mountain there.

Suddenly, as I stared at Ama Dablam, I had a burst of recognition: "This is Sue's mountain! This is the one she sent the energies to during her past life as a high priest in Peru! This is where the power came when the rock mountain near Lake Titicaca could no longer hold the energy she was transmitting into it!" In that instant I also knew that this was the same mountain that Mark had warned contained the doorway to the Gates of Hell.

This was the place where we were supposed to do the special meditation process for healing the Earth of the negative energies stored in the core of the Himalayas. Mark had told me that now was the time to use our consciousness and the high spiritual energies available to release negativity, and to replace it with vibrations of Divinity. I didn't know how we would accomplish this, only that it was our job.

Our group at the Thengboche Monastery

Meditation in the Monastery meadow

Trekking the Himalayas

It was early spring. Barely blooming rhododendrons fringed the meadow and the land around Thengboche Monastery. The thin air held the distinctive smells of yak dung and wood fires. Young, maroon-robed monks struggled to lay a water pipe. A sense of timeless well-being prevailed. In a yak pasture beside the monastery, our trekking group gathered to do our spiritual work. The spectacular peaks of Everest, Lhotse, Nuptse and Ama Dablam held dominion above us. I channeled Mark in a meditation that took us on a mystical journey to the rocky root of Ama Dablam. There we witnessed the Gates of Hell that Mark had shown Sue and me back in Denver. Clothed in Light and protected by the ancient Masters of the White Brotherhood, we faced the darkness. I once asked White Eagle, "How strong is the darkness?"

His answer: *Darkness is as strong as your fear of it.* We had no fear. Those of us with the gift of inner sight witnessed the opening of a portal deep within the Earth and the transmutation into Light of the negativity stored there. By assisting in the energetic healing of the Earth, we helped heal ourselves that morning. But had we accomplished our spiritual mission?

Mark told us before we left for Nepal that the sign to know we had successfully released and transmuted the negative energies at the Gates of Hell would be a black bird flying overhead. We must have completed our mission with flying colors because all of nature conspired to celebrate our accomplishment. While we sat meditating in that high Himalayan field, we could barely hear Mark's channeled words for all the ravens around us! At no other time on the journey had we seen so many ravens. A flock of at least twenty big, black and boisterous birds swooped above us, perched on nearby branches, or curiously tiptoed within inches of our tarp. The Masters wanted to assure us that even though we didn't know what we were doing, we did it!

Our next meditation in the meadow brought us to experience a 'stargate' or powerful energy portal, also within the core of Ama Dablam. After we had helped release the negativity held there, we felt a strong presence of cosmic love. We were enveloped in a wordless and holy rapture that transported us far beyond the limits of this life. Infinite bliss poured through us, awakening dormant seeds of grace within each of us. We accessed a transcendental doorway that connected our hearts to cosmic goodness. Mark explained that the energy gateway of Ama Dablam is one of the main receiving centers of higher dimensional frequencies for the Earth's energy meridians or grid. This is the Himalayan meditation that activated our hearts to a higher level of experience:

Om Mani Padme Hum

Allow the chant to take you on the wings of sound into the mountain—Ama Dablam. There is a stargate there in the fifth dimension.[10] You'll know it by feeling the essence of geometric forces and patterns. Move yourself powerfully into the heart of those geometries. Deep in the great mountain Ama Dablam, there is a transmitting and receiving station for energies and stargates outside the Milky Way.

Move your awareness into the energy transmissions themselves. You may experience them as patterns. You might even get a sense of the source that transmits to this place from outside the galaxy. Then this portal, in turn, transmits to the Earth and atmosphere. We ask you to adjust your own vibrations to be in harmony with the patterns that are being continuously transmitted here. That will put you in alignment with the energy for transformation that comes to the Earth.

You might call this Himalayan portal the Mother Stargate—the conductor of all the other stargates and portals on the planet. They all communicate to this main stargate. Simply ask to align and resonate yourself, your being, your knowing to the activity here. It is important that we open this today—on the full moon. It will continue to touch you and to calibrate itself to you. Whenever you feel the speed of transformation going too quickly and creating disharmony, imbalance, or chaos in your life, connect back to this central transmitting station. Recalibrate yourself back to this for this is the master fifth dimensional stargate on Earth. Once you are aligned to it, the chaos and disharmony will seem to melt away.

Feel how important this is in conjunction with the release work you just completed. There is nothing else you need to do. We needed to introduce you to this place so you can find it, resonate to it, adjust yourself to it, and listen to it. The integration will take place forever. When you have difficulties climbing these mountains, and in life, this connection will make your ascent easier.

I still feel a physical movement in my heart when I connect with the power of this awesome mountain. The most significant gift from the journey is that the higher frequencies now resident in my physical heart are able to be a catalyst for automatically activating the hearts of others.

Thengboche Monastery

During our stay at Thengboche Monastery, we joined the Buddhist monks in the unheated, main temple for their chanting, once early in the morning and again at 3 o'clock in the afternoon. We sat on the bare floor bundled in our high-tech alpine gear, teeth chattering in the bone-numbing cold. The community of monks, each clothed in a simple, woolen robe, seemed impervious to the environment as they gently rocked to and fro during their trance-like recitations. After the prayers, one joyful, young monk laughingly mocked Larry Cooper, who, like all of us was wrapped to the hilt in warm layers. The monk fully opened up his robe to reveal that he wore nothing at all underneath it!

While we camped there, we had the good fortune to have an audience with the High Lama of the entire Everest region, the Abbot of the Monastery, Ngawang Tenzin Jangpo. It was fortunate because he had only returned from wintering in

Kathmandu the same day as we arrived. Our guide, Pema, who knows the Abbot well, was able to arrange the meeting.

Rimpoche Ngawang Tenzin Jangpo

The Abbot was born in Namche Bazaar, Nepal to a Tibetan family in 1935. As a youngster he insisted that his real home was at the Thengboche Monastery. He was taken to meet with a High Lama in Tibet who recognized the boy as the reincarnation of the founder of Thengboche Monastery. The boy was given the name Ngawang Tenzin Jangpo and spent years of study and training with great teachers in Tibet. Known as the Thengboche Rimpoche, he is the spiritual leader of the Sherpas. The title "Rimpoche" is given to a person who is the acknowledged reincarnation of a previous Great Teacher or Master. Not all Abbots are Rimpoches and not all Rimpoches live in monasteries.

In Nepal and Tibet there is a beautiful custom to show respect when meeting someone new. For instance, Krishna Lohani,[11] our friend and tour guide in Kathmandu greeted us at the hotel with an age-old ceremony whereby he draped a white or gold silky, kata scarf around each of our necks. Then with his hands together in a prayer position, he bowed his head repeating the universal blessing and greeting "Namaste," translated as "My divinity greets your divinity." Our kata scarves served us well. We were instructed to present the Abbot or High Lama of Thengboche with a silk scarf with a few dollars or some rupees folded in it as a donation. The Abbot then blessed us, one at a time, and returned the now sanctified scarf back to us. My husband, Ed, and many of us were in tears merely being in the Rimpoche's presence. Although he spoke little English, his radiant smile penetrated all language barriers.

The Everest Base Camp Trek

Our typical day on the trek started with tea served in our individual tents by the cook-boys at 6 a.m. This was followed by a bowl of warm water for washing, although it was usually too cold in the morning to feel like washing any more than the essentials. We packed up our duffle bags and went to breakfast. Meanwhile, the porters took down our tents and loaded up their baskets and yaks with all the gear. Breakfast was cereal and often eggs. By 8 a.m., we started hiking, dressed in all types of layers to keep out the cold. Of course, once we got walking and the sun came over the peaks, it became so warm we had to make numerous stops to remove layers. Due to the altitude and the varying abilities within our group, we proceeded slowly. The trails were rocky and steep, winding through hills and valleys. "Himalayan flat," Pema called it, because all the hiking up and down resulted in no net gain of altitude. The most treacherous part of the trail was watching out for the loaded yak trains. We were reminded to walk on the inside of the trail so we wouldn't be pushed off the side of the mountain by a yak with faulty brakes.

At the lower altitudes, the footpaths wound through tiny villages of terraced farms and trekker's lodges. April coaxed out some flowers and blossoms on the fruit trees. People plowed by hand, stooping to plant potatoes, cabbage and greens. On most days, we hiked for three hours then rested along the trail while lunch was prepared by our cooks over kerosene camp stoves. We generally trekked another three or four hours each afternoon. During midday except at the highest elevations, it was warm enough to wear shorts and light shirts. However, by midafternoon the clouds rolled in, bringing frigid, wet weather. We stopped along the track to add back all the warm layers of clothing which we had shed earlier.

Nephew John, Ed and Jonette, Ama Dablam in the background

By the time our group dragged into camp each night, the porters had already erected our tents. We became very lazy campers. We traded in our dusty trekking clothes for somewhat cleaner and warmer camp clothes. Our much anticipated teatime was at 4:30. Dinner was at 6:30 in the dining tent. We were all too cold and tired to stay up much past 8:00 p.m. Since I loathe the cold, I was happy to have brought the warmest, down sleeping bag I could find. On several nights of heavy snow, we woke to the sounds of our tents being thrashed by the Sherpas. They were clearing off the snow so the tents wouldn't collapse on top of us.

We trekked a total of fourteen days on the roundtrip between Lukla and the Everest Base Camp. Our highest camp at the tiny settlement of Lobuche was 17,000 feet. Our group spanned in age from seventeen to the late fifties, with most people over forty-five. We represented all levels of fitness, no one with alpine experience. We fell into a rhythm of life on the trail, fitting in meditations when we could.

As might be expected, our group suffered various illnesses. Most of us had some sort of intestinal problem; one became quite serious. We had to leave Ralph Johnson, a fit and strong man from Stockholm, at Pheriche, a village with a clinic that serves the Everest expeditions. He was better after antibiotics and a few days of rest.

Fortunately, one member of our group, Yolanda Groeneveld, was a medical doctor with a specialization in acupuncture. She was always busy making tent calls. Pema, our lead Sherpa guide, watched with wary interest as Yolanda used acupuncture to treat altitude sickness, intestinal problems and leg pains. When Pema's own dry, hacking cough worsened, Yolanda offered to treat him with her needles. Fear flashed on his face as he stammered, "No thank you. I'll be just fine."

We kidded Pema mercilessly, "You mean you've *summited Mount Everest* three times and you're afraid of these tiny needles!" He wouldn't capitulate, so we shared our cough drops and vitamin C.

It was a personal victory for each of us who painstakingly climbed those last few rocky feet to Kalapathar's 18,200-foot summit! From the top, we looked down onto the Everest Base Camp spread out like colored specks on the Khumbu glacier below. We were there for the 50th anniversary celebration of the first ascent by Edmund Hillary and Tenzing Sherpa. Large numbers of climbers from around the world were camped on the ice. Across the valley loomed the highest point on the planet, Mount Everest. Its white crown was majestically silhouetted against an impossibly blue sky. A perpetual pennant of snow blasted off its peak.

Khumbu glacier, nearing Everest

Mt. Everest from the summit of Kalapathar

The Yeti

From then on, the trek brought us gratefully back down to a lower elevation, though not without several more tough ascents. Our breathing became easier, our appetites returned, our headaches diminished. By then we were seasoned veterans of the trail. On our return trip to Lukla we stopped overnight at Pema's village of Khumjung, where his wife ran a small guest-house as part of their home.

Khumjung is noted for the yeti or abominable snowman skull kept in a padlocked, glass case in the local monastery. We paid our rupees to have a look at the skull. It wasn't much to see, a lot of black hair and some dried skin. If you were skepti-cal about the existence of the fabled Himalayan yeti or ape-man, you would remain skeptical even after seeing this evidence. But after hearing an amazing story from my nephew John, I had reason to believe in the existence of an elusive spe-cies of bipedal primates, known here as yetis.

In every society there are conventions, norms of belief around which people group themselves. Stray too far from the mean and you run the risk of being labeled a deviant, or at least a little eccentric. This works pretty well most of the time. We can simply choose not to see something or at least not believe it, if the acknowledgment of it threatens to cast us into the outer fringes of the bell curve of what is considered normal. I was thinking about this as I listened to John tell me an incredible tale about what he discovered in the wild Colorado high-coun-try the previous summer.

He and his Dad, my brother John, were doing an endurance hike in the Rockies between Redstone and Aspen, covering twenty-six hard, mountain miles, over three passes, all without stopping. As sometimes happens in the mountains, the dashed line that seemed so clear on the topographical map ceased to exist in the alpine reality.

John described it: "We were way off the regular trail, making our own path in the middle of nowhere, when we noticed a big, old stump that looked like it had been pushed over. The dirt around it was soft, and pressed in it was a *huge,* human-like, bare footprint... *Big Foot*! The footprint was clearly defined, even to the toes. We looked around for other prints, or tufts of hair snagged on a branch, but didn't see anything. We put our walking stick next to the print for perspective and took a couple of photos. The print was over 18 inches long!"[12]

I was excited by John's story! I love the apparently impossible becoming probable, and the probable becoming proven! It was marvelous to think that there are gigantic, hairy, and unbelievable creatures that have coexisted with us, and yet with all our science, we have missed them. In fact, such things usually remain overlooked until someone breaks from the conventional path. It reminded me of something a friend once said, "I love to wake up in the morning to find out that I've been absolutely wrong about something I've always believed."

The Ama Dablam Heart Activation

As we flew back to Kathmandu and the world of roads, electricity and toilets, we were all a little wistful about what the Himalayas had given us. In Kathmandu we were blessed to spend time with another reincarnated Tibetan Lama, Choki Nima Rimpoche. He spoke English, delighting us with his clear wisdom and light-heartedness. I personally felt a special soul connection to this Enlightened Master. Several times since meeting him, I have felt him come to me in my meditation, to greet me with his blessing.

Our trek together through the Himalayas bonded our group into a wonderful family, a team. Everyone supported everyone else with expressions of encouragement and compassion. Living in the moment with kindness was our greatest learning. We were well cared for by each other, our expedition crew, and Pema—our head Sherpa, who has become a friend. In the glorious mountain, Ama Dablam, we found the place to which Sue, in her life as an Incan High Priest, had sent energies of wisdom and power, when the massive rock at Lake Titicaca could no longer contain it all.

Just a few weeks after returning home to Colorado from Nepal, I attended the Crimson Circle's monthly spiritual gathering in the Colorado foothills. Over a cup of hot tea at the break, I introduced myself to Josh Roach, who was also new to the gathering. Still full of my trip to Nepal, I jabbered, "I just got back from a spiritual expedition to the base of Mt. Everest… There was an incredibly beautiful mountain called Ama Dablam. It has a cosmic stargate portal that activated our hearts into higher levels of love and light…" I would have continued talking, but as soon as I mentioned Ama Dablam and the heart activation to this complete stranger, I could *feel* the energies jump from my heart to his! My eyes opened wide in amazement, "You feel this too, don't you?" I asked him, shocked.

Josh's hand sprang to his heart as an incredulous look crossed his face. I held my breath, waiting for his confirmation. "Yes, yes, something *is* happening to my heart… but… how did *you* know?"

For that question, I had no response. How could I *not* have noticed? The shift in Josh's heart was just so *huge*!

Bewildered, Josh puzzled over how a bubbly stranger *knew* what was happening in his chest, while I was ecstatic that I could transmit the heart initiation just by mentioning the name of the mountain!

Later Josh described his experience. "When the stargate portal activation moved from Jonette's heart chakra into mine; I knew for the first time what my life's work was. My whole body flushed with goose bumps, my hair follicles tingled. I could feel the cellular structures of my body resonating to the most robust, delicious, and inviting energetic vibration. It was an energy I hadn't experienced in this incarnation, but one that caused me to re-member."

Since that afternoon, Josh and I have become spiritual buddies. Sixteen months later he was one of the twenty on the Inca Trail in the Andes. Since that first experience with Josh, I have transmitted the powerful Ama Dablam Heart Activation to hundreds of people in my classes, on teleconferences and through webcasts. In turn, people are able to use their intention to transfer these high energies of love into the hearts of others.

Sue

I had so much to share with Sue Burch about our experiences in Nepal. She was excited to hear about our expedition since she was with me when Mark told us about the "Gates of Hell" portal in the Himalayas and our group's mission to open it into the Light. Weak with cancer, my dear friend now resided in a hospice.

I brought her my silk kata scarf, blessed by the High Lama of the Everest region. I had the strong feeling that Sue and he were connected somehow in a past life. I pushed her out to the garden in her wheelchair, a blanket over her thin legs, her blue eyes shining brightly from her hairless head. I showed her my photo of the Buddhist Abbot of Thengboche Monastery. She grasped the scarf to her face, looked at the photo, and broke into the sweetest smile. "He was once a wonderful husband," was all she said.

As we poured through my Nepal photos together, Sue was curious about everything. I told her how the ravens surrounded us when we meditated. When we turned to the photo of Ama Dablam, I explained that in our meditation we cleared the negative powers at the mountain's base, and afterward, experienced a powerful portal of expanded heart energies. She was moved by the grand peak's beauty, confirming that this was indeed the mountain she had seen in her vision. It was the counterpart to the stone mountain in the Andes that she and I had visited in our consciousness journey the year before.

In addition to the kata scarf, I brought Sue, the woman-who-talks-to-rocks, a small, ordinary looking stone from near Ama Dablam. She sent her daughter Becky out to have it set into a necklace. For the last months of Sue's life, the golden scarf was by her bedside in the hospice and the Himalayan stone was on a chain around her neck.

9

Peru Calling

ue died a few months later, in August 2003, a great loss to me and all who knew her. Sue Burch faced death unafraid, looking forward to finally getting answers to all her spiritual and metaphysical questions. Although she never made it physically to Lake Titicaca, the place in the highlands of Peru and Bolivia where she felt she had important spiritual work to do, she and I were content that we had done what we could during our solstice meditation the year before.

At the time of Sue's passing, I had no intention to go to the Andes. It didn't matter to me that the energies Sue encoded into a rock at Lake Titicaca had a direct link to Ama Dablam, or that many people believed the Himalayas were energetically linked to Lake Titicaca. The next adventure I had in mind was to lead a spiritual group to Africa to climb that continent's highest mountain, Mount Kilimanjaro. However, the Universe had other plans. When logistics didn't fall into place for my dream trip to Kilimanjaro in Tanzania, friends encouraged me to lead a group to Machu Picchu. "Everyone does trips to there," I argued, "and I don't like to do what everyone else does." The fact was, I had been to Peru once before and I wanted to do something new.

In my early twenties, I fell in love with another graduate student. Gustavo was from South America. So for Christmas 1980, I traveled to Cali, Colombia to be with him and his family. The visit and the relationship didn't go well, so I popped into a travel agency, asking naively, "Since I am already in Colombia, where else should I go in South America?"

"Many people like this place," the agent replied, pointing to a wall calendar featuring a dazzling photograph of Machu Picchu. I had never seen or heard of it before.

"Yes, I'll go there," I answered. On my own at age twenty-five, I journeyed to Ecuador and then to Peru on a whim. Even then Machu Picchu's magic pulled me to her in a most illogical way. However, this time, 2004, would be different. I would learn that I have a very special connection to an Andean shaman. I would spontaneously remember past lives and see into other dimensions.

Your Andean Brother

Once I relented and agreed to organize a group tour to South America, I contacted my friend, Asa Levine, in Stockholm. She led trips to Peru annually and highly recommended her tour guide and travel agent, Mallku. "Nothing bad ever happens when Mallku is around," she reassured me.

I emailed Mallku Arévalo in Cuzco. His itinerary fit my plans; his price was fair. He is also on a spiritual path so as an added bonus he was willing to conduct special Andean ceremonies. His emails to me were straightforward and clear, signed sweetly, "Your Andean Brother." His website was well done.[13] His photo showed a strong aquiline nose and the high cheekbones of a Peruvian Indian, thirty-something, quite good-looking in an indigenous way. His straight, black hair fell well below his shoulders. The photo showed him dressed like a shaman, wearing a headband and ceremonial costume with the emerald green mountains of Machu Picchu in the background.

Mallku, an Andean shaman

He had published several books on Machu Picchu and Andean spirituality. He was also an artist and professional photographer. I was convinced. He would be our guide in Peru.

Deep within me something else was stirring. I could *sense* Mallku. It started when I first saw his photo on his website. His *energy* came to me when I read his emails. He was prompt and thorough in responding to my endless logistical inquiries. There was never anything personal in the correspondence yet I felt powerfully and personally connected to him. When he signed "Your Andean Brother," I knew his soul! He truly *is* my brother. My heart was opening in a most surprising way. I had never experienced anything like the feelings I had for Mallku. It wasn't like me to have a crush. I began kidding with my friends that I was in love with our Peruvian tour guide, whom I had never met. Did I say that I had just turned fifty and was happily married? I told my husband Ed what was happening. "I promise not to run off with him," I said as we both laughed.

10

The Fifth Buddha

en months after we returned from Nepal and six months before we were scheduled to leave for South America, my father, John Crowley, passed away. His death brought another piece to the puzzle of the Incan prophecy which I only understood in hindsight.

At the best of times, Dad expected to be waited on. At the worst of times, as he recuperated from heart by-pass surgery, he became relentlessly imperial. "Bring me my cane. Put my peaches there on the little table. No! Not there! See, where I'm pointing. Where is my testing kit? Clean my glasses. Clean my dentures." He hardly ever said please and he rarely said thank you. Yet, Dad came to his regal bearing honestly. He had an IQ that left merely smart people far behind in his wake, remembered everything he had ever heard or read, and was used to being the boss—Chairman Crowley of this Board and that. On first name basis with governors and senators, he was sought after for his wisdom and soaring vision in land planning, urban transportation, community building and more.

Mostly, Dad was too busy to do the usual things fathers did with their kids. Because of that, my siblings and I seesawed between resentment and forgiveness. Yet we always loved and respected him as a visionary, a man with compassion for the world, a man with larger-than-life integrity and commensurate pride. Dad wasn't religious and never talked about spiritual things. He accepted all people for who they were and actually endorsed the fact that I was a channel, occasionally sending a friend or acquaintance to me for readings. He asked White Eagle questions himself when Mom was dying of cancer two years earlier.

It was February 26, 2004 when we got the word from Dad's in-home caregiver that he had taken a bad turn and was rushed by ambulance to the hospital in Tucson. Two brothers, three sisters and I flew to Arizona, not knowing that a systemic, staph infection was chewing up his life. He died on February 29, Leap Day, without ever coming out of the coma. He was seventy-four. While we were sitting vigil at Dad's bedside, a group of his friends convened on the top of the desert mesa Dad loved. Chief Woableza, a Lakota medicine man who had come to know and respect my father, conducted a ceremony for Dad's transition.

After leaving the hospital, my family drove to the southern Arizona town of Tubac, where Dad had lived. We gathered at the home of his close friends, Todd and Lisa Harrison, to hug, mourn and have a glass of Merlot—Dad would have ordered the red wine himself if he could have. Chief Woableza was there too. He made a medallion necklace for Dad out of beads and a flat, round, golden shell. He presented it to me, as the eldest child. According to Native tradition, the necklace signifies a leader. It ensured that Dad would be recognized as a Chief on the other side. I cherished the precious gift.

Lisa, her eyes as puffy as mine, needed to talk. "Jonette, when Todd and I were speaking to John he told us that his shoulders were getting heavy because of the weight of all his chakras."

"Dad knew what a chakra was?" I was astounded by the thought.

"Yes," Lisa continued, "He then told us that he was the Fifth Buddha. I thought you would want to know."

Shocked, I stammered questions, "My father said that? Was he serious? Was he drinking?" She assured me that he was quite clear in his assertion.

Bewildered, I thought, "How did Dad even know there was more than one Buddha?" From my time in Nepal, I knew that there were twelve acknowledged Buddhas, which means Enlightened One. This wasn't commonly known. My mind raced, "When did Dad start believing in past lives? I had never heard him mention Buddhism or any spiritual philosophy. How could this be?"

Suddenly, I flashed back to a long-forgotten experience in the late 1980s when rebirthing and past life regressions were the tools de jour of the human consciousness movement. I had joined some friends for a weekend workshop by Henry Leo Bolduc, a noted hypnotist, author and international teacher.[14] Henry presented an easy process to lead a whole roomful of people to discover a significant individual past life and see what lessons could be brought forward into today.

Eighty of us followed Henry's soothing voice as he instructed us to relax, regressing backward through this life, then to the time before we were born. I recalled being directed through a blue mist until we were supposed to find ourselves plopped in the middle of one of our past lives. Henry asked us to open our inner eyes and imagine looking down at our feet and legs in that previous incarnation. Mine were bare, skinny and brown. My clothes were white homespun. I was fourteen or so, a boy in a great temple or hall in what seemed to be India, a scribe, sitting at the side of a platform busily writing down the words of a Great Teacher. There were hundreds of people, all sitting cross-legged on the floor listening to the guru. My gaze moved over the audience to the dais. As I looked at the guru, I recognized him as my father in this life!

The shocking realization that my Dad had been a great teacher and I had been his scribe jolted me right out of that past life, back to my chair in Henry's class. How could this be? It was not quite the John Crowley I knew. That past life recognition lay buried in my memory until the night Dad died.

I came back to the present with Lisa. At another time I might have replied to her, "Hmm, that's interesting," and finished my glass of wine. However, that night, with Dad dead only three hours, I *heard* what Lisa said. I *knew* that Dad told her the truth: he *was* the Fifth Buddha. I knew it because I remembered him from that lifetime!

Incremental learning, knowledge that merely expands on what you've always believed is nothing compared to knowledge whose very presence renders meaningless all previous ideas.

This is what happened to me regarding the idea of enlightenment once I accepted as true that John Robert Crowley, with all his human foibles, could have been a Buddha. Prior to this, my merry, new-age belief was that we work toward some level of personal enlightenment, and once achieved, we're cut from the chains of karma. We are somehow perfected; spending eternity being prayed to, or in some other way, serving the still-striving masses. I had always thought that enlightenment was a one-way ticket out of our human suffering. So why did Dad come back to Earth and why wasn't he perfect? Perhaps we need to let go of everything we think we knew about enlightenment. What if we can be light and dark, great and flawed and still be a Buddha? This was just the beginning of my understanding that we are all much more than we think we are.

11

Dreaming Path

une 2004. We had been back from Everest for a year and would be leaving for a spiritual adventure tour to Peru in mid-August. I was in Amsterdam teaching a workshop called, "Universal Enlightenment: Initiation into Power." The name was suggested by my spirit guide Mark, who picked that title for a reason that would soon become apparent to me. During the workshop, I channeled a meditation process that Mark called "The Dreaming Path." The term is used by Australian Aboriginals to describe the sacred trail they walk as their way of praying and connecting to Mother Earth. Each clan follows the route of its ancestors; men and women always walk different paths. Walking along their special, sacred path takes the people into a deeper part of themselves and into the vast dimensions of 'Dream Time.' Australian natives, and most indigenous people, see themselves as part of the Earth and the entire universe in a way most of us find difficult to comprehend.

I remembered an encounter I had with some Aboriginal women in 1992. I led a group to Australia's Outback to learn from the native people who lived near Ayers Rock or Uluru. We sat in the powdered, red dirt around the women's fire, asking questions about their spirituality. This strident group of Aboriginal women tried to enlist our support to fight the proposed construction of a dam on one of their sacred rivers. The section of the river that was to be dammed was on their ancient dreaming trail. They explained that the Australian government just didn't understand. "The sacred river *is* our body. If the river's flow is stopped, we will die," one elder said grimly. There was a true sense of terror as they described their situation. As we listened, we felt a kinship with these people of Australia's desert center; we began to understand the importance of their dreaming path and our true connection to the Earth.

Sunday morning in the Amsterdam workshop, Mark guided us on a dreaming path of consciousness. I channeled a series of destinations that we visited in our meditative journey. Some of the places were physical and related to the Earth—such as the root of Ama Dablam in the Himalayas, or beneath Lake Titicaca in the Andes. Some were multidimensional—imaginary stops such as the magnetic center of the Milky Way. Together, we wove our awareness through a cosmic version of the Aborigine's prayer path.

When Mark finished guiding us around the universe, we were supposed to return our awareness to our bodies. I've come back easily from distant meditative journeys thousands of times before, but this time was different. On my way back to normality, I reached a sharp fork in the road. One way was the path to the same old me. The other was the path to a whole new me. It seemed that I was being presented with a direct path to enlightenment, a goal I had always pursued. But was I ready? I had been a spiritual *seeker* for so long, was I ready to abruptly become a *finder*? Was I ready to confidently choose what I had always wanted?

Of course, I *thought* I was ready. The choice itself wasn't hard to make. But *how* would I be different? *Who* would I be? Did I need to let go of my personality? If so, how do I act? It was a complete impasse. I wanted to move to the new, improved, more enlightened Jonette but I couldn't figure out the first step. The part of me that takes action was gone. So I sat empty and numb. I could feel my face become vacant. This concerned the class who had finished the meditation and were patiently waiting for me to return from the channeling space and continue to teach.

Without opening my eyes, I dismissed the class for an

extended lunch. They filed out, probably looking over their shoulders at the change in their usually animated teacher. I sat unmoving for an hour and a half. Several friends came back from lunch early to see if I needed anything. With eyes still closed and a face that now shined with deep contentment, I heard myself reply, "I am perfect." And at that moment, I *knew* I *was* perfect! Grasping my perfection was what it took to break the impasse! I could move again.

In that moment, I realized that enlightenment isn't earned, learned, or given. It is *chosen*. When the participants returned from lunch, a different person sat in the same chair in front of the room. I held them all in a space of infinite love. I was softer and stronger. It surprised me how much of my personality was left after this remarkable shift. I realized that our personality is a means of self-expression. It can express either our soul or our ego. We choose at every moment which it will be.

My previous spiritual initiations had taken place privately, with the admonishment not to tell anyone until it was time for me to initiate others. So why did this breakthrough happen so publicly, while fifty people watched me? Because I was *supposed* to tell. Because they were ready to choose too.

I used to think of someone with an ego as a person pretending to be *greater* than she is. After that experience, I realized the more dangerous side of ego is pretending to be *less* than the greatness we are. Perhaps our reticence and humility are the ego's last stand in trying to control us as we march forward to our greatness. What kind of leaders are we in this new world if we listen to our ego cautioning smallness? We don't need to be taught or healed. We simply must *choose* to move forward into the miraculous. I know it was this spiritual breakthrough in Amsterdam that set the stage for what would happen to me in the Andes just two months later.

12

The Secret of the Andes

hile I was in Holland, my friend Berdine DeVisser, who had been with us in the Himalayas and who would go with us to South America, gave me her copy of a dog-eared paperback book from 1961, *The Secret of the Andes*.[15]

George Hunt Williamson, claiming to be the Prior of a monastery hidden in a remote valley of Peru, wrote the book using the pen name, Brother Philip. I was intrigued by the book's amazing legends, and by the theories that have launched much speculation and countless expeditions to search for the mysterious monastery.

It all began more than 30,000 years ago. Before the now-lost civilization of Atlantis reached its height in the Atlantic Ocean, there was a continent in the Pacific known as Mu, often referred to as Lemuria. The massive planetary disturbance in 28,000 B.C., believed to be the period of the Great Floods, led to the final destruction and submergence of Lemuria. According to Williamson, in the land of Mu there was a Temple of Divine Light which housed a gigantic Golden Disc of the Sun. It held secret power from the early star races on Earth and represented the Great Central Sun, which itself symbolized the Creator. The Disc was a scientific instrument containing knowledge from the Universe, stored in magnetic fields or codes. Williamson wrote that due to the imminent submergence of Mu, the Master Teachers of Lemuria gathered the precious documents, Discs

The Eagle and the Condor

and crystal records preserved in the libraries there. The Master Teachers, who were part of the Great White Brotherhood, took the precious objects and spiritual teachings to different parts of the world where they established schools of this hidden wisdom. These schools were to remain a mystery; their teachings and meetings secret, until the inhabitants of the world were spiritually prepared for the knowledge to be disseminated.[16]

The Secret of the Andes states that Lord Aramu Muru, (sometimes spelled Amaru Muru or Meru) one of the seven Great Masters of Lemuria, was selected to take the sacred scrolls and the enormous Golden Disc of the Sun from the Temple of Divine Light to the Andes in order to save the objects from the eventual sinking of Lemuria. The book asserts that the Sun Disc was eventually placed in the Monastery of the Brotherhood of the Seven Rays in a hidden valley near Lake Titicaca. There it stayed until the Incan leaders and priests had achieved a level of spiritual development so that they could use the Disc to benefit all people. Williamson wrote, "The Inca Emperor at the time was a Divine Mystic or Saint, and he made a pilgrimage to the Monastery at Lake Titicaca, and there Aramu Muru gave the Disc to the Emperor."[17] He took the Disc to the Incan capital of Cuzco and placed it in the Coricancha or the Temple of the Sun where it was sacred to the Incas. With the Spanish arrival in 1533, in order to protect the Sun Disc from the invaders, it was removed from the Temple in Cuzco and returned to the Monastery of the Seven Rays near Lake Titicaca.

There is independent evidence that supports George Williamson's theory of a secret abbey hidden away in Peru. Sister Thedra, an American woman, was directed to the hidden monastery in the 1960s by the physical appearance of Jesus Christ, who introduced himself to her by his esoteric name "Sananda Kumara." Sister Thedra spent five years studying at the Monastery of the Seven Rays in the Andes. After returning to the United States, she founded the Association of Sananda and Sanat Kumara in Mount Shasta, California.[18]

The legends in this 1961 book by Williamson, known as Brother Philip, seemed so fantastic: the lost continent of

Lemuria; Lord Aramu Muru bringing a golden Sun Disc to Lake Titicaca; the Sun Disc containing divine truths stored in magnetic codes, later given to the Incas, then hidden again to protect it from the Spaniards. As incredible as it all sounded, could it be true? It certainly reminded me of the mystical, inner journey I did with Sue Burch on the June solstice two years earlier. She was a High Priest in an ancient lifetime standing on a rock mountain, pouring energy, wisdom, and power into the Earth near Lake Titicaca. In that past life, Sue did this to protect the ancient mysteries from foreign invaders. Sue felt the power go through the Earth to connect also with the mountains in the Himalayas. Was it the power and coded knowledge of the Sun Disc itself that Sue, in an Incan past life, transferred into the Earth? After reading Brother Philip's book, the adventurer in me silently hoped that our tour group would be led to the secret monastery in Peru to catch a glimpse of the Sun Disc of the Incas.

13

Grand Chief Woableza

 month before we left for South America, Dad's friend, Chief Woableza visited me in Denver. A Lakota Sioux from South Dakota, Woableza is a native healer, teacher, keeper of prophecies and member of the Council of Spiritual Elders of Mother Earth. The vision of this Council began in 1999 when Don Alejandro, a thirteenth generation Quiche Mayan High Priest, dreamed of connecting spiritual elders in South and Central America with those in North America. He sent the sacred Staff that his family had held for generations to help North American elders unite. The Staff guided the elders to unite with the respect, knowledge, wisdom and courage of the people.

In accordance with this vision, the first meeting of the elders occurred in the canyon lands of the Navajo Nation in New Mexico. At the second

Grand Chief Woableza

meeting, Woableza, whose given name is Robert LaBatte, was honored to be named as the second and youngest Grand Chief of the Council of Spiritual Elders of Mother Earth. The Council's goal was to seek out the prophecies of the indigenous people and bring them forth. They believed that now was the time to use the Native knowledge to create a new 500-year calendar, as many of the old ways of reckoning, including the famous Mayan Calendar were reaching their end times. An article on their website states: "Now, we must prepare for and take possession of the next 500 year journey just as our ancestors, wisdom keepers, time keepers, medicine people and elders did for us in accordance with the Great Laws and traditions."[19]

I had initially met Chief Woableza in Arizona in early 2002, two years before Dad's death. Several months after that first meeting, I had an amazing vision during a meditation. I saw myself in a circle of high spirit beings where I received a white robe or cape that was draped over my shoulders. I was told in that vision, "Woableza is your student." I didn't understand what that meant but assumed that he was to attend an upcoming workshop that I would be teaching. However, I understood that I should not contact Woableza to personally invite him or give him details about the seminar. My intuitive voice said, "He will know and will respond to the inner call." I didn't think that was possible, so I was amazed when Woableza phoned to say that he and his sister were driving to Colorado from Mississippi and would be at the class. He *really did* follow an inner call to be at my doorstep!

While Woableza was at our house, he told me more about the Council of Spiritual Elders of Mother Earth and their goal to create a new, multidimensional calendar to replace the Mayan one when it is supposed to end in the year 2012. A few weeks later, I emailed Woableza with an audacious message. I wrote him that I was to assist his group in creating the energies to help build the spiritual calendar for humankind's future. My fingers typed this offer absolutely in spite of myself. My mind was thinking, "How could you, Jonette, a white woman from suburbia, without a single drop of Native blood, have the gall to offer assistance in something you know absolutely nothing about to a group of acknowledged Native Spiritual Elders?" I pushed "Send" before my rational self could stop it. When Woableza's gracious reply came back, I knew that I had done the right thing and that somewhere in my greater self I must have known what I was doing.

Ceremony in the Yucatan

From 2002 until the summer of 2004, we heard little from Chief Woableza, as he was recuperating from a serious head injury. One evening in July 2004, just weeks before our expedition to Peru, Chief Woableza showed up at our house unexpectedly. Woableza is a master storyteller. He travels around the country performing sacred ceremonies and sharing stories of indigenous myths and legends. He is a gentle man, short of stature, soft-spoken and always smiling. No matter what challenges he faces in life, and he has had many, he greets each one with compassion and love. He arrived on a Monday night and so joined our weekly Mark meditation class. Many pieces fit together for me as he enthralled us with a magical story of how he had participated in an ancient ceremony led by a high priest of Incan descent:

I was invited to the Yucatan in Mexico for the Spring Equinox in 2003 to be part of a gathering of Native spiritual elders of the Americas. On the second day, a man from the Andes appeared amongst the people. He was dressed in the most awesome ceremonial clothing. You could tell he was a very important person because everything appeared perfect with him. Around him was a very wonderful and powerful Spirit. He wore huge, blue macaw feathers. He stood about five-foot eight but with the feathers, they made him appear seven feet tall. He said he was an emissary from an ancient path. In his homeland in Peru there are four high priests who remain hidden from the outside world. This man is one who is sent out to share knowledge with the world when the time is right. He told us that there was *going to be a very important ceremony in the next few days and he invited everyone who could come. Only seven of us went because we had only one van. I was one of the people who got to go.*

This Holy Man said he needed people to help with the ceremony. He had a whole intricate format of activity they needed to do. We were told that they had waited thousands of years to dance this ancient ceremony. We went to a Mayan site, Mayapan, not far from the famous pyramids and archeological site of Chichen Itza.

It was a beautiful place, perfectly restored. Some were to do a dance while four of us held the place for each of the Four Directions. I was honored to be one of the four. In the center the other people danced in two concentric circles; one group danced in one direction, while the others danced the opposite way. To me it was like someone twirling all the combinations to open a safe. It was an old, old ceremony and we could feel that every move we made was changing everything around us; and everything inside us was changing. It was so powerful!

Our Andean spiritual leader wore a large, circular disc of gold on his chest and a headdress of bright parrot feathers. At the end of the dance he said that we needed to take a sacred bundle up to the top of this very holy site. He explained that this is a Wellspring of Life that had not been opened for 2,000 years or more. Our ceremony was unlocking those sacred places. When the holy place was opened, people with spiritual sight saw a huge geyser coming out of the pyramid—reaching all the way to the blue sky! When this geyser hit the sky, the sky became like a domed glass shield covering the Earth. The water went all different ways like we just shot a hose up at glass, scattering the water in all directions.

We understood that this was Sacred Re-Seeding Water; to re-seed the Earth with the beautiful, powerful Water she con-

tained in the beginning. Now it is time for Earth to reclaim her power, to rebalance. Now is the time for people to be healthier, to live longer lives and to evolve. With our spiritual eyes we saw this geyser spread over our entire world. It was a very, very important ceremony that needed to be done. I was really in awe that I was there and participated. People may not believe this, but I am telling you this is a true thing that happened. So many great things have been happening all over the planet.

People there talked about the Prophecy of the Condor coming to the Eagle. Well, on one side of that pyramid is a very ancient, beautiful carving in stone of a great big Eagle... and on the other side is a great big Condor. They are walking toward each other. In the middle of these two is a man standing there. Where the man's head should be is huge block of stone, like someone intentionally left the head missing. What this says to me is that for a time while the people are split apart they will forget about whom they are and their purpose on Earth. This is depicted by the man walking around without a head. He does not recognize what is true in life, or the true things humans are supposed to do for the Earth and for all beings within our Universe. This is a very powerful image to see.

My own thought is that this man's head needs to be put back. This will show that now we know. It is time for us to know that we have all the greatest knowledge of the World and our Universe. We have been shown and given these things through many, many various ways. So this is a place where events have already been set into motion for what is soon coming... Thank you.

Woableza's words, especially about the Incan priest who wore a golden disc on his chest, intrigued me. His story brought to mind the legends about the Sun Disc of the Incas from Brother Philip's book. Somehow, I too had a spiritual connection with a golden Sun Disc.

Just two weeks before Chief Woableza showed up at our house to share these stories, I was a featured speaker at the "New Energy Conference" in Santa Fe. With the help of my guide Mark, I was able to create for the 350 people attending one of the holiest, most transcendent spaces of consciousness I've ever experienced. While I stood on the stage channeling Mark's words and the energies that enabled such power, I felt myself wearing a radiating disc of golden light on my chest! Since the Inca symbol of the sun had nothing to do with the words I was speaking, I dismissed it. In fact, I completely forgot about my personal experience of a sun disc until Woableza described the Andean priest.

The Wisdom of the Grandmothers

The last thing that Woableza shared with us that evening has haunted me ever since. He unrolled a three-foot by five-foot painting on canvas that was a copy of a mysterious petroglyph found in a cave on Navajo lands in New Mexico. The origin of the petroglyph predates Navajo history in the region. Though uncertain who drew it and what it means, the Navajo Elders guard it fiercely as a sacred site. Recently they gathered to pray and study the mean-ing of the ancient cave

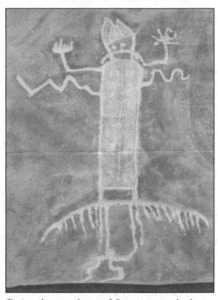

Painted copy of a pre-Navajo petroglyph

painting, knowing that it was a timeless prophecy to be unrav-eled. It was of a stick-figure human with no mouth, but had eyes, nose and what looked like a handlebar mustache pointing down, and a body made of two side-by-side, long, narrow rectangles. The arms were bent up at 90 degrees with the hands facing palms out, the fingers distinct. The figure was standing on and rooted to a partial sphere that probably represented the Earth. On his head was perched a double-pointed hat. The most evocative part of the drawing was a wavy line outside and to the left of the figure that hits the rectangle body in the chest area and an identical wavy line that intersects the right rectangle also at the chest.

Woableza explained that the native Elders say it is a prophecy in the form of a timeline that is read from top to bottom. They believed that the pointed hat, looking a little like the Pope's hat indicated the troubles in the Catholic Church regarding pedophiles and sexual abuse within the priesthood. The outreaching arms symbolized the worldwide reach of the scandal. The wavy lines hitting the two upright conjoined rectangles represented the two planes crashing into the World Trade Towers. The roots where the figure's feet go into the half-sphere looked to the Elders like flames coming out of a missile. This part of the message was of grave concern according to Woableza, because it represented eminent disaster or destruction.

Yet every prophecy of doom also contains an answer of hope, according to the Native Americans. If you look at the drawing upside down, the roots become the upward arcing branches of the Tree of Life. The double pointed hat symbolizes the breasts of women. Woableza's last words summed up the meaning that was communicated through the centuries to us today: "The women have the answers. In order for humankind to be saved, men must step aside and listen to the wisdom of the Grandmothers."

All the while Woableza spoke, pointing out the aspects of the painting and the understanding of its message given to him by the Navajo Elders, my brain kept saying, "That's not right! Their interpretation is incorrect!" I felt strongly that this prophecy was so much larger and more universal than events in our modern civilization. I couldn't imagine that an ancient oracle, painting a message in a cave for his descendants would care about our World Trade Towers or a scandal in our religious institution. Perhaps, because Woableza had just finished telling us the story of the Eagle and the Condor, I felt certain that the wavy lines weren't planes hitting the Towers at all but the coming together of two worlds symbolized by two birds flying into the figure's heart, healing the separate rectangles of his body—the Eagle and the Condor.

My mind argued vehemently with itself, "Who am I to disagree with the wisdom of the Navajo Elders who have deciphered the painting found on their sacred land? I must be wrong," I thought. "I've jumped to this conclusion only because the prophecy of the Eagle and the Condor is so fresh in my mind." As much as I tried to dismiss my version of the painting, I could never get it out of my thoughts. We'll never know for sure what the ancient cave artist intended to convey, but I now see this episode as a personal test. "Am I willing to trust my instincts even if they run counter to the words of authorities?"

If I really listened to Woableza's summation, the painting itself was giving me guidance. "The women have the answers… we men must step aside and listen to the wisdom of the Grandmothers."

14

Preparing for Our Mission

hen Woableza finished speaking to our class that night, I called in White Eagle to channel guidance on the significance of the work we were to do in Peru, and to find out more about Chief Woableza's connection to the people of the Andes. It was one of the strongest and most powerful spaces from which I had ever channeled. I had to lift my consciousness beyond my normal limits in order to hold the energy and form the words. I hardly recognized my own voice. This sometimes happens when I must speak with great truth and not allow any of my personality to get in the way of the translation. As White Eagle spoke, I saw a vision and felt the intense power of four giant beings—the Keepers of the Four Directions of the Incas. It was truly as if all four of them had *physically* entered the living room! It seemed so real; they *were* with us. I later learned that the Incan Empire was known as Tahuantinsuyo, or Four Lands of the Sun.

This is White Eagle. We speak for the Brotherhood of White. This is a Council meeting, you all are invited. Twice the man you know as Woableza lived in the Andes; once before the great explosion that tore the world apart, once after. Before the great explosion, he understood the magic and power of alchemical gold. This was a highly evolved society, all remnants of which

are gone under the sea. The second time he was of the Condor
People. He was the guardian for two portals that have not been
re-activated. It is now time they are reawakened and opened.
One of the purposes of your group's journey to Peru is to
rebalance the Earth's core. There is a magnetic wobble in our
Mother now that must be healed. The calendar that you seek
will not be possible until the Earth is steadied. You must also
open the two portals. This will begin to bring in the energies of
the new calendar. When the serpent leaves the den, the healing
must be complete. The timing is of GREAT IMPORTANCE.

White Eagle's message was incredibly enigmatic, but
because of the power by which it came I knew it was true and
needed to be taken seriously.

My Twin Soul

I had one more major surprise before our trip began. While
dining out with Brad Johnson, a dear friend who was also
going with us to Peru, I admitted to him that I had unfounded
and inexplicable feelings of love for Mallku, the man I had
employed to be our tour leader in South America. As I tried to
explain my feelings, Brad remarked, "He's here."

"What do you mean?" I questioned.

"He's here. Mallku's energy just came in." In that moment, I
felt the spirit of Mallku's powerful presence in front of me in
the restaurant. Tears streamed down my cheeks as an immediate and full knowing pierced my consciousness like a lightning
strike. In one single flash of illumination I remembered everything about Mallku and me.

"He is of my soul, he is my twin!" were the words I blurted
out. Overcome with emotions of indescribable love, yet afraid
of what this might mean, I shook my head and vehemently
exclaimed, "Oh, no! I don't want this!" For five minutes, using
up both our napkins and two from another table, I cried, holding Brad's hand for comfort and to steady me.

What could I do with Truth like that? How do I accept absolutely knowing something I didn't want to know, something that might disrupt everything I have so carefully set up? I didn't even want to believe in the existence of twin souls or twin flames. The only information I had heard about them was from Shirley MacLaine's recent book *The Camino*.[20] While she walked on a solo pilgrimage for 500 miles on Spain's Camino Santiago de Compostela, she received visions. MacLaine wrote of a time in ancient Lemuria in which luminous, genderless beings split into perfect counterparts, male and female—twin souls or twin flames.

What do you do when you come face to face with the truth that it *is* a bear paw print in the mud? Ignore it. After all, you've only seen the bear print, you haven't seen the bear.

The Eagle and the Condor

PART III

Secrets in the Andes

"We didn't have to know what we were doing—or how to do it—for something to happen. It was the knowing, not the knowledge that was important."

The Eagle and the Condor

15

Twin Souls in the Amazon

ugust 2004. Twenty-three of us from the United States and Europe came together for the South American adventure, including nine of the same people who went on the trip to Nepal. I was delighted to have my middle sister, Erin Crowley along too. Our journey began with three days in the Amazon rainforest upriver from the Peruvian town of Puerto Maldonado.

My first glimpse of Mallku, our Andean tour guide, was when he boarded the plane in Cuzco for the final leg to Puerto Maldonado. He was short, yet with the powerful build of an athlete. He faced the other way as he walked down the aisle looking for his seat. Recognizing his long, black hair from the photo on his website, I called out his name. As he turned and smiled, the brown skin crinkling softly around his eyes, my heart flooded my chest. I remembered.... something... everything. In that moment of deep soul recognition I *knew* then that the insight I had in July about Mallku was true: "He is my twin flame!"

I could no longer ignore the bear print in the mud, pretending it was something else, because in front of me was the bear! Tears came unbidden into my eyes, streaking down my face. As I took a seat beside him on the plane, I quickly apologized for my surprising emotions. "I'm so sorry for crying... umm... it's nice to meet you, Mallku... this isn't like me... I'll be okay and back to myself... just give me a moment," I stammered. He seemed understanding; of course he didn't have a clue about what was going on for me. In a few minutes, I willed the vast feelings to pass.

Once we arrived in Puerto Maldonado, an old bus was waiting to take us to a pair of wooden boats for the trip upriver to our lodge. As the group leader, I had much to organize—luggage, rooms, meals and a late afternoon nature walk through the jungle. The Eco Amazonia Lodge had clean, quaint, thatched huts with no electricity. My husband, Ed, couldn't come to the Amazon but he planned to meet us later in Cuzco. At the very last minute, the woman I was to share a room with cancelled. I had no roommate. Mallku needed a room. No problem. We could share.

Huts at the Eco Amazonia Lodge   *Photo by Mark Brindel*

Very Married

Fine. My armor was up. I was totally businesslike, showing none of the emotions that had escaped earlier on the plane. Single beds. I wore shorts and a tee shirt to bed. I chatted a lot. I had so many questions for Mallku about Andean spirituality: "Do traditional people here believe in star origins? Is there evidence of Lemuria? What's the connection to the Himalayas? What kind of ceremonies will you be leading for us?"

While I was talking nonstop in the dark, Mallku spontaneously sprang out of his bed and came to mine! It happened so quickly! He simply asked if he could hold me. "Is this okay?" he queried as he pushed my pillow to one side.

What could I say? It felt wonderful. It felt infinite. It felt perfectly ancient to have this man next to me... but this was not the Jonette I knew. She immediately piped up, "I am *very* married."

There was some silence, then Mallku's voice, "I am very divorced."

"Oh, great," I thought. "Where do I go with a comment like that?"

He assured me that I was safe. He respected me. I knew to my bones that this was true. Safely enveloped in his arms, I remembered simultaneously every life I had ever had as a brown-skinned woman in the embrace of a dark skinned, black-haired man. At that instant I accepted that he was with me for a much higher purpose than either of us understood. It was too well orchestrated from Above. I checked in with my inner wisdom and heard, *This is beyond karma. All is as it should be. This is a moment of choice that is offered only once in many lifetimes.* Before the reasoning part of me could catch and edit it, a thought exploded fully formed from my subconscious, a thought that scared me more than anything I've thought for many years. It was an inner statement unadorned with either emotion or rationalization. "I would give up everything to sleep in these arms every night." In an instant, my normal self regained control of the situation and pushed the errant thought back into the unexplored recesses of my soul, slamming the door shut with the non-negotiable ego command of, "That's just not in my plans." Period.

Whatever the metaphysical ramifications, it all boiled down to one question, "Do I allow him to stay?" My inner voice seemed unequivocal; *This is a window of spiritual growth that will not open again for at least another 500 years.* I could choose the path of my soul or be limited by my guilt and fear. Here we were, against all odds—I, a married businesswoman from the United States and Mallku, an Andean shaman—twin souls lying next to each other in a thatched hut in the Amazon rainforest.

An Initiation of Leadership

He stayed. I rested my head on his shoulder, smiled at the blessing this was, and closed my eyes. The intimacy was simply that he held me—that and nothing more; yet it was everything. Did it last a moment, or was it lifetimes? With no prelude or explanation, I heard the voice in my head say: *You must initiate his third-eye.*

"Okay," I thought, dreamily, "Lake Titicaca will be a good place to do that." I had no intention of rousing my sleepy self from Mallku's arms.

Now! came an inner command. I've learned that it's better not to ignore such insistent guidance. So I leaned over, and whispered to Mallku that I was supposed to give him an energy initiation. Half asleep, he assented with a nod. I touched the center of his forehead; sending power and light through my hands into his third-eye chakra, his spiritual power center. He became comatose… he didn't stir… for hours. Finally, when he moved I whispered, "What happened?"

"I went on a journey," he mumbled, only half present, "Some kind of confrontation…" and he drifted off again. Mallku slept deeply, his back to me, my arms around him. Holding him I experienced electrical currents weave through my chakras, spiraling into his energy centers then back into mine in a continuous tying together, as if we were one being. It reminded me of shoestrings lacing in and out through the eyelets. Each of my cells seemed to become magnetically polarized in a new way. Our proximity alone was bringing a profound and vital change to my body. It was an energetic as well as a spiritual transformation. It was a communion of twin souls. This was his gift to me.

I initiated Mallku with the symbol of the eleven-pointed star and the energies of spiritual leadership. I wish I could say that I felt galaxies of suns or rainbows of colors moving from my palms to Mallku's forehead, but as often happens with these powerful but extremely subtle high energies, I didn't feel anything moving from my hands. I simply *knew* that something life changing was being transferred through me to him. And I knew when it was complete.

Initiations, such as the one I administered to Mallku, frequently mark the next level of spiritual growth. Most of my initiations have occurred spontaneously during my meditations. Fourteen years before I was taken on an inner, mystical journey in which I was told that I was moving from the path of teacher to a path of greater responsibility—the Way of the Leader. At that time, I perceived, between my brows, a golden, eleven-pointed star, which is a symbol of transcendence.

Mark once explained that in order to continue to grow spiritually, we must graduate from understanding things based only on our senses—what we can feel, see, touch, hear or experience. He said that our reliance on feelings or experiences alone keeps us in the third-dimensional reality. The higher worlds cannot be experienced through our senses. According to Mark's teaching, the first and most common level of understanding and learning is based on our own *experience*. The second developmental step is to *trust* our intuition. This is because at the higher energetic or vibrational levels sensory experience may be non-existent, so we must rely on trust. The third step, beyond *trusting*, is to *know* that something is so without any evidence. I *knew* that I had given Mallku the gift of a high spiritual initiation. I also *knew*, without the need for proof or confirmation, even from him, that Mallku was my soul's twin or other half, much closer than even a soulmate.

In the cosmic sense of masculine and feminine, Mallku and I played out our roles when he first held his protective arms around me. He made me know that I was safe. It was that knowledge that enabled me to move into the divine feminine role of initiator. The woman brings spiritual knowledge and energy into the world and then gives it to the man, who helps bring it into action or form. The most powerful initiations on Earth are from a woman to a man; especially if they are twin souls. Some spiritual breakthroughs are so intense that they cause shifts in the physical body. People may feel achy, ill, or out of sorts for several days following such an initiation.

For the next day and a half, Mallku was sick. He later confided to me that he had never before received an initiation that had made him ill. No doubt, the aftermath of my touching his forehead surprised him. On a conscious level, he knew me only as a woman who hired him to guide a tour group through Peru. That night he skipped dinner and was in his bed by 6 p.m., with his clothes on, where he stayed unmoving for twelve hours. For several minutes I stood watching him as he slept. So much tender love and compassion poured from my heart to his. I was all at once his mother, his sister, his daughter and his lover.

We Are the Eagle and the Condor

Ever since meeting White Eagle in the mid-eighties as I meditated in Sydney, I carry the energies of the Eagle. To the North American Natives the White Eagle is the highest creature in our world: It is the "Messenger of the Gods." I casually asked Mallku, whose birth name is James, what his spiritual name "Mallku" meant. He said it was given to him to mark a higher step in his spiritual evolution—it means "the Spirit of the Condor."

"Oh, my God," I thought, as the legend of the Eagle and the Condor that Chief Woableza had shared, burst into my mind. "Was Destiny rearing her head into my well-organized life? Do Mallku and I have something to do with the prophecy?"

More than a week later, Mallku and I had a rare moment to talk privately as we sat together on the long bus ride to Lake Titicaca. I asked him, "Why did you so suddenly jump into my bed that first night in the Amazon?" I was trying to ascertain if he did it because he consciously felt a soul connection to me.

His immediate response was, "Because I sensed your power." Then he elaborated. "That night you were talking about many things and asking many questions. I recognized your power and understood that even if you knew many things and were so sensitive, you didn't know about another kind of power that belongs to you. This is a power most people do not realize. I am talking about the conscious sexual power. So after all that time listening to you, I said to myself, 'This is a powerful woman who does not recognize this power that is within her, so let's teach it to her.' Of course, I didn't mean a sexual approach or sexual activity. I meant to provoke in you the awakening of that power by only being close to you. I have been on the tantric path for more than half my life and know what it is about. I could see where you will go once you realize how this power moves within you."

Mallku's Story

Born in a traditional Catholic family near the coast in northern Peru, James Arévalo was the fourth of seven children. His mother is Native, of the Mochica society, a pre-Incan people. His path always was different from his siblings. At nine years old, he took groups of his friends for entire days up into the mountains. "My friends' parents hated me," he chuckled in telling me of his past. "You see, I've always been a guide. It is just part of my nature." At twelve, he became a strict vegetarian, a radical stance in his family. By fourteen, he was going into the desert alone to fast. "I was sixteen when I told my parents that I was leaving. They thought it was for the weekend. I never returned."

James traveled around Peru, sometimes staying in ashrams, taking up yoga, where he mastered difficult asanas or postures. He made his own clothes by hand, wore sandals, and grew his hair. The teenager who thought he was so adult went to the mountains and the rainforests of the Amazon to live as a hermit; gathering fruit and living off the land. At seventeen his intensity and his intellect were inspired by eastern philosophy and ideas of equality. He and his companions traveled to town plazas to preach against the greed and structure of organized religions, especially Peru's Catholic Church. People gathered to listen. In order to support himself, he sold books on the street. "I was absolutely on my path. This was the basis for who I am now," he told me.

This was in the 1980s when the Shining Path—the ruthless, Maoist-inspired guerilla movement—terrorized Peruvians. The government was corrupt; police and military behaved much like terrorists also. James, then seventeen, and a nine-teen-year-old friend, were traveling on a bus in the Amazon region. Police stopped the bus. Suspicious officials searched the boys and their luggage. "We were jailed as terrorists and thrown in prison. For eight days we were given no food or water. I drank water from the toilet. For three of those days, we were thrown into a tiny, damp cell, completely dark, with ten other prisoners. We couldn't get help because no one knew where we were. After eight days, they released us. I hated police. I became more of a revolutionary."

James discovered the traditions of the Andes, feeling a spe-cial kinship for the ancient spiritual ways and reverence for nature. He went to school to become a tour guide so he could share what he learned about the Incas and earlier Andean soci-eties. He continued learning and growing on his spiritual path, eventually taking the name Chaski, which meant messenger. On the March equinox of 2000, as he was meditating on a sacred island in Lake Titicaca, he was given "Mallku" as his new spiritual name. It means "Spirit of the Condor. It is a role of leadership," he told me.

Mallku is a leader, an accomplished businessman, owning a travel agency, a vegetarian restaurant, and a partnership in an exquisite tourist hotel in the Sacred Valley. Although I have referred to him as a shaman, Mallku would only say that he "is on a shamanic path." He believes that the threshold for truly being a shaman is forty-nine years of age; he was thirty-eight at the time.

16

Some Slithering Things
and One that Charges

That first night in the Amazon while Mallku slept motionlessly, I lay awake listening to a magnificent rainforest storm. Lightning and thunder tore through the sky. The rain pounded the thatched roof relentlessly. I presumed that the waters would rise to the top of the stilts on which our hut, the Escaribe, or beetle, was perched. The power of nature unmasked was as joyful as it was terrible. It was all too wonderful to sleep. I was safely under the same roof as my ancient Beloved, a man who in this life was still unknown to me.

I hoped the immense storm would cancel our early morning jungle walk and the scheduled 6 a.m. wake-up knock that went with it. "After all, how can we discern that knock from the many thunderous poundings?" I asked myself.

Mallku mumbled something about using his shamanic powers to tell everyone telepathically to stay in bed. He yawned and slept again. That didn't work for me. Some of the group would stay in their huts, but others—good tour group citizens—would be ready with raincoats and cameras for our scheduled dawn jungle walk. I got up and dressed, then roused our fearless leader.

The Garden of Eden could not have looked as mystical as the Amazon basin on a rainy morning. Clouds crept through vertical slots in dense vegetation, levitating the tree tops on a ghostly base of foam. High leaves broke the brunt of the falling rain. Only faintly scattered water droppings persevered down to our Gortex-hooded heads. The rainforest, abundant with leaves of every shape and size, emitted a tangible feeling that was primeval, even sensual. The jungle floor was merely muddy most of the time, but in areas prone to flooding, we walked on wooden paths set on pilings above the water. "This is dry season," my sister Erin reminded me. The glistening beauty of water droplets diffusing the early morning sun was something special. Mallku, who usually carried a backpack with at least twenty pounds of photographic gear, lamented that this was a day in a thousand—and he didn't have his camera equipment with him.

Trudging on, carefully watching the path for the ubiquitous roots and vines that could snare our ankles like leg traps, the group suddenly halted. In the center of the muddy trail was a strange sight—a small mountain of perhaps eighty to a hundred individual, black, hairy caterpillars. They were mounted on top of each other, ever so slowly inching their way across the path en masse. Cameras flashed. The significance of such teamwork was evident. Alone they were nearly invisible, but together they were a single creeping, leggy creature. There must have been a tribal consciousness that ordained which caterpillars would ride on top and which would be the legs. It seemed there was some switching of roles going on as we continued to study the anomaly. It made me think of the teamwork we would need a few days later when we trekked the Inca Trail.

I realized then that the jungle, as a whole, was a perfect ecological system, with nature elegantly balanced. Yet, no bit of it looked perfect to my eyes. The most beautiful tree was host to strangling vines and trails of creeping termites. The floor was littered with dead, decaying things; messy. A gorgeous leaf, its edges delicately filigreed, was riddled with holes from lunching bugs or beetles. "Maybe our world is perfect after all," I thought, "and death and dying are all part of the greater cycle of creation." The thought allowed me to relax in my endless endeavor to make my life perfect, healthy and organized.

The rainforest gave way to small lakes, marsh and vegetation-choked waterways. We needed a boat. After half an hour of tireless bailing with a plastic jug, Apollo, the naturalist guide from the Lodge, prepared the wooden dugout canoes that were stashed there. Our group was ready for our sojourn through the swamps. It was idyllic to paddle through green, pungent glades. Birds with clacking, chattering songs called to their friends, "They are coming." A pair of macaws with the distinctive screech of parrots flew high above the towering treetops and us.

Using paddles and a pole, Apollo nosed the boat deep into the overgrown swamp. Suddenly he stopped and pointed five feet ahead of us. The excited message that whispered through the boat finally reached the ears of those of us seated near the back: *Anaconda!* One at a time we gingerly moved to the prow, cameras poised, eyes popping in awe. Only six feet of this inspiring reptile showed itself above the water. Head, tail and the mammoth remainder of the serpent lay submerged. It is no exaggeration to report that the circumference of this particular specimen was at least five feet around. "Snake" was too discounting a word for such a creature. "Serpent" was closer in its connotation.

When my brother John heard I was going to the Amazon, he did his best to prepare me. Ever so thoughtful, as only brothers can be, he emailed me a series of photos entitled "Lunch in the Amazon." I've suffered through John's sick humor for over forty years, so I should have just clicked "No" in the box on my email that says, "Do you know who sent this attachment?" and be done with it. However, squelching my curiosity has never been my strong suit, so I opened the sequence of captioned photographs. The report indicated that a native worker in the jungle couldn't be found. His searching friends located a gigantic anaconda with a suspiciously lumpy midsection. The first photo was of the snake. The second was of ten men lifting the snake, presumably dead, into the back of a pickup truck. Try as I might to forget them, those pictures were seared in my brain and resurfaced again as I stared at the anaconda in the swamp in front of me.

We were all very, very careful standing up in our tipsy canoe photographing the anaconda. There was just no way to know if he had already had lunch.

On a later jungle walk, our group took a boat across the wide expanse of the Madre de Dios River to Monkey Island. Mallku told us that our local guide, Apollo, would actually call the monkeys down from the trees. Cameras were readied as we waited to hear whatever ancient animal call was capable of summoning wild monkeys from the canopy. In his firm voice and his loudest Spanish, Apollo called, "Plátanos, plátanos." Bananas. He was telling the monkeys that in his rucksack he carried bananas! It worked. They came. We laughed and took photos.

Jonette and Mallku in the Amazon

Back at our compound, we enjoyed late afternoon pisco sours, the typical Peruvian drink made from fermented grapes, limes and egg whites. The group had unanimously created a new rule earlier that morning. Whoever was late and made the rest of us wait had to buy drinks. Amazingly, with only two exceptions, the group became very prompt. Bill and Ann Hines were that night's hosts for cocktail hour.

As we were settling down in the large, screened area with our drinks, Larry Cooper came running in, shouting that a strange, pig-like beast was stampeding around the huts. Cameras at hand, we cleared out of the bar to see a tapir charging about the compound. Apparently, the sun's setting gave him the cue to hurtle into the midst of civilization. He was a friendly chap though, posing for photos and graciously allowing us to pet him.

17

The Spirit of the Water

ur first group meditation in Peru was in a spacious, thatched hut, romantically lit by candles and set in the rainforest at the edge of the lodge property. Groups experimenting with ayahuasca and other sacred, psychotropic plants of the jungle most often used the hut. We did our meditations sans plants, but then we have my spirit guides White Eagle and Mark to help us along. In the first guided meditation, we connected our thoughts to the Incan Keepers of the Four Directions, whom many of us had experienced at my house the night Chief Woableza spoke. Twenty humans gathered, but countless millennia of guides, teachers and wisdom were present with us.

White Eagle had told us that an important mission for our stay in the Amazon was to use the power of this formidable river basin to heal the waters of our planet and within all living things. Such a task made sense to me based on a book by Japanese researcher Masaru Emoto.[21] He was able to photograph single water crystals and demonstrate the difference in the crystalline structure between water from pure, clean streams and water from polluted lakes. The first showed the lacey, snowflake patterns you would expect. Polluted water photographed as disfigured, ugly, non-symmetrical crystals. Emoto photographed similar differences in single water crystals in vials showered with love, compared to water that received negative energies and intent. His work demonstrates that thought and intention can alter the structure of water crystals.

Healing the Waters

It followed that if we could bless the water of the largest river system on the planet and imagine holiness expanding to all rivers, lakes, ice and seas, we would be doing a great service to the Earth.

Here Mallku demonstrated his uncanny connection to our work. Without knowing that we were planning a meditation ceremony for "Healing of the Waters," he informed me that he had organized for us to take a motorized canoe up one of the small tributaries of the Rio de Madre de Dios (The Mother of God River) at sundown that evening.

When we had motored far up the narrow waterway, the boatmen cut the engine. I channeled a meditation as we floated downstream to the main river. It was humorous attempting to meditate while we ducked our heads to avoid low branches. Several times we struck mud with the bottom of the boat while the boatmen, trying to stay quiet, maneuvered us back into the flow. No one actually burst out laughing, though several would-be meditators were close. Bill Austin remarked that everyone "was positively saintly not to laugh, and we never even got credit for being so good!"

The healing energies were sublime as we drifted to the sounds of birds and insects and Mark's channeled words. We touched into the life force of the water. As I dangled my hands in the river, I could feel them tingle with the vitality of life. The Andeans believe that the entire world is comprised of living energy. We were on the river to connect to it.

By the time we merged back into the main river from its shallow tributary, nightfall had seeped into the twilight sky. Mallku and the two local boatmen were nervous. Navigating an unlit dugout upriver at night was not their idea of fun. When I got back on shore, some doubt crept in: "Did we really accomplish anything in our meditation?" My inner voice said all was fine. "You just have to show up and do your part."

That night in the Peruvian jungle, it was my turn to be exhausted. I was not centered after the meditation process on the water, feeling like when I've had one too many glasses of champagne. I evidently was looking spacey because Henriette Reineke and others volunteered to do some energy healing to help me get grounded. I also had the help of our expedition doctor, Yolanda Groeneveld, who came to our hut to do acupuncture on me. I was the one who went to bed fully clothed at 6 p.m.

As I lay there, I felt as if I had popped through to a new level of conscious awareness. That night my visions showed that I had entered a world where I could see the ebb and flow of divine energies before they became form. For the next few days, I could barely touch a living thing without having to pull my hand away because the energy coming from the object was too intense. I experienced the life force energy, even in inanimate things.

Flow

The river held us to her for an extra day. A constant cloud cover shrouded the airport, canceling all flights in and out of Puerto Maldonado. The group remained good-natured. We sat all day on the floor of the crowded terminal, hoping the weather would change so we could fly to Cuzco as planned. It didn't happen. No planes arrived or departed that day.

Mallku found a decent hotel for our unanticipated layover. Between checking in and going out for pizza and lasagna, I channeled a remarkably helpful meditation on "Flow."

Welcome again travelers, this is Mark. Find within your veins the Spirit of the Water. Move yourself into Oneness with Flow. Experience the timeless flow of your breath, of your blood, of the water in the world, of the clouds in the sky. Let go of permanence to become one with Flow.

The more Flow becomes a presence in your life; the more powerfully you will create the visions you desire. You may think that Flow is just the space between permanent markers, an unimportant aspect that gets you from one event to the next. Please consider yourself as Flow, as movement; your breath is liquid, your thoughts are liquid, your beingness is motion itself. There is no such thing as static being.

In the next few weeks you will be experiencing gateways between the physical and the spiritual. You'll be able to understand and experience spirit in matter and matter in spirit. Flow is the line between spirit and matter. As you master Flow in your life you will begin to transfer your matter-based world to the understanding of that which is spiritual. Then Flow, which is the boundary of each, dissolves and you have spirit and matter as One.

Put your attention on your solar plexus, that area below your ribs, by touching it. From the solar plexus chakra you perceive the world as black and white; as singular events; as solid. Your heart however, knows the world of Oneness; knows the world beyond form. Feel Flow as you visualize breathing into and out from your solar plexus. Then let that go, and have no differentiation between in and out. This opens your greatest block to flow, which is the black and white way you process your life.

So first breathe in and out... then breathe simultaneously... in and out at the same time; in a way that can't logically be followed. Breathe in all directions from your solar plexus—not simply in the front. The Spirit of Water that you connected with last night on the river is also the Spirit of Flow; ask its help. You might imagine the waves on a seashore coming in while others recede. All is perfect; all is flowing.

Now let the feeling spread throughout the rest of your body, up and down until an easy rhythm begins to establish itself between you and the external world. Your form begins to soften, your being, your expectations, your thoughts all soften. As they do, notice that you strengthen. There are no hard quali-

ties about you; only a streaming in all directions. There are no rules now. Connect to the great Amazon River, to the river of life. As you master this, you're indeed traveling along the edge between matter and spirit. Allow yourself to know Spirit every bit as well as you know physical matter. So much of what you will experience in the sacred Andes will require this new perception. Imagine the blinders coming off so that you can know things differently. Know the world as a timeless flow so that you can sit on a rock in Machu Picchu and feel the past and know the future. Allow your consciousness to reorganize itself in a way that easily grasps the whole rather than the part, the flow rather than the event. It takes a different set-up in your mind.

Begin to be comfortable with the infinite… the water, the weather, the clouds, the air… anything that flows. Watch for Spirit to come into you. How does your heart center feel now? How has it changed? Call forth this flow—this in and out movement simultaneously. It's not give or take; it's give and take. It's in and out, all at the same time. Feel your life loosening.

For the last few minutes listen to your Presence, your Inner God. The powers in this world are wind and water. The reason they are powerful is because they move. Imagine that you are listening, that the experiences of the next few weeks will easily come to you. Imagine that by doing this you are opening yourself to so much more. So much more…

This is Mark. Thank you.

The Healing Shaman

On our last morning in the Amazon, I woke up feeling sick and slightly feverish. With sweet concern, Mallku opened his shaman medicine-bag and instructed me to stand with my eyes closed. Shaking his Amazonian rattles and chanting a special invocation, he performed a healing ceremony. I had read about Andean healing traditions so I was at least forewarned. I remembered two unusual practices from my reading. First, a shaman might use a guinea pig for diagnosis and divination. He will slap the patient repeatedly with a guinea pig until the animal expires. The shaman would then perform an autopsy on the animal to discover the cause of the patient's illness. The second healing practice I read about occurs when a shaman takes a drink of strongly perfumed holy water and spits it out onto the patient. Thank heavens I was only a little unwell and Mallku didn't have a guinea pig handy. I got only the overly fragrant spray that he spat on me.

All of us loved being in the Amazon. It was a gentle introduction to the strength of the Andes. The next day the Puerto Maldonado weather was again too nasty for planes to arrive. Our group spent long hours at the terminal waiting, buying trinkets at the kiosks and drinking lots of tea. Finally, the clouds broke long enough for *one* plane to take off. Fortunately, thanks to Mallku's extraordinary efforts, we were on it! Although short, it was a rough and bumpy flight. A momentary hole in the clouds appeared; our plane threaded through mountain peaks and dropped precipitously onto the landing strip at the Cuzco airport. One glance at Mallku's ashen face told me how lucky we were to be safely on the ground.

My husband, Ed, and two others who didn't come to the Amazon met us at the Cuzco airport to join the group for the rest of the journey. I was truly excited to see Ed's smile as I ran through the crowds to greet him with a big, welcoming hug. Yet my heart felt that, in welcoming Ed, I was saying goodbye to Mallku and the love I had for him in my soul.

18

The Inca Trail

bus was waiting at the airport to take us winding down the roads from Cuzco's 10,900-foot elevation to the area called the "Sacred Valley" below. Now it was time to embark on the journey we had been waiting for: a four-day trek to Machu Picchu on the Inca Trail. Our group had one night in a lovely hotel where we organized our gear into duffle bags for the porters to carry, and daypacks that we carried. Gathering together, we called in White Eagle for his words before we set off on our hike.

Our group in Peru

White Eagle's Blessing

This is White Eagle. We are called to do the Blessings of the Trail. The White Eagle is the northern image of the Condor. Together, Eagle and Condor, we meet to bring messages from the gods. Now we ask you to bow your heads so the energies from your crown chakras can merge. Your Christians have assumed that a bowed head means submission to your God. The truth of the bowed head is that it connects the crown chakras of the group. So bow your heads and feel your power touching, head to head. Receive the energy. You are weaving the consciousness of Oneness. Bring it through your spine, down your feet into the Earth. Let it flow from all of you. The blessing goes through your feet and into the trail. It is your energy that blesses your trail.

In our time together, you will dream a journey for the future of humanity. The trail has been worn by thousands of feet over thousands of years. The trail you will walk is not the Incan stones; it is a trail of stars. At every moment be aware of receiving from the stars, connecting to all the other star-beings and to the hearts of humankind. Be aware of connecting to the hearts of the animals and the plants, the hearts of the waters and the stones. We ask you to enter into a shaman's world. When you wish for power, when you wish for insights... connect to the White Eagle of the North and the great Andean Condor. Call in the ancestors to walk in front, shoulder to shoulder, and behind you.

We ask blessings on your journey from Pachamama—Mother Earth. Feel her lift her blessings into your soul. We ask for blessings of our Sister Moon and all she controls. We ask the blessings of our great Father Sun and the Cosmic Sun beyond, and from the Great Spirit, the All-That-Is. By your humble actions bless your ancestors and gift your descendents in this circle of life. May every step you take lead you back to yourself. This is White Eagle with our brother the Condor. We give you great blessings.

The Trek Begins

After a short bus ride, our band of twenty eagerly disembarked at the trailhead for our hike through the mountains to Machu Picchu. It was significant that nine of us had been together in the Himalayas. In some ways this journey in the Andes was the other half of our spiritual mission in Nepal.

The Incas thought that the Sacred Valley of the Urubamba River was a reflection of the entire Milky Way. This coincided with White Eagle's blessing that we *would walk a trail of stars.* So while our boots stepped on the well-worn stones, our souls were traveling the Milky Way.

Trekking the Inca Trail   Photo by Mark Brindel

The ancient Andean people were amazing engineers. The Inca Empire, which extended to include most of the length of South America, was tied together with a vast system of over 14,000 miles of roads. These were pedestrian trails only, as the Incas did not use the wheel. The grandeur of the snow-covered Andean peaks and the soft brown of the hills in dry season transported our consciousness to many dimensions at once.

The first day was arid and cool, the climbing easy. After all, porters carried the gear. We carried only our daypacks. Desert succulents and sharp grass lined the track, while far off mountain vistas of the Vilcanota range sprang spectacularly into view. We especially loved the snow covered peak—Veronica (known to locals as Wakay Willka), which overlooked the beginning of the valley from a height of over 20,000 feet.

White Buffalo Calf Woman

For part of the first day on the Inca Trail, I walked next to Josh Roach, the bright, philosophical man in his thirties, with whom I have had a special spiritual connection from the first moment we met. When I mentioned to Josh at our first meeting about the powerful portal at Ama Dablam in the Himalayas, he spontaneously felt the energies active in his own heart. He had a unique way of dramatically experiencing my energy field, and I his.

The Andean landscape through which we walked that afternoon was partially covered by eucalyptus trees that thrived in the high, dry air. Their weepy leaves and unmistakable fragrance reminded me of my magical hike in the Australian Blue Gum Forest two decades before, where I encountered the silver-haired Spirit Woman. I told Josh about that previous mystical experience, describing the woman. "She wore only white and had the most beautiful, wise face. Her eyes were accentuated by long, rich, silver hair, falling over her shoulders to the middle of her back." I shared with him how she told me that I must proceed without my gear and without a defined road to follow. Her words, *Your path is made by walking,* are still clear guidance for me today.

Relating to Josh about my vision in the Blue Gum Forest took me once again to that altered reality. I felt like I was back in the Australian clearing with the ethereal woman sitting on her rock. Suddenly, I was struck by an energy wave of knowing, rocked by a cosmic blast of truth. I grabbed Josh's arm so I wouldn't fall as my knees gave way underneath me. Recognition poured through me in a momentous flash. I instantaneously knew who the silver-white haired woman was! "She is White Buffalo Calf Woman!" I exclaimed excitedly to Josh. I knew her as a legendary figure, beloved by so many North American Natives.

More than that, in an electric rush of recognition, I knew that I was her! Incredulously I blurted out to Josh: "Oh my God! I am her and she is me!" The knowledge seared into form in a sudden understanding much larger than words. In the flash of a moment, my former identity was obsolete.

In a most amazing way, Josh literally shared my experience. He described it: "Immediately upon that realization... a very warm and powerful heart chakra energy exchange occurred between us... the energy radiated through my body meridians while we were timeless in that experience. I was captured by the most amazing sight... not a meditative vision, nor an imaginary thought, but in front of my eyes was White Buffalo Calf Woman superimposed over Jonette... as if the two figures were actually one. Simultaneously, while I was witnessing this, Jonette witnessed her own actualization, that she was White Buffalo Calf Woman."

In tears, Josh and I hugged. The truth stood. Against all my logic, it sank in that the apparition I had seen in Australia was White Buffalo Calf Woman, and most significantly—that she is me.[22]

As I continued walking the Inca Trail beside Josh, I watched the Spirit Woman again in my inner vision, just as I had seen her twenty years before. This time she turned her full face to me and smiled. Josh too felt this acknowledgment from her. She was joyful that, after two decades, I finally knew the truth about myself and about her. The truth would have been too big for me to consider, much less accept if it had come to me in a less dramatic, less physical way. Often I know something is true because I get goose bumps, or truth-bumps. This was goose bumps times a million. All my logical resistance to what Spirit was presenting was instantly blown apart by this revelation.

My Lakota Sioux friend, Chief Woableza, who was the first to tell me of the ancient prophecy of the Eagle and the Condor, also told me the story of White Buffalo Calf Woman. According to legend, she was the great Medicine Woman who brought the spiritual teachings and the sacred pipe to the Sioux people over 500 years ago. She was revered and given the name of the White Buffalo Calf, the most rare and sacred animal for the people of the Great Plains. As a Lakota Sioux, Woableza and his people are students of White Buffalo Calf Woman.

Woableza's spirit traveled with me that afternoon. When I communicated to his spirit about my revelation that I am White Buffalo Calf Woman today, I heard in my mind his matter-of-fact reply, "I know."

Maybe this is what was meant when an inner voice told me two years earlier that, "Woableza is your student."

Meanwhile, on the Inca Trail, we all stopped at a tiny enclave of houses for water and rest. Local women squatted on the ground beside the track. Bottled water and warm cans of Coke were spread out for sale on blankets before them. Mallku bought a cup of chicha, the foamy, native brew of the Andes. "It's not safe for you to drink," he warned those who wanted to taste it. Pigs, dogs and bare-bottomed toddlers crawled under-foot. The "facilities" were in the field — wherever.

Still stunned and transformed by the revelation of White Buffalo Calf Woman, I shared my experience with the group. They could feel how momentous this insight was for me. My sister, Erin, interjected levity, "Jonette... White Eagle... Mark... now White Buffalo Calf Woman. I can't wait to tell our brothers this one!"

That night I meditated, coddled in my sleeping bag. I still envisioned the woman with long, white hair as separate from me, even though intellectually I accepted the truth that we were one and the same. 'I am her and she is me.' As I continued my focus on her, I began to experience us walking toward each other. Standing face to face and holding hands, she and I spun and spun and spun, becoming a spiral of stars that lifted us into the higher worlds. Now we *are* one.

I tried to embrace the energy and the power of White Buffalo Calf Woman, though I desperately wanted answers to the questions: "What does this mean to me? What am I supposed to do with this knowledge?" The insight came with no 'how to' manual.

Three Steps of Growth

I've noticed that there are three steps I move through whenever I make a spiritual quantum leap: The first is recognition; the second is acceptance; and the third is the coming together of my new power with a new or greater mission. In this case, recognition occurred on the Inca Trail with the shocking realization that I am White Buffalo Calf Woman. The second step, acceptance, happened as it all sank in. It was important for me to be neutral in accepting my link to White Buffalo Calf Woman. It was as wrong for me to think, "Isn't this great?" as it was to feel, "Oh, no, this can't possibly be me." I would be undeserving of my mystical experiences if I doubted them. The knowing itself was indubitable; the translation into what it meant in my life was impossible to know. Remembering my Dad as the Fifth Buddha enabled me to consider that I really might be White Buffalo Calf Woman, since strange, spiritual lineage evidently runs in my family.

The third step in integrating the growth, which was to use the new ability and power to face a need or a mission, was yet to come. For me, new spiritual abilities never make themselves known until just prior to the moment of need. When I move forward and trust, the gifts and abilities are there the instant a mission is undertaken. All I knew was that the acceptance of being White Buffalo Calf Woman came because I would soon be facing a spiritual mission that would require her abilities.

I believe that the answers to our spirituality lie in the present and the future, not necessarily in the ways of the past. It is not for me to channel White Buffalo Calf Woman or become immersed in the traditional ways of the Native North Americans. Although the Native American myths have almost made her into a goddess, in truth she was a human woman with the gift of knowing. She carried messages relevant for her native people. Those of us awakening in this epoch are accomplishing the same thing now for our people.

Only two things in my life have presented themselves to me with such a physical explosion of knowingness. First, realizing, even before I laid eyes on him, that Mallku was the masculine counterpart of my own soul—my twin flame. Second, that I am the current aspect of White Buffalo Calf Woman. These revelations crashed like meteors into my world. They collided with, and shattered, so much of what I had thought was true about myself. The ideas could not have come gently; otherwise, I would never have accepted them as true. Two life-altering realizations came together as we hiked the Inca Trail. They must have revealed themselves to me for a reason.

19

The Pass Where Women Die

he second day on the Inca Trail was difficult, the third day was even more so. It had been a cold, soggy night. No one slept well because the tents were set up on a lumpy, slanted pitch. The start of the trail was a boot-sucking bog of slimy mud. Mist muted the scene with gauze-like softness, protecting our senses from the rugged sharpness of the landscape. Light snow powdered the mountain. The first of the three passes on our hike today, known as the "Pass Where Women Die," was at the top of an incline that went straight up from our campground to almost 14,000 feet. Once we began trekking, the group splintered; the faster walkers plowed ahead, leaving the others to their slower pace.

Ed was feeling especially energized and fit that morning. With no effort, he found himself in front of the others. He was on top of the pass before anyone else, yet he wasn't tired. He told me later that while he waited on the summit he closed his eyes and silently asked Mother Nature for a sign that he was indeed connecting to the Earth. Ed has often been frustrated that he doesn't see or feel anything spiritually. So he was profoundly moved when he heard an instant thought response in his head, *Who do you think has been giving you all this energy?*

Meanwhile, Gloria Barschdorf, one of the physically strongest of the team, was rendered weak with intestinal problems, nausea and sulfuric belching. Four of us, including our doctor,

Yolanda, stayed with her. When Gloria could walk, it was slow. She had to stop often, finally vomiting with the force of a volcano. The majority of the group stood at the top of the pass, sending loving energy to help her ascend. Ed felt a powerful connection to Gloria as he watched her struggle up the trail. He resolved to accompany her on the train if that was required. This was a breakthrough for him in experiencing deep compassion. The spiritual magic that was part of this adventure for all of us opened Ed's heart creating a permanent change. I've noticed, and he would agree, that he has been a much more compassionate and loving man since then.

When Gloria, and those of us who stayed with her, finally made it to the top of the pass, having taken three times longer than we should have, we had a difficult decision. Should we send her back to take the train to Machu Picchu or continue on at a slower pace? None of us wanted Gloria to miss her goal of completing the trek. She had trained too hard and too long. However, Mallku couldn't take the risk that a continued delay would prevent us from reaching our camp by dark. We still had two more passes to climb. Twenty people stranded on the trail as night fell wasn't our idea of a safe journey.

Yolanda gave Gloria a quick mountaintop acupuncture treatment and administered an antibiotic tablet. Three people did Reiki healing as we pulled EmergenC vitamins and Rescue Remedy from various daypacks. Gloria summoned all her courage and strength, and within fifteen minutes she experienced a dramatic shift in health and energy. Mallku tested her by taking her 200 feet down the mountain to see how well she could make it back up. He decided that she could continue with the group. Hurray!

Gloria later reflected, "I knew I was clearing and transforming into a whole new self. My spirit has not been the same since. I know my life purpose is just to *be* and to love everyone unconditionally since we are all connected." Gloria's gift to us that day was an illustration of courage and surrender. As the group supported her, we all truly bonded as a team.

The second pass of the day still loomed before us on the Inca Trail. The landscape had become stark and strong. Vegetation was sparse at altitudes above timberline. The mountain sky turned dark and ominous as lightning slashed the thin air. Fierce hail lashed at our exposed faces as we neared the top of the pass. Thankfully, the hailstones were small, but they stung our faces as we climbed. Yet, even in the throttle of a sudden storm, it was unspeakably beautiful to be on top of the high pass, enshrouded in clouds, with white pebbles of ice hurling around us. The rapture was fleeting. We had a long, long way to go to our lunch stop, and it was well into the afternoon.

After a short break, the strenuous, high-altitude trail extracted its toll on us exhausted trekkers. It took all the strength some could muster to keep climbing up and down. Others helped by carrying daypacks or walking beside the weary ones to offer encouragement. Darkness fell quickly. I hiked alone somewhere near the middle of the pack. The Inca Trail had opened up to overlook a magnificent, green valley. Higher, snow-covered Andean peaks created the far perimeter in a spectacular panorama. As the sun set, I could see the profile of people at our intended campsite on top of a mountain, still a forty-five minute walk straight up from where I was. There would be enough soft light of dusk to make it. I wasn't worried, at least not for myself.

I rested, waiting for some of the others to catch up. Three women of our group reported that there were six others behind, but one of our English-speaking guides was with them. "I'm the group leader," I thought. "Should I go back? But what help would I be?" I pondered. "I don't even have a flashlight." I decided I should pray.

We Have Waited to Be Commanded

I sat on a stone ledge on the Inca Trail, the valley's green unfolded below. I didn't want to pray in the traditional way, rather I would powerfully command the outcome I wanted. I remembered a story from an old Aboriginal woman I had met in the 1980s in Australia. Molly Craig and her cousin Daisy sat at our dining room table in Sydney, sharing tales far into the night about a time before the white men came to their people in the Outback of Western Australia and changed everything. Molly narrated:

> When I was just a little girl, I went with my uncle and brother out on our raft to fish. A dangerous wind and storm came up, tossing our log raft in the waves. Suddenly my uncle jumped into the biggest wave and shook his fist to the sky, shouting to the spirit of the storm, "God, don't you recognize me? I am here with my family. You must stop the storm, now!" The ocean calmed and my wet uncle climbed back onto our raft. We were safe.[23]

As the sun set on the Inca Trail in Peru, I thought of Molly's story. I stretched out my arms to encompass the pristine valley, the mountains and the moon that would soon be rising. I proclaimed aloud to the Universe: "I command safety and light for our fellow pilgrims."

Only a few seconds passed when I heard a response! It came from the highest, grandest, snow-covered mountain that guarded the valley. I heard it in my mind as clear as any voice: *We have waited to be commanded.*

To the Andean people, all mountains are sacred. The protective deities of the mountains are known as apus. This great and beautiful spirit of the mountain, or apu, had spoken to me! It seemed to be saying that even with all its power, it was waiting for us humans to wake up, to be in the role of commanding for the good of all. I was moved beyond words as I sat on the stone seat watching the sun set to my right and the first rays of the moon, which was almost full, appear from under the clouds to my left. I had commanded from a place of Oneness with the mountains and all of nature, not from a place of domination. Love commands form. I walked in silence in the darkness up the last slope to camp, knowing that the others behind were safe. The reason I felt powerful enough to consider commanding safety and light from the Universe, was that I had integrated the essence of White Buffalo Calf Woman into my present identity. Two days earlier, I had recognized and accepted that she was me. This was the third step in my spiritual transformation. My new ability appeared when I undertook a mission to protect my fellow trekkers in the darkening night.

Later, Berdine de Visser, one of our Dutch travelers who had difficulty with the altitude and was with the group that was behind, shared her experience of the last hour of their walk. "That last uphill climb, when we were all so tired should have been grueling, but it was the easiest walking of the day. It was as if the stones on the path itself were lit for us."

My People Have Suffered

The experience with the snow-mantled Andean mountain propelled me into an expanded state of consciousness. Ed and my sister, Erin, had already organized our tent. Dinner was still a couple hours away. I climbed the highest rock overlooking all the campsites to watch the moon rise. Below me were the sounds and smells of the many cooking tents. There were at least six different groups camped there, with tents pitched on any flat area on the mountain perch. Tomorrow we would descend through the Sun Gate to the top of the sacred city of Machu Picchu.

The Southern Cross constellation barely peeked up over the horizon. It felt as if I slipped into another incarnation, another reality as I sat upon that high rock, looking down at the lights shining through the nylon of many tents. Perhaps it was a village of teepees I was gazing at in some distant time and place. Or was I an Inca, looking down at the suffering of her people? I found myself saying aloud to the wind, "My people have suffered and died too often." I felt the surge of so much compassion. Yet as I spoke, I knew it was more than just a past life memory. It felt as if a greater part of me was making a solemn statement of resolve, a firm and clear commitment to do something about suffering. That simple sentence reverberated through my being, becoming a point at which my life quietly and irrevocably pivoted. At the same time a tremendous sadness took hold of my heart. The pain was real; the anguish seemed endless.

Mark's words at the Amazon proved prophetic: *Know the*

world as a timeless flow so that you can sit on a rock in Machu Picchu and feel the past and know the future. I was certainly seeing into the past as I sat on that rocky pinnacle. So many things I could not understand as I tried to sleep that last night on the trail.

The One Who Cannot Be Tamed

At 5:30 a.m, I was compelled to get up to meet the rising sun in praise and gratitude. Inside the tent, I stepped on Ed and Erin each a half dozen times as I tried to locate all my layers of fleece, hat and gloves. I completed my attire with the large medallion Chief Woableza had made to help Dad in his transition from this life. Again, pieces came together in hindsight. Only then did it dawn on me that the necklace was a large, golden, circular shell—a Sun Disc. Woableza had given it to my father to recognize Dad as a chief. That morning I also wore it as a chief.

Scrambling up to the highest promontory in the area, I had plenty of time to myself in the receding darkness. I prayed to the Four Directions, giving thanks for our journey. The first rays of the morning sun hit the tallest peaks, setting the snows on Salkantay, the mountain that had communicated to me the evening before, on fire. After half an hour, a tour guide from another group joined me on the mountaintop. He offered me a cup of steaming tea made from coca leaves, which are

Jonette with the sun disc   Photo by Mallku

legal and plentiful in the Andes because they help the body cope with the high altitude. As I gratefully sipped it, I pointed to the majestic peak to the south and asked, "What does its name, Salkantay mean?"

Salkantay mountain, "The Wild One"   *Photo by Mallku*

"Ah," he said, "It means The Wild One or The One Who Cannot Be Tamed." I was speechless that Salkantay, at over 20,000 feet, the most untamable mountain of the Andes had communicated to me the evening before, *We have waited to be commanded.*

20

Machu Picchu: The Sacred City

fter breakfast, we performed a ceremony to thank the staff of twenty-eight porters, cooks and guides, who would be turning back now that we were in sight of Machu Picchu. They all worked especially hard the previous night to prepare a Peruvian tradition—roasted guinea pig. (Many of us became vegetarians for the evening.) With Mallku as translator, we told the cooks and porters what we appreciated about them. They sang for us in return. Wilfredo, one of the English-speaking guides commented, "This group is different from most I work with. I can tell you all really care about the Earth and nature."

That day we agreed to proceed in silence. It was a stunning walk, descending down into the emerald cloud forests. Vegetation became dense with varied shades of vibrant green. As we approached the Sacred City, the trail was constructed of handsomely carved stone steps. We rested at a semicircular, agricultural terrace named Wiñay Wayna, meaning "Forever Young." Perfectly engineered stone walls separated narrow plots of land. Incan farmers had painstakingly carried fertile topsoil from the river valley up the steep mountain to plant their crops of maize, potatoes, grains and avocados. Today green grasses, sprigs of hardy wildflowers and native orchids claimed the Inca's curved gardens in the sky.

Walking in silence for what seemed like eternity through undulating, moss-covered slopes, we were each embraced in feelings of holiness and connection to the great Mother Earth, known here in the Andes as Pachamama. Ann Hines felt the "Angels of Joy" beside her as she trekked. Larry and Tryna Cooper experienced Mother Mary's presence with them. Ed was still ecstatic that Mother Nature was inspiring him.

After five hours of knee-wrenching descent, our weary group reached the long, steep steps up to the famous Sun Gate—the stone archway that in ancient times was the official entrance to the holy city. Below us at 8,000 feet, grazing on the dazzling green terraces were llamas. The round topped mountains of Machu Picchu (the elder mountain) and Wayna Picchu (the younger mountain) seemed to defy the sky. A thin mist broke apart to reveal the dramatic vision of the famed ruins below. The peaks languished in clouds, making it appear that we were high up in the heavens, yet we were fully 3,000 feet lower than the elevation of Cuzco.

One of our group, Elizabeth Boersma-Wentzel had tears in her eyes when she first saw Machu Picchu spreading out beneath us. She ran down the steps from the Sun Gate exclaiming, "I am coming. I am coming." She told me later, "When I arrived on the platform overlooking the city I cried and automatically spread my arms out, feeling the energy between the Universe and Machu Picchu. After hundreds of years I was back to help restore this connection."

Judi Slaughter, who gave herself this trip as a sixtieth birthday present, had an astonishing transformation during the four days on the Inca Trail. Before we started, she was anxious and worried. She had never even camped before. Now she bounded down the Incan steps with the exuberance of a filly running free on a fine morning. She positively radiated joy and confidence. "After making it up Dead Woman's Pass and then down into Machu Picchu, I know I can do anything in life!" she told us.

Once we entered the amazing archeological site, Mallku described how it might have been if we had arrived during the Inca's time. He showed us the Ceremonial and Offering Table where ancient pilgrims brought stones to offer in thanksgiving. We rested, absorbing the iconic panorama before us. In his book, *Machu Picchu Forever*, Mallku wrote: "Everything here exists in harmony, not only through man's creation of the structures, but also because the Earth appears as an intelligent living being. Nature is brilliantly presented, like a divine dance with beauty as its main character."[24] Of all the places in the world I've seen, Machu Picchu is by far the most spectacular. It is the astonishing result of nature's magnificence complemented by human architectural achievements.

The Incas

The Incan Empire, though grand, was short lived. As an empire it existed for barely a century. From 1100 A.D. to 1430 A.D., the Inca's rule was limited to the area immediately around Cuzco. Around 1430 A.D. they won a major military battle, which began the rapid rise of their dominance. From pre-Incan societies, they inherited a rich religious, agricultural, architectural, and engineering culture, and then added to it with their unique ability to unify and administer a far-flung empire.

The name "Inca" was for the ruling elite of less than 40,000 people who conquered and administered an empire of hundreds of different tribes. The more than ten-million people they ruled were mostly Aymara and Quechua Indians. Although it is now referred to as the Incan Empire, the vast majority of people were not Incas. The Incas were the rulers. The empire was wealthy and the Inca rule was generally fair. Within a hundred years, the Incas overcame all armies who opposed them to create the world's fastest growing civilization.

Without the use of wheels for transportation or iron tools, the best Andean artisans and engineers constructed Machu Picchu, a mystical citadel in the clouds. It has 600 terraces, each only about ten feet wide, that provided flat areas for growing food. The terraces kept the mountain stable enough to hold 170 buildings, solidly constructed of white granite. Fresh spring water still flows through the city in the stone-lined channels and fountains designed and built by the master craftsmen. The city has steps for streets and God as a neighbor. At its zenith,

Machu Picchu was thought to be home to between 300 and 750 residents.

The original name and purpose of the city have been lost. However, the quality and beauty of the structures have led many archeologists to believe it was built as a royal, spiritual retreat for the last great Inca emperor, Pachakuti. He came to power in 1438 A.D., beginning the period of Incan expansion in religion, architecture, art and government. Some Andean people including Mallku believe that Pachakuti was an enlightened Master, a solar being.

Not all scholars agree that Machu Picchu was founded by the Incas in the fifteenth century. Some research, based on astronomical evidence, concluded that the original layout of the site must have been accomplished between 4000 and 2000 B.C.[25] One theory holds that the use of gigantic, sometimes irregularly shaped stone blocks, some weighing between 80 and 150 tons, indicated that it was originally built by pre-Incan people and was later enlarged and updated by the Incas. The Incan construction style most often utilized smaller, rectangular-cut stones. Throughout the area, the precision stonework, much of it done without mortar, allowed buildings and temples to stand for centuries, even in the face of earthquakes. Mystery surrounds Machu Picchu and the Incas.

We do know that less than a hundred years after Machu Picchu was first inhabited by the Incas, it was abandoned. Because it was a holy city, used by the high Inca royalty, officials, and priests, the common people didn't know of its existence. Self-contained, it was invisible from the river valley below. In that way, it remained untouched by the conquering Spaniards and unknown to the world at large until it was rediscovered in July 1911 by an American explorer and geographer from Yale University, Hiram Bingham.

Bingham had no idea he had stumbled upon such a treasure. He and his party were in search of the lost city of Vilcabamba, the last stronghold of the Inca warrior Tupac Amaru. A local Indian showed him the jungle-covered ruins. During that initial visit, Bingham spent only a few days exploring and photographing the ruins before moving on. He returned in 1912 and again in 1915 to continue clearing and excavating the site. He described Machu Picchu, "Like the Great Pyramid and the Grand Canyon rolled into one."[26]

Today over 300,000 visitors per year travel to Machu Picchu, making it one of the most popular tourist destinations in South America. They arrive either by train from Cuzco, or by walking the Inca Trail. There are no automobile roads to the Sacred City.

21

Realigning the Earth

he next day we could spend exploring the archeological wonders, but now, after four days on the Inca Trail, nothing sounded better than a hot shower and clean clothes. We bused steeply down the mountain on a narrow dirt road with dozens of hazardous, hairpin turns. Aguas Calientes, (Hot Water in Spanish) the small village along the Urubamba River was our base for the two days at Machu Picchu.

The August full moon was certainly not evident as we splashed through town in a drenching rain. Clean but hungry, we convened in a warmly inviting room upstairs in the Indy Feliz restaurant. In July, White Eagle had explained the evening's spiritual task. We were to *heal a magnetic wobble in the core of the Earth by the time the serpent leaves the den.* Friends around the world were meditating with us on this night.

I channeled Mark, who led us into a process of expanded consciousness in which we visualized an initiation portal at Machu Picchu that connected the poles of the Earth with the magnetic poles of the Cosmos. Mark told us that this realignment of just a few degrees would *heal an instability that would have led to a shift in the poles. There is enough light and consciousness now so a pole shift does not need to occur.*

I experienced a stronger sense of flow and vitality when we reached the part of the meditation where Mark told us to feel the Earth's ley-lines and meridians adjust to the magnetic north and south of the Cosmos. Ann Hines said she actually felt a 'pop' as we worked to realign the Earth. Ann's husband Bill relayed, "I was asked to go into the inner orb of the Mother Star and to approach a large, spherical crystal. Upon touching this crystal I found myself standing at a doorway with my arms spread wide to receive and to direct the energies of joy, love and immense support from the higher beings there. I have no words to describe it. It felt as if I touched into all wisdom, all truth and knowledge when I touched that crystal orb. Yet I know there are many more doorways and many more higher beings."

Like often happens on these spiritual journeys, I didn't really feel or see much. I merely trusted that by showing up with clear intentions we were doing our part. We did not have to know what we were doing, or how to do it, or even believe it, for something to happen. It was the knowing, not the knowledge that was important.

Pole Shifts

Did I believe what Mark said about a magnetic wobble in the Earth's core that could result in a pole shift? It didn't matter. I proceeded as if I did. I used to think that my believing something was related to its veracity. The only new beliefs I was willing to entertain were ones that fit my existing thought patterns. If it was comfortable to believe something, I did and I defended it as true. If it upset my old beliefs too much, I would not believe it, and I'd declare it as untrue. I've come to realize that what I choose to believe has little to do with its truth. After all, my brain is a limited instrument for adjudicating what is so in the Universe. Over the years of reading hundreds of books, listening to scores of speakers and reading thousands of emails, I have simplified my thinking and I now believe that *anything is possible!* It isn't worth my gray matter to attempt to figure out if something is true or not. I either believe it, or hold it in the 'I don't quite believe it yet' bin.

Take for instance the idea of pole shifts that Mark had mentioned. I'd heard of this phenomenon before but frankly I had more immediate things to worry about. This was in the 'I don't quite believe it yet' category. I have another helpful basket as well: 'Who cares?'

Evidently, many people do care about planetary wobbles and pole shifts. I met a young German geologist at Lake Titicaca who had just returned from Siberia where he was studying the crystallization patterns in some of the Earth's most ancient surface rocks. These indicated the magnetic orientation of the planet at the time the rocks were crystallized. He explained to me that the uneven weight of the polar ice caps creates instability in the rotating Earth much like an unbalanced load of laundry in the washing machine. The Earth's axis moves between 21 to 24 degrees. Today its tilt is 23.5 degrees. The magnetic poles migrate until a point when the inclination becomes so skewed that the planet's magnetics go crazy, like a spinning top that begins to wobble as it slows down. The geologist explained to me that there was a time when the Earth had many pairs of north and south magnetic poles. Eventually it settled down into a new pair of poles in entirely different positions than the previous ones. Mallku believes that Lake Titicaca is the feminine pole of the planet and a place near Mount Everest is the masculine pole. It is interesting to speculate that perhaps these two spots may actually have been the Earth's North and South poles at one time.

Could such catastrophic Earth changes such as pole shifts have caused the legendary oceanic civilizations of Atlantis and Lemuria to disappear during the Great Flood of 28,000 B.C.? Did this send highly evolved immigrants to Central and South America to found mighty civilizations like the Incas, the Mayans and the Aztecs? The various pieces of this interesting theory were beginning to move into my 'anything is possible' category.

22

Out on the Edge: Ed's Story

The next day, we had an entire afternoon to explore Machu Picchu, which Mallku called the "Crystal City." Every corner, every stone wall presented geometric perspectives of unparalled grace. The physical beauty of the natural, high mountain setting alone could elicit the finest from a poet's pen. Yet all of this was crowned by human architectural artistry conceived and executed with elegant precision. Machu Picchu was a world of co-creation between man and nature. Rather than scarring and dominating the landscape, humans had managed to improve it.

Besides leading our sightseeing and teaching us about the Incan culture, Mallku had several spiritual exercises planned for our day. One was a test of fortitude, balance and trust that involved standing on a sliver of rock that protruded out exceedingly high above the entire Urubamba Valley.

As an organizational consultant, my husband Ed is always thinking about how to understand leadership better. In Machu Picchu, he faced some of his own fears and came to a deeper understanding of leadership. Later, Ed wrote about his experience that day:

Standing on a cliff towering over Machu Picchu, Peru, twenty-three trekkers watched our tour guide Mallku step out onto a very narrow rock. This precipice jutted out into open space, just wide enough for Mallku's feet. Quite simply, if Mallku fell, he would die. Some watched in awe, while others of us were petrified! My own fear of heights raised its hideous head.

When safely off the rock, Mallku invited volunteers to repeat what he'd just done. I was terrified that he would ask me to volunteer, so I quietly hid myself behind the group. After Ann and Elizabeth walked out on the rock with protective assistance from Mallku, I was shocked to hear Jonette say she wanted to do it also. I watched in horror, as Jonette stepped out onto the slender rock slab. You can imagine the frantic mind-chatter and emotions the intensity of my fear stirred up inside me. I was a mess.

Of course Jonette was safe. Yet, as she stepped back off the rock, I somehow knew that this tribulation wasn't over. I was right. Jonette walked directly to me and took my hands in hers. She looked me in the eyes with such a loving gaze. When she finally spoke, what she said was incredible. "You do not have to do this." The love in her eyes was evidence to me that whether I walked the rock or not wasn't important… because she honored whatever choice I made. I tear up even now as I recall those incredibly empowering moments. She continued, "And… you have the opportunity to deal with your greatest fear." She went on sharing her personal power with me as we softly held each other's gaze. I gradually felt strength welling up inside me from her. Perhaps twenty or thirty seconds passed before I let go of one of her hands. While holding the other tightly I moved slowly toward that object of my fear. Then, I was standing on the rock perch, perhaps not as far out as the others, but I was on the precipice and by myself! She stood just behind me. This incident became for me a huge moment of personal growth and empowerment.

The key to my breakthrough was Jonette's leadership. She demonstrated the maxim, "You will follow a leader to a place you wouldn't go by yourself." She didn't nudge or push me into doing something I didn't want to do. She simply invited me to do it, while her actions demonstrated her total belief in me that I could do it. She showed that she fully accepted and respected me regardless of my decision, while lovingly inviting me to step up to another level of personal growth.

Mallku, the condor, on the edge *Ed on the edge*

Ed, the Last Inca?

The history of Ed's apprehension started just before our late August departure to South America. We went together to have a joint session with James Pinkel, our friend and a gifted healer in Denver. James does body work, helps remove people's energy blocks and so much more.[27] During the session, Ed mentioned that he wouldn't be going to the Amazon. James immediately asked, "Why not?"

"Two reasons," Ed replied. "One is that I have a business

conference I don't want to miss. That's the reason I've been telling people. Second is I'm afraid."

I looked at Ed, more than a little surprised. I could think of nothing that would make him afraid of going to the Amazon. He had never mentioned a fear of it before.

"Ahh," James responded, "Let's see what that's about." James and I are both clairvoyant, so between us a full picture began to emerge. James started, "Something terrible happened to you in a past life in the jungle."

From my inner vision I added, "You were a leader, engaged in a war or a battle. You were a good leader, a good man and you did everything right militarily…"

James completed the scenario, "But you were betrayed by your brother, causing your defeat. You were captured and died a gruesome death at the hands of your enemies."

"It was so awful that you vowed never to be a leader again," I said, seeing the cost of that long-past decision.

"Who is that brother in this life, do I know him?" Ed queried James. Ed then listed off some names of close business associates.

James responded, "No" to each of them.

"Was it my father, Garland?" Ed asked.

Again, James answered, "No."

"Was it Beulah, my mother?"

After a moment's reflection, James answered, "Yes. The brother who sold you out and caused your death was your mother in this life."

Tears filled Ed's eyes as the significance of this became clear. His mother died when he was a two-year-old infant. In some ways, he was betrayed again. For the remainder of the session Ed worked on forgiving his mother and clearing all the painful remnants of that life as a defeated leader.

Ironically, Ed's story had a strange twist, which could help explain his irrational fear of the Peruvian jungle and tie him to the history of the Incas. In 1572 A.D., the Spanish viceroy in Lima declared war on the last remaining rebel Inca leader Tupac Amaru in his jungle stronghold called Vilcabamba. Tupac burned and abandoned the city before the Spanish army arrived, then he fled with his men deep into the Amazon basin rainforest. He was betrayed by his half-brother and consequently captured by the Spanish. Tupac, known as "The Last Inca" was taken to Cuzco where he was beheaded. Could Ed have been Tupac Amaru? Who knows? But I am now the first to admit that we all may be so much more than we think we are.

23

Initiation in the Temple

B efore our journey, Marlene Tuttle, one of our group, also had a session with James Pinkel, the Denver healer who helped Ed. James told her, "You will be initiated into your divine feminine power by Jonette. This will take place where the four directions come together." Marlene had also been part of our team that trekked to the Everest base camp. In many ways, that expedition to Nepal was a completion for her, a way of honoring her climber husband, who had died a decade earlier while summiting Mount Rainier. Coming to Peru was to be another major step in her growth.

We spent most of the day exploring Machu Picchu. In late afternoon, we entered what Mallku called "the magical time," when the day-tourists have left to board the train that winds along the Urubamba River, taking them back to Cuzco. Mountain shadows stretched out to claim terraces and temples alike, gobbling the warm afternoon air and making it chill. Mallku was in his finest form sharing history and spiritual knowledge about Machu Picchu's most glorious place, Intiwatana, also known as the Hitching Post of the Sun. This is a solar astronomical compass carved in stone that sits on top of the Pyramid of the Sun, dominating the city and the green, cloud forest valley.

As the group ascended the last of the seven, gray granite stairs to the temple, Larry Cooper, who knew that Marlene was to be initiated into a higher level of power sometime during the

Machu Picchu, Pyramid of the Sun

trip, spoke up. "What do you think, Jonette? This feels like the place."

"No, I don't think so. I'll bet it's at Lake Titicaca." I answered. I was enjoying just being a tourist.

Mallku instructed the group on theories and history of the Intiwatana, created out of a massive piece of living stone. He had written several books on Incan spirituality, including a gorgeous volume of his photography of Machu Picchu. He believed that this was a place where, on June 21st, disciples became solar initiates or the new "Messengers of the Sun." Mallku informed us, "This is where the four directions come together."

I didn't hear Mallku's lecture because I was drawn to walk through a stone archway to another large deck or platform of the temple. Alone, I enjoyed the peace and the breathtaking view of what 500 years before was a bustling, royal retreat and religious center for the chosen of the empire. I was simply a tourist circling the platform, wishing I had our camera that was in Ed's daypack.

In an instant, I felt a shift. I noticed it first in my body and in how I walked. My head was erect; my shoulders were back. My tourist loll changed to strong, purposeful strides. I felt regal, a person in charge. I knew this feeling… *I remembered this place!* Suddenly I knew that I was a priestess of power in another world. It was time to initiate Marlene. Back through the arch, I strode to fetch her from the midst of our friends. I could tell that she too knew the time was now, because tears tracked down her face. I requested her to follow me through the stone archway to the edge of the open platform overlooking the Sacred Plaza.

How could I do something I had never done, never seen, and didn't know anything whatsoever about? I didn't think about it. I followed my instincts. Empty of all notions, I was a ready vessel for the remembrances. I recalled how to walk out on the prow of the temple platform, holding my hands palm up to the sky. I didn't know the actual words of the Incan incantations but the feelings were there. Tapping into a deep well of ancient, wordless knowledge, I touched Marlene's shoulder and the crown of her head as she knelt before me. Larry seemed to know that he should stand guard at the arched entrance. His wife, Tryna, held a small vial of aromatic oil that she knew to bring, as she took her position behind Marlene. No one said a word. No one needed to.

Something beyond description transferred through me into Marlene—a sacred ordination, an opening of power into the initiate. Standing up, Marlene faced out over the ancient city, her arms outstretched to the heavens. "I felt tremendous energy flowing through me," she told us later.

The veils between dimensions are thinning, many channelers write. Time/space isn't to be reckoned in a linear, logical sequence, quantum physicists all agree. Dusk at Machu Picchu, the world held its breath between day and night. Marlene and I, white women from Colorado in the year 2004, were somehow the newest initiate and the elder priestess. Without a doubt as we stood at that altar to the Sun, we were Incas.

Shamanic Ceremony: Calling the Moon

The sun dipped below the horizon as we all waited at the summit of the Pyramid of the Sun. Mallku had two friends assist him to prepare a sacred place for our ceremony to honor the full moon. It was in the Sacred Square, a small courtyard below the pyramid and beside the Temple of the Three Windows. Out of his woven, alpaca-wool bag, Mallku pulled the tools of a shaman: flutes, drums, bells, sage, condor feathers and a conch shell. The sky changed from pink to marbled gray. Magic whispered herself around the well-wrought Incan stones as the thin mountain air became cold. Mallku summoned us to sit in a circle on the stones in the courtyard. Through music and prayer he invoked Mamakilla, Mother Moon.

It was a cloudy night. The moon remained well hidden, her silvery light escaped only now and then to give us a hint of her location. The invocations complete, we cheered when the full face of the lunar disc momentarily crept out from behind the clouds. White Eagle added a prayer that I channeled as we gathered under the stars on top of Machu Picchu:

Welcome brothers and sisters. This is White Eagle. At this time the passage is open—the pathway to the Milky Way.

As the moon comes up over the horizon:

Imagine the Milky Way becoming stairs and humanity walking upon those lights to dimensions and worlds untold.

Imagine that you will remember when to begin and how to walk those stairs.

Imagine that everything you will ever need, you will know in the moment of your requesting.

Imagine that there is nothing you don't have.

Imagine there is no heart so far away you cannot love it.

Imagine there is no star so far away it cannot brighten you.

Imagine the web you live becoming closer, becoming One.

Imagine all ancient knowledge remembered.

Imagine all future knowledge remembered.

Imagine your lives a clear reflection of beauty.

Imagine your ego serving your Spirit.

Imagine your Spirit serving the One.

Imagine that you know how to bring it all together.

Play your part, be aware and walk that Milky Way pathway to forever. You are all Great Ones. In the greatness that you recognize, may others remember their greatness.

May you all, in united human spirit, find the glory that is meant to be.

I sent a personal prayer out to the heavens to Sue Burch, who had passed away exactly a year to the day before we stood on Machu Picchu under the full moon. I knew her spirit was with us. Had we accomplished our spiritual mission explained to us in July by White Eagle? We couldn't know what we had achieved, but we did what we could with the help of Mark and White Eagle. Parka-wrapped and silent, we left Machu Picchu to the night.

24

Return to Cuzco

My emotions used to be easier to understand. I would experience a feeling then look to see what personal, recent event had triggered it. This recipe didn't work as automatically for me in Peru. Our time at Machu Picchu was over. My sister Erin and I, and just about everyone in our group, tore through the tourist bazaar of Aguas Calientes to purchase silver jewelry and alpaca sweaters before boarding the train to the Sacred Valley and Cuzco.

Our luggage made it on board; we all sat together in the first class car. There was nothing whatsoever upsetting about how the day was transpiring. Then why did I feel so emotional? Clingy, I needed to have Ed put his arm around me. Sad, I was leaving something cherished behind. "What is this about?" I thought.

As our group rode in the train toward Cuzco, the centuries fell away and I experienced myself back in another time. The modern tracks and train morphed in my vision into a well trampled, dirt trail. I remembered being a priestess at the Pyramid of the Sun in Machu Picchu when we received word from our leaders that an enemy was marching to the heart of our empire. We were being called back to the capital of Cuzco.

In that past life in Peru, I walked in simple robes, heavy hearted, eyes downcast. I was a high priestess, leading the people of the temple—the priests and priestesses, the newest initiates, away from the only world they had ever known. We left the great temples where we could give praise and hold the wisdom of the Universe. Behind us was everything we knew, everything we had trained for. Our rulers were not afraid to lose gold and silver; they were afraid of losing the greatest secret of the kingdom, which was the mystical wisdom of the people in the temples.

I saw through the veils into the past, that for our safety as Inca holy ones and for the protection of the sacred knowledge, our spiritual community had to be dissolved. We were permanently exiled to live as common people in far-scattered villages. An unfathomable enemy marched from our shores to the mountains. In that life, everything in me was defeated. Our gods, our faith, our wealth and our wisdom failed to keep us safe. Now I would meet with our Ruler to follow his instructions for the dissolution of the temple. In my current life, as I sat on the train holding onto Ed, I cried soft tears of remembered pain. My sorrow was no less poignant for its having aged for centuries.

In 1532 A.D. Francisco Pizarro, the Spanish conquistador, invaded what is now Peru with 180 men, horses, guns and canons. He had heard stories of the riches of the Andes, of royalty who ate from plates of gold. As he and his men marched toward Cuzco, the Inca capital, he met the Inca Emperor Atahualpa. The emperor commanded his 30,000 warriors not to attack the Spanish because he believed that the Spanish, with their white skin and beards, were the fulfillment of the prophecy of the return of the god Wiracocha. Atahualpa assumed the Spanish were gods like the Incas—the Children of the Sun.

Pizarro's men held Atahualpa prisoner and easily overpowered the unresisting Incan armies. The emperor promised the Spaniards ransom in return for his life. He had his subjects fill a room once with gold and twice with silver. The greedy Spaniards took the wealth and killed him anyway, marking the beginning of the demise of the great Incan Empire. Spanish priests and missionaries followed the conquerors and began the conversion of the people from their ancient religious practices to the Catholic Church. Within fifty years, hundreds of

The Eagle and the Condor

thousands of natives who had been part of the Inca Empire, one of the greatest civilization in the New World, had died of war, smallpox and measles.

25

Cave of the Serpent

e departed the tourist train in the town of Ollantaytambo in the Sacred Valley, where Mallku had a surprise for us. He was planning a ceremony and meditation in the Cave of the Serpent, Amaru Machay. I got goose bumps when he told me this. White Eagle had channeled in July about our task to help heal the Earth. *When the serpent leaves the den, the healing must be complete. The timing is of great importance.* How had Mallku known to take us to the den of the serpent? I had never shared any part of our spiritual mission with him. Was Spirit silently orchestrating Mallku's itinerary to fit our group's higher purpose? Were Mallku and I partners in some greater plan? Was this why we had come to Peru?

Our group filed one by one into the cave's opening in the rock, folding up coats and new alpaca sweaters as cushions and taking up positions along the cave's cramped inner corridor. I couldn't go in. It wasn't time. Near the cave entrance was a ledge, just a small niche in the rock. A few pulls brought me up to it. Instead of sitting on the shelf facing out toward the local women who were arranging their trinkets to sell, I stood chest against the rock face. My arms and hands embraced the cool, smooth surface of the stone and I began to cry. The tears were so much more complex than mere sadness. In them was the acceptance of a commission to undertake a difficult but consciously unknown task.

Only Mallku remained outside the cave. "You've been here before?" he said, both a statement and a question.

"Yes." Then I followed him into the cave where my friends were waiting.

Mallku, the shaman, lit sage to cleanse the space with its purifying smoke. The still life beauty of that moment in time was painted forever in my memory. Horizontal rays of sun from the cave's entrance struck particles of smoke from Mallku's burning sage, resulting in direct and reflected light that shone gold on the peaceful faces of the meditators. The rhythm of Mallku's drum, his flute and his rattles lifted us as if in a trance that belonged to our joint consciousness. He prayed aloud to the Spirits of the Cave and to Pachamama, Mother Earth, and Wiracocha, the Creator God of the Andes. He called out our gratitude, our oneness with Nature, our readiness to serve Spirit. Mallku's ceremony perfectly choreographed time and space for the words I was to speak. The holiness of the place, the perfection of the moment was palpable as Mallku finished his offering and I was to begin.

Seated in the Cave of the Serpent, I was ready to hear the familiar "Welcome journeyers this is Mark," pass from my lips. However, it was not Mark who spoke. With a strong, clear voice, I said, "I am Kumaru of the Incas. I am the Woman of the Buffalo People." This was me! I was speaking as a greater version of Jonette, not merely channeling a spirit guide. It was time to step past my beloved guides and to speak for myself.

Jonette in the Cave of the Serpent

I am Kumaru of the Incas. I am the Woman of the Buffalo People. I wear the face of the Mother and the power of the center of the Universe. In the Den of the Serpent, in the womb of the Mother, I invite you to face your death. When you walk through that threshold, there will be the meeting of the masculine and feminine and the unity beyond that, which is what we seek. Put yourself deep into your heart, deep into the heart of the Mother.

Move backward into time to your death before you were born. I invite you to move into that void—that darkness; to disappear all form and need of form; to disappear all self and need of self; to walk to the death of self... and then to walk more; beyond your fears, beyond your darkest hiding places... walk more. Walk into the Den of the Serpent in... in... in! Walk into the coldest, darkest places without form, without self, until you have met the stillness in the eyes of the Serpent and are reconciled with Death. Move into the eyes of the Serpent, the stillness. As you do, you are beyond the pain of fear, of death and darkness.

Find Nothingness here and know Nothingness as your friend. The eyes of the Serpent are the doorway of Death. From there, you will know a small fire, a single flame. Put your soul there. From the flame is a thin, blue wisp of smoke. This is the Masculine Principle. Follow that thin, blue line of smoke upward... as it moves into the world of the Earth, creating the masculine polarity. Embody all that this means—the power and the wisdom. This fine wisp of smoke becomes the coding of one side of your DNA. Embody it fully and cleanly. Take everything of yourself into the divine Masculine Principle, and everything of the Masculine Principle into you; in its pure power, in its pure intention.

Feel this masculine energy in the middle of your spirit, in the middle of your spine, in the center of everything. Accept, embrace, hold and birth the masculine—the Light of the Fire. From our consciousness we send this pure light of fire, the pure Divine Masculine, into the planet, into our brothers and sisters, into nature. I ask now for the masculine in everything to be presented free and clear as the gods intended. From your soul spread the fire of the masculine into every living thing; spread it into the DNA of life.

Flood the world with this knowing from your soul—from the soul united, from the fire in everything. Feel the fire of the masculine in Pachamama, in Mother Earth, in Gaia. Claim also the masculine in our great feminine symbols. Feel the masculine power of the moon. When the masculine has spread you will know it; there you will find stillness. When all is sated, when all is filled with the balance of the Divine Male, you will find quiet.

Yet the resonance so full and so complete is missing its complement—the complement that makes the resonance of the masculine something special, something powerful. That is the resonance of the Divine Feminine. Look up now into the stars until you find a star that sends a thin, silver thread through the cosmos to the Earth, into form. Bring the Divine Principle of the Feminine, the other side of your DNA into you, down your spine. Feel the complete, the pure and the powerful Divine Feminine entering you now, fully, directly. She comes and spreads the power through you, through all consciousness. Through her she gives meaning to the masculine by bringing the presence of the feminine. Feel the completion, connection, concordance as she softly moves her silver starlight into all things and all parts of things, into all life and all thought.

As the Divine Feminine spreads, you feel softness, stillness, completion. What was the fire and the smoke combine with what is the star and silver light—whole, twirling around each other in spiral and helix, balanced perfectly. Both are powerful. Both define the other. Through the Earth now, through all life, through the mineral kingdom, through everything... the Divine Feminine brings her power.

As the light, the essence of the Divine Feminine and the Divine Masculine spiral together, there is once again a Serpent. This is not the Serpent of Death, but the Serpent of New Life, of Unity. The Rainbow Serpent of myth is born and balanced within you, within consciousness. Feel the power of the birthing, again aligned and balanced—the Rainbow Serpent, the New Life. Know yourself beyond male and female, beyond opposition of any kind. Know yourself as self-United.

Feel the consciousness of the birthing of the Rainbow Serpent together. The Rainbow Serpent is all diversity in One. Gather that energy here in the Den of the Serpent before we give it birth to the world. Feel the energy growing in the womb of Mother Earth, the birthing place of the Rainbow Serpent.

Feel the power build in this cave, in this den. Our intention is so holy and so ancient. The power coils and spirals around us, within us, between us, and when we are ready, the Heavens will open and draw out the Rainbow Serpent from the den, up into the Universe to be made manifest, to bring balance for all humankind when it is ready. Feel the Heavens open and the Serpent emerge.

Balance beyond masculine and feminine, the divine Oneness is apparent in form in our world. We ask with our strongest intentions, our greatest of prayers that the power of the Serpent will help brush away those things of imbalance that have come to be part of our world. We pray to bring the great balance of

Earth and stars together into the heart and soul of man and woman, into our children and theirs. As we accepted death ourselves, with our intent on behalf of the human community, we accept death of that which no longer serves the One. We humans, on behalf of those still awakening, accept death of the illusion. We understand what we are asking for and we will not be deterred.

This message is for the Buffalo people, the people of the Puma, and all children of the stars. Allow your hearts to break open into a billion rainbow pieces so that you will know that it is done and it is good. I am Kumaru of the Solar Temple. I am the woman of the Medicine Wheel. I thank you!

My words, not channeled from outside me, but spoken from the part of me that is Kumaru and White Buffalo Calf Woman, were as powerful as they were beautiful. Unknown to me at the time, the message of balance between the masculine and feminine principle was to become the reason Mallku and I met—the unification of the Condor and the Eagle.

26

The Pyramid of the Sun Disc

n the bus back to Cuzco, my spirit still reeled from the power of the ceremony in the cave. I was bewildered. Who was Kumaru? Why didn't I channel Mark or White Eagle, as I have done for years? What had changed and why?

We arrived to the bustle of Cuzco. The evening plans called for shopping at the stores on the plaza. Following that, Mallku invited all of us to his apartment just off the city center for a ceremony.

Ascending three flights of stairs, we entered Mallku's home. It wasn't like any apartment I'd ever seen. The main room resembled a shaman's cave: giant crystals, Tibetan singing bowls, flutes, drums, bells, rattles, conch shells, condor and other feathers, and so much else. Rather incongruently, there was a bookcase with stuffed animals and a couple of Barbie dolls. A two-person tent was fully erected in the living room. Mallku is a single father with three daughters, ages eighteen, eight and six. The tent was the bedroom for the youngest two. I asked him, "Why did you get the girls full-time in your divorce? Is their mom not a very good mother?"

His answer was politically correct. "It's just that I'm a better father."

May My Path Be Illumined

Somehow, there were enough cushions and small stools for all of us to squeeze in. For me it was a relief to relax and meditate without having to be in charge or to channel. I was going to enjoy this immensely. Mallku, his long, black hair in a braid, donned a woven headband, and became, once again, the shaman. In his deep voice and accented English, he invoked the Spirits in prayer. The only thing I really remembered were his words, "May your path always be illumined." Knowing how I love paths, I liked this mantra. So as Mallku drummed and chanted, I repeated, "May my path always be illumined." I relaxed, letting the sounds, the vibrations, the holy setting take me on an inner, mystical journey.

Mallku, ceremony at home

The music dissolved into my body, the notes vibrated in my bones. I started moving, uncontrolled by my mind, in perfect rhythm to the drumbeat. My hands and arms danced to a spirit they seemed to know. All the while I repeated, "May my path always be illumined." The normal side of my consciousness was impressed that my body, usually so tight and controlled, that knew no rhythm, that could not even dance with a dance instructor, was moving so naturally with the sounds. The setting was safe enough so I let the rather apoplectic movements go with the flow, to see where this would all lead. I hoped my motions weren't disturbing Vicki Staudte, who sat on a little stool to my left. In my consciousness, I traveled on an inner journey to the front of an etheric, other-dimensional pyramid. Its steeply stepped sides and flat, rectangular temple on top reminded me of Mayan architecture.[28] In my vision, I stood in front of the pyramid and asked, "Who guards this place?" No one appeared. I asked three times very sternly, "Who guards this place?"

I've come to understand that the mystical world has its own protocols, and it's not always a good idea to go through a doorway or portal even if it shows up in front of you. Just because I can stumble into some higher realm doesn't necessarily mean I belong there or that I know what I'm doing. But in this case I knew I had to find the guardian-being to ask permission to enter the pyramid. After my third time asking, "Who guards this place?" there slowly appeared, surrounding the base of the pyramid, many small, ephemeral beings. My instinct told me these were inner-earth beings. They didn't seem to be in charge so I demanded, "Who leads these guardians?" No answer. Again, I asked, "Who leads these guardians?" The normal part of me smiled at this variation on the cliché, "Take me to your leader." The entire time my body still rocked and rolled to Mallku's ceremonial music and chanting.

The small beings disappeared, replaced by a single, colossal, kingly Guardian—Incan, Aztec, or Mayan, I didn't know which. He wore a cape of feathers and other adornments of gold. I fleetingly recalled that Maori kings wore cloaks of woven feathers; perhaps it was the style for Lemurian leaders. His skin was dark, his nose prominent. He held tremendous power in his presence.

Codes of the Sun Disc

He stood before the pyramid's main door. Apparently, the higher part of me knew what I was doing, because I was not intimidated. In this mystical, parallel reality I demanded, "I am

Kumaru and I request entrance." I thought, "Here I am calling myself that name again, *Kumaru*. At some level, I am she." I repeated again, with Kumaru's confidence, "I must enter. It is time." The Guardian moved aside.

As Kumaru, I found myself standing alone inside the center of the pyramid, facing seven luminous steps. The chant, "May my path always be illumined" brought me to this place beyond time and space. In my inner journey as Kumaru, I ascended those seven steps of light. At the top was the golden Disc of the Sun, holy to the Incas and other civilizations. How can I even begin to describe the power of the Light that radiated from this interdimensional, circular disc? It emanated wisdom and truth, and seemed an endless source of energy. It communicated its very essence, its knowledge in tiny bursts of geometric shapes or codes. I was awed by its magnificence.

"My people are ready for the next level of activation. I have come to receive the codes for our people," I heard myself say in the vision. My physical body trembled. My conscious mind kept asking, "Will I be okay? Can I handle all this power?" The answer was "Yes." And it was given to me. Energy codes of light poured into my body in an exquisite spiritual electrocution. Universal wisdom embedded itself into every cell of my being. It was as if an Infinite Intelligence was directly communicating with my DNA.

Mallku finished his ceremony. The piercing sound of the conch shell jolted me harshly back from the mystical reality. My friends opened their eyes to stare at me, concerned. They wondered what was happening to me while I shook uncontrollably. Several people put their hands on my head and shoulders to help me get grounded. Bill Austin gave me his water bottle.

In the present time, in Mallku's tiny apartment the Universe was still coursing through my body. I was breathless and my voice shook with energy and emotion as I told the group where I had gone and what had happened. "It's flowing now. The codes are flowing everywhere. A seal on the Sun Disc has been broken. My heart is broken into a million rainbow pieces and they all hold the new codes. I am Kumaru and we have waited.

The inner Light shines immensely from all life, from our Mother Earth. The power of the Light is being restored: As it should be; as it always was."

Kumara

Mallku came over to put his hands on my feet to help me fully return to my body. "Welcome Kumara," he whispered.

Mallku said "Kumar*a*." How could he know that? I had actually said "Kumar*u*." But that morning in the Serpent Cave and again just then, my Spirit had wanted to say "Kumar*a*" and at the last second when it came out of my mouth I changed it to Kumaru. I must have thought it sounded more Incan. When Mallku addressed me with the correct name, Kumara, I knew he was right. He, as my twin soul, knew me as *Kumara*.

I didn't understand any of this, but I remembered the inner words that came to me after our meditation on the boat in the Amazon. "You only need to show up and do your part." If I just accept it, the purpose will be revealed. So far, my connection to the Sun Disc of the Incas had shown itself to me piecemeal. First, the golden medallion that Chief Woableza presented to me at my father's death; then the experience of a radiant disc shining from my heart as I channeled in front of hundreds of people in July; and now, as Kumara receiving an energy 'download' from a Sun Disc on an inner journey.

I believe that I found the Sun Disc that Brother Philip had written about in *The Secret of the Andes*. After reading the book, I had hoped that our group would somehow be led to the actual secret monastery where a physical Sun Disc was hidden. I hadn't imagined that I could look for it in the higher dimensions—and that I would find it! Later I learned that my personal relationship to the Sun Disc extended to ancient Lemuria and beyond.

Once I could walk, which took some time, we all went out for pizza, and probably too much wine.

27

Lake Titicaca: Interdimensional Doorway

It was a day's drive by bus from Cuzco to our destination of Puno, a town on the shores of Lake Titicaca. I hoped to find the rock outcropping that I had envisioned two years before on my shamanic, inner journey with Sue Burch. In a past life as an Incan high priest, Sue had hidden the Universal codes and energies of the initiates into a massive rock near Lake Titicaca in order to protect the knowledge from invaders. I wasn't even sure if the place existed in this reality, or if I would recognize it, if it did.

Although Sue had felt compelled to visit Lake Titicaca, she died before she could complete this important part of her life's work. It was left to me and to our group; that is, if we could find the place and if we were spiritually ready to unlock the energies encoded in this portal. Logically, the chances of recognizing Sue's rock somewhere around a 3,200 square mile lake didn't seem that good. But then, there was nothing logical about this adventure, one that was millennia in the planning.

The Doorway of Aramu Muru

According to Mallku's plan, the day's highlight was to do an Andean ceremony at a pre-Incan rock structure, or interdimensional gateway, often referred to as the Doorway of

Aramu Muru. It was named for Aramu Muru, the legendary spiritual Master who was said to have originally brought the Sun Disc to the Lake Titicaca area from his homeland in Lemuria. Mallku didn't know that I hoped to find the stone mountain which I had witnessed in a meditation with Sue two years earlier.

In 1992, Jorge Luis Delgado, a Peruvian tour guide and friend of Mallku's, stumbled across a mysterious structure with three doors carved into the solid face of a gigantic stone outcropping in the Hayu Marca (sometimes spelled Ajayu Marka) mountain region near Lake Titicaca. Its shape resembled the pre-Inca Gate of the Sun at Tiahuanaco in Bolivia. Locals called it the Doorway of the Demons and avoided it, treating it with suspicion; though native people of the area have a legend that in ancient times, great heroes passed through it on their way to immortality.

Jorge Luis told a local reporter, "When I saw the structure for the first time, I almost passed out! I have dreamed of such a construction repeatedly over the years. I also saw that the smaller door was open and there was a brilliant blue light coming from what looked like a shimmering tunnel. I have commented to my family many times about these dreams, and so when I finally gazed upon the doorway it was like a revelation from God. How does one make order of such a strange occurrence?"[29]

We didn't know any of this background information when we hiked through dusty fields and around sage-dotted hills to the stone outcropping Mallku had chosen for our meditation. As we rounded the last of the hills, the Doorway of Aramu Muru, carved into a massive red rock formation, appeared before us. My heart stopped in recognition: This *was* the place in which Sue had hidden the "codes of the Knowledge of the Universe!" This *was* the place Sue and I had journeyed to in consciousness on the solstice two years before! Every other part of this trip had been magical; I shouldn't have been surprised.

In Peru 2004, our group gazed at the stone mountain, three doors nested within the other, carved into the rock. It stood alone in a windswept field of the high plateau south of the

The Doorway of Aramu Muru, Lake Titicaca   Photo by Al Taylor

town of Puno. The carved structure included an outer door twenty-three feet in height and about the same width; with a smaller, more deeply engraved second portal that measured six feet high. At the bottom of the smaller door there was a niche or keyhole, only about a foot high, which to me represented a third gate. On either side of the large, outer door were deep indentations carved into the rock. Mallku told us that the niche on the right was for us to ask the Guardians for permission to enter, and the one to the left was where we give thanks when we move away from the doorway. We all sat in a semi-circle in the fine, red dirt, facing the stone wall, a gathering of Masters, each bringing his and her own spiritual gifts.

My gift was inner sight and the remembrance of being here before. I was to lead a shamanic journey through the doorway into other dimensions of consciousness. It was not to be channeled. These steps of healing and growth needed to be from a human perspective. My spirit guides, White Eagle and Mark, had brought us this far. Now they watched as I took over. We

Jonette in the inner door

knew we were surrounded by the Elders, the White Brotherhood, the Ancient Ones, the Ones without form. We prayed
that everything they had taught us we had learned well and
that we were ready to move forward. It felt that we were the
elders doing what we could to create peace, love and harmony
to pass down to our children. Mallku began the ceremony by

calling forth the sacred fire. The blue of the fire stood for power, the pink for love, and the gold for wisdom and clarity. Grazing donkeys watched us from the field nearby.

Unsealing the Portal

I began to speak as Jonette, leading our group into a timeless, multidimensional state of consciousness. Together we accessed the vibrational codes of the Sun Disc. This was the most important spiritual process of our entire journey.

As we approach this sacred Gateway, please let go of your separateness and let your soul emerge. Receive each other into your hearts with the recognition of mastery remembered. Each one of us has carried a torch through millennia, even when it wasn't safe to be a torch bearer. Together we move our awareness to the right side of the great stone door and ask permission of the Guardians of the Gate. Access is granted. We move our awareness into the Cave of Crystals inside the rock. The intelligence of the crystals touches us deeply, opening us, tuning us into Oneness. Your ability to hold energy and knowing has expanded in the crystal cave.

We're at the gates of history. Feel the eleven-pointed star of leadership on your forehead. Now we are at the large door, which I see as the Gate of Venus. I see the code to open this door is the Incan square Cross. Instead of the normal three-tiered cross it is a cross of seven steps. There are twenty-eight steps total in this cross... the Esoteric Cross... the Cross of the Seven Rays. Feel this cross in your heart and in the door, until there is a vibration that opens the door. Notice that we are in a different reality, one that feels strongly magnetic... dynamic. Notice how much of humanity is following us... perhaps hesitantly at first. Feel this reality expanding to hold everyone who is ready. Experience the wisdom here; it is something wonderful beyond words.

Now we are ready to move through the next gate, the smaller portal. Go into what Mark has called the seventh dimension by allowing your consciousness to explode into a hologram. Move from one specific perspective to take on perspectives from everywhere. Follow the energy of that exploded heart, the Rainbow Serpent that we experienced in the Cave of the Serpent. Move yourself to vast consciousness where you are centered everywhere. Once we have expanded, the inner gate opens into yet another world, a world beyond understanding.

This is the higher reality that now holds the energy of the Solar Disc of Mu or the Sun Disc of the Incas. Imagine this multidimensional Disc radiating light and vibrations that have only rarely existed on Earth. In this Disc the vibrations, codes, and templates are concentrated; they open up our holographic beingness to a download of Universal Wisdom. We are now receiving the codes and vibrations that we've been seeking. They will be activated as our personal path initiates us into the next level. For now we are simply absorbing everything in a mystical way.

Some of you can now sense a third-level gateway. I'll call it the "Ninth Solar Initiation." It is not an Initiation that you are currently ready for, but an Initiation that will be next upon the path of humanity and certainly upon the path of those Crystalline and Indigo Children of the newest generation. It's not appropriate that we move further. There are some keys and codes for this Ninth Solar transmission that will go into your heart for the future. These are Codes of the Cosmos. These are codes of wisdom beyond comprehension. They are codes for the destiny of mankind. Our human DNA has been created to do so much more than has yet been awakened. We are doing our part by imagining these Ninth Solar Codes moving into us, through our children and our children's children, and into nature herself. These are seeds for the future. Nature, the mountains, the clouds, the lakes, the forest, the jungles, the deserts can all hold aspects of these codes.

When you're ready, move out of the threshold of this small third gate and close the door lightly. It's not appropriate that it stays open. It is closed with a film that those who can find it and open it are welcomed to push through. Acknowledge once again those souls of humanity who have joined us and made it through that second gate, the Gate of the Seven Rays. Now gather with these people and move back out the second door, leaving this gate open.

Now reconnect with the millions of souls who were able to join us through the first door but couldn't go further. Touch them with what you now know because someday they will also be able to enter the second door. Now that you feel deeply changed, exit out the first great door, the Door of Venus. Find waiting for us all the Beings, Archangels, Masters who supported us, feel their jubilation. Feel the Light of the throngs of humanity who aren't quite ready to enter any of these doors. They can see us and feel our love and our wisdom. They can feel their future, their hope in our eyes. We stand now, facing the sun in the east and we love… and we love… and we love.

Before we walk away with all our gifts let's turn back to the great stone. See through your third-eye that we have broken the Seal. The mysteries unveiled are free now. We are ready to lead the next level of our destiny. We have been listening, we have been learning, and we are courageous.

Something great surely happened as we sat there together on the terra cotta earth near the shore of Lake Titicaca. I doubt if we will ever know what we did, or how, or why. I was there for my beloved Sue Burch. The words Mark had spoken to us years before finally made sense:

With this encoding the true Brotherhood of Man and nature and stars will begin to be realized. The veils will be dropped. In many ways this is the remembering of the unified field in which everything is One. There is no longer separation and therefore amnesia between the human race and all the other parts of One-ness. It is an acknowledgment of the higher dimensions of non-separation. The world was not ready for more energy before. Now there are enough humans awake who can under-stand the higher purpose and can work with the Earth so that this rock alone does not have to hold all this wisdom. There will be phases of activation in partnership with the Earth and stars, for this is a huge interdimensional opening.

Time melted around us in the altiplano of Peru. It felt to me as if our souls were fulfilling promises we didn't remember making, to help humanity create a future we were unable to comprehend.

The Sun Disc as a Key

Once I returned to Colorado, brimming with unanswered questions about what really happened in Peru, I stumbled on a fascinating article on the internet by Paul Damon. It expanded on the legend of the Doorway of Aramu Muru.

One Incan priest of the Temple of the Seven Rays named Aramu Muru fled from his temple with a sacred golden disk known as the key of the gods of the seven rays, and hid in the mountains of Hayu Marca. He eventually came upon the door-way which was being watched by shaman priests. He showed them the key of the gods and a ritual was performed with the conclusion of a magical occurrence initiated by the golden disk which opened the portal, and according to the legend blue light did emanate from a tunnel inside. The priest Aramu Muru handed the golden disk to the shaman and then passed through the portal never to be seen again.[30]

Excited, I barely breathed as I read on. This story brought together several elements of my experience. First, the stone portal of Sue's vision years earlier was connected with the Sun Disc that I encountered on the inner planes while in Cuzco. The article mentioned that the golden disc was the key that opened the interdimensional gateway in the rock mountain. I asked myself, "Was this the reason I was shown the Sun Disc and given energetic codes, just two days before we arrived at the Doorway—so I would know the secret to opening the portal?"

Another element that Damon's article brought to light was the idea that the golden disc was known "as the key of the gods of the seven rays."[31] Without consciously knowing any of this, during the meditative jouney I led at the Interdimensional Doorway, I said, "The code to open this door is the... cross of seven steps... the Cross of the Seven Rays."

How did I know all this? Coincidence?

But the final piece that tumbled into place as I read the paragraph on my computer screen was about the high priest Aramu Muru, for whom the doorway was named. It was he who first opened the mystical portal in the stone mountain, handing the disc to a shaman and then disappearing forever.

The questions had to be asked: Was Sue the Incan High Priest, Aramu Muru, who came from Lemuria? Were the codes of the Sun Disc that downloaded through me two days earlier some of the same energies that Sue had hidden in the rock? Was that disc the key? Did the legends spring from what she had done and I had witnessed in our past lives? Why else would I recognize this place? Why else were we here? I knew that I was here in part to fulfill the prophecy Mark had told Sue in my living room in 2002:

In that life you did it alone; there was no one who dreamed what you dreamed and knew what you needed to know. Jonette is an apprentice to you. She is here to be with you and to help hold the power of this Wisdom, this Light, this encoding, that is now to be released.

28

Fertility Temple

ollowing our meditation at the Doorway of Aramu Muru, we had a picnic lunch on the shores of Lake Titicaca. The tour day ended with a sunset stop at the small village of Chucuito to see the remnants of a fertility temple. Next to a Catholic Church was a walled courtyard that was littered with forty or so two and three-foot, upright stone phalluses, dominated by one gigantic penis. Mallku explained that when the Spanish came they destroyed the temple, using what stone pieces they could for building their nearby church. Mallku remarked jovially that there is a rock penis used as a building stone that thrusts right into the church! When the natives saw that the friars didn't appreciate these monumental male organs, the locals carted them away and hid them for centuries in their homes. With the renewed interest in archeology and Andean culture, many of the phalluses have reappeared to once again hang together in the courtyard of the fertility temple.

I envisioned that the men and women in our group should pursue different rituals. The women's ceremony involved a transfer of maternal energy and strength from the women who had borne children to those of us who had not. We created a circle where the mothers surrounded the childless females. Everyone shared what came to her to speak. The sweet, spontaneous convocation brought tears to our eyes.

Meanwhile, I had exhorted Ed to demonstrate leadership

with the men so that they could come up with a meaningful ceremony in that sacred courtyard of human reproduction. He gathered the men together in their half of the temple and began a discussion on the leadership role of men. From what I was told, that conversation lasted less than a minute before Mallku turned the discussion to the importance of tantric sex. You can guess where everyone's attention went. There was just no contest.

Bill Austin of our group observed, "Most of the guys with the exception of young Trent looked fairly uncomfortable." Bill added, "If I had some of my gay friends along they would have all cracked up. Straight guys are so funny about sex." I did notice the men looking at their feet as Mallku, hand on the head of the king penis, talked about the history of the place.

My never-shy sister Erin wouldn't let us go until she had dragged at least one other unmarried female to bow in exaggerated homage to the alpha phallus while we all took pictures. Her personal goal in coming on this journey was to prepare herself to find Mr. Right. Less than three weeks later, she met

Vicki and Erin at the Fertility Temple   *Photo by Al Taylor*

Ken. "When people ask me how I met Ken I tell them I met him through the Incas!" Erin told me, "I believe that finding him was the result of my fervent praying at every sacred site. While everyone else was opening portals and receiving codes, I concentrated on finding a wonderful mate, good sex and a lifetime of happiness. All the meditations and the cleansing work, and the love and friendship with everyone in the group opened my heart up so much that when Ken stepped in a few weeks later, I was ready for him! I feel nothing like the 'Before Peru Erin' and that is a wonderful thing!"

After seventeen days in Peru, we left with spiritual breakthroughs that would take us months to understand. We were a powerful group who had shared magical, mystical adventures.

Mallku already had another tour group waiting for him at Lake Titicaca. Before he left us, I found a private moment to ask him, "What has been the most significant part of this trip for you?"

I wanted him to answer that he enjoyed our group, that he appreciated meeting me, that he recognized a special bond, that he hoped I would bring other people to Peru. He might have said so many things to summarize his time with us. What he did say was hardly what I wanted to hear. With animated voice he exclaimed, "The most amazing thing for me was when our plane finally landed in Cuzco through that storm. I thought we were going to hit that mountain! I can't believe how close we got to it!"

There were so many *other* things he might have said.

I was leaving with the truth in my heart that Mallku was my twin flame or twin soul, not because he agreed with me, but because I couldn't doubt my strong knowing. Courage is believing one's own truth, irrespective of external validation.

PART IV

So Much to Understand

"It is the spirit of flight that we are addressing—the freedom to be supported by that which is unseen. So we ask you to unfold your silver wings, lead with your heart, and jump into the sky. For the sky will catch you and carry you to universes unknown."

White Eagle

The Eagle and the Condor

29

Twin Souls

I believe that the incredible spiritual awakenings I experienced in Peru were in part a result of my recognizing Mallku as my soul twin. Throughout the trip, I found myself watching Mallku with pride, pride in what the masculine side of our twin soul had become. Every time I looked at him, I felt unnamable and uncontrollable energies and timeless emotions.

Mallku was a fabulous coordinator—handling a myriad of details gracefully, a strong and balanced leader, a man passionate about sacred knowledge, and a researcher dedicated to uncovering deeper truths.

Most of the time I successfully kept a shield up between Mallku and myself so feelings wouldn't escape my confused heart. One day as Erin and I were shopping in the tourist market in Aguas Calientes, Mallku appeared at the next stall to buy something for that evening's full moon ceremony. I wasn't expecting him there so my heart's protection wasn't engaged. His presence, even in such an innocent setting, slammed me full force. I felt my knees weaken, my pulse sputter and my hand flew up to cover my heart. Damn. How could this man, whom I hardly knew, have such an effect? Everything about this bypassed my thinking mind, and thus my ability to control it rationally. The connection wasn't one of feelings or romantic emotions; it was inescapably energetic. It felt physical like the ends of a stretched rubber band snapping back together.

My friend P. J. Deen had previously taught courses on

"Awakening to Your Twin Flame," so once I was back in Colorado, I sought her guidance to bring some answers to my bewilderment. This is what she wrote:

Twin flames go well beyond soulmate-type relationships to the point of being practically indescribable. You are essentially part of the same energy and this can create an almost overwhelming, magnetic attraction.

Twin flames are consciousnesses that have been one, and then split like the first division of a fertilized cell, growing separately in their own search for existence and occasionally crossing paths and merging once again to share the other's experiences and exalting in the joy of that, raising the growth of each other in an exponential fashion. This rise in growth through the multiplication of experiences results in the ecstasy and extreme joy in these relationships. In this blending there is the opportunity to experience unity and the One, triggering remembrances of the state of bliss and union with all things. The compatibility of twin flames is great. It is almost like a coming home. For indeed it is in a way. It is a coming home to oneself, a coming home to the remembrances of total union with oneself and God.

One of the most important things that characterizes twin flames is the work they've agreed to do together in this lifetime. Your coming together, especially at this time of wonderful acceleration, holds great meaning for the success of humanity's expansion into light and greater consciousness. And the time is now.

I spent the first several days back home on the phone talking about my experiences in South America. I found only a few friends, besides P. J., who had actually met their twin souls. For each woman the truth of the relationship was undeniable. Not one of them said, "I *think* he *might* have been my twin." They all just *knew*.

Patricia said, "I met mine in the Yucatan; he was Cuban. The attraction was so unbelievable that I would have left my young children and cut off my arm if he had wanted me to."

Dayle, a friend from Canada told me that she's known her

twin flame for over forty years. "He's a Jesuit priest in Ireland. Our connection is so strong, though it probably bewilders him, that every few years I fly to Ireland just to spend an afternoon in the rectory talking with him. I could write a book on all those years." She added, "What's interesting about truth is you just can't hide it."

Kristine, from Holland, emailed me a beautiful description of meeting her twin soul at a workshop. "I was drawn as by some magic hand to talk to him. As I came near him my heart center started vibrating tremendously. When he gave me a hug I was transported to another level of connection, like there was only one of us. The state of bliss was beyond any of the normal senses... My heart was taking over... I had no more body or emotions. It almost felt painful to withdraw from that embrace and state, like when you're born as a baby and are suddenly thrown out from the beautiful womb into the cold world. My gift at this time was not the *re*union itself but the *re*membrance of the union."

P. J.'s twin flame, in feeling the power of her connection to him probably stated it best of all, "You scare the hell out of me."

Deborah Bergman, another friend who writes and conducts workshops on the Divine Masculine and Feminine, just laughed when I phoned her after the trip and told her about Mallku, asking her the question: "What am I supposed to do now?"

Her answer: "It's a good thing you don't live on the same continent," delivered with a tone of knowing mirth, wasn't exactly the answer I was looking for in helping me deal with the Pandora's box I had inadvertently opened. Deborah and I chatted a long time; after all there aren't too many people to whom a happily married woman can talk about an inexplicable, energetic attraction to a younger man who just happens to be an Andean shaman.

At the end of my conversation with Deborah, I dropped the bomb that no doubt both she and P. J. could have predicted: "I'm going back to Peru... in December... for the solstice." It took me another two weeks to break the news to Ed and even longer to tell Mallku that I was returning to the Andes.

Girlfriends

It is important in everyone's life to have a balance between the spiritual and the ordinary. That is why we have long-time friends. We were back from Peru a month when I joined four college sorority sisters for a vacation in Cape Cod. We arrived in Boston from Denver at midnight. At 3:00 a.m., we were still looking for the right town on the Cape. Deborah Deeg was at the wheel; conversation was lively as we tried to keep her awake. "Jonette, tell us everything about your trip to Peru from the beginning and don't leave out a thing," came the opener from the driver's seat.

I started with Mallku. I skipped the twin soul stuff, going right to the part they would find most interesting—sharing a thatched hut with a thirty-eight-year-old Peruvian tour guide. I told them that he held me in his arms and that it felt lovely. They *really* listened to this part. Even Barb Scripps woke up from her nap in the very back of our rented minivan. I told them of my declaration to Mallku that "I am very married." They were relieved as they all adore my husband and wanted to make sure I hadn't lost my marbles.

We've been best friends since we were eighteen, long before anything spiritual started happening to me. They remain skeptical about the channeling part of my life and they love me anyway. Then I made a fatal mistake in my storytelling. I told them that I heard a voice telling me to initiate Mallku by touching his third-eye. As one, they hooted, they howled, they roared with laughter. The minivan slalomed as Deborah, the driver, shook with hysteria. All four of them had questions: "You touched his *what*?! Where exactly *is* a man's third-eye? What *kind* of initiation was it?"

Sidney Friend summed up the general sentiment with her question: "*Whose* voice in your head told you to do this?"

There is nothing like close girlfriends to keep you in check. I changed the subject and we finally found the cottage on the beach.

30

Answers from White Eagle

ur mystical, adventurous journey to the Andes was so much more than any of us had hoped for and certainly more than we could easily process. Ed told people, "The trip to Everest was an experience of a lifetime; none of us thought the breakthroughs could be equaled, but Peru was so much more."

Berdine de Visser from Holland wrote, "I have been thinking about Peru and what happened personally and as a group, but I still find it hard to put it in words. I really am changed."

"It is difficult, if not impossible to describe the feelings, the energies, and the experiences from this journey," Brad Johnson emailed. "All I can say is the trip was a life changing event."

I talked to Larry Cooper who said that from the traditional view he was going more and more insane since he had been back from South America.

"I guess we all are. Sanity isn't what it's cracked up to be," I replied. I too felt different: stronger, lighter, more loving, more approachable.

My Relationship to White Buffalo Calf Woman

The transcendental moments in the Andes left me with a great deal to digest and understand. I channeled White Eagle for some higher answers. One thing on my mind was my relationship to White Buffalo Calf Woman. White Eagle explained:

Jonette holds the energy and wisdom of White Buffalo Calf Woman, though some of it is still behind the veils. They are the same soul. In this life Jonette is awakening to her mission, vision and power. There is no doubt that she is a spiritual great one. There is only doubt if she will awaken fully or not. Quickly she must fully grasp the power of the spiritual awakening so she can help others. If not, others will be afraid to grasp their own Light. The extent to which Jonette can hold and accept this Truth, is the extent to which she will break through the barriers that she and other humans have—barriers that also keep them from their greatness. She is asked to accept greatness. So are all. It is hardest to accept greatness before the others have.

Who Is Kumara?

Besides understanding my connection to White Buffalo Calf Woman, the other looming question I had was "Who is Kumara?" It was the name I called myself in the Cave of the Serpent, and the name I used to seek admittance to the mystical pyramid that held the Sun Disc. I did some internet research and found that the Sanskrit scriptures refer to the holy Kumaras. Reference to Sanat Kumara, or the Highest Kumara, who is said to be the Lord of the Earth, and seven other Kumaras were mentioned in Buddhist teachings, in the Hindu Puranas, and in the Theosophist writings of Alice Bailey. It was said that the Kumaras were great beings from the planet Venus. Supposedly, there were great mystery schools on Venus that were the training ground for the hierarchy of Brahmanism, Hinduism, Lemurian and pre-Lemurian avatars or Masters. The mention of Venus struck a chord because of my experience at the Interdimensional Doorway of Aramu Muru. When I first saw the gigantic outer door, carved into the stone, I reflexively stated, "That gateway has to do with Venus."

However, the idea of mystery schools on Venus was far-fetched, even for me. It was time to ask White Eagle his opinion about Kumara. He had a way of making things easy for me to understand.

Jonette, White Buffalo Calf Woman and Kumara are the same
soul at different levels of awakening. Kumara is at an extraordi-
narily high level of awakening yet is still Jonette. Kumara is so
much more because she embodies a huge Enlightened One, both
male and female; yet Jonette is more comfortable with the female
side for now. Kumara is the energy of a Divine Human. It is a
name, a field for a human awakened at a high dimension. Every
human has the possibility to have the power of Kumara. As
Jonette claims this energy she will open the path for others to be
fully enlightened. She is claiming the Universal power that
should belong to everyone. She is claiming it, not as a deity, but
as a human claiming divinity. In that highest name Jonette is
still human and can claim the power of the Sun Disc.

The Power of the Sun Disc

I wanted to know more about the mystical pyramid and the
codes of the Sun Disc that I had received in the ceremony at
Mallku's apartment. White Eagle continued:

Mark and White Eagle are closely related to Jonette's soul. The
energy, power and wisdom of Kumara and White Buffalo Calf
Woman are Jonette's soul. She is opening the vessel of herself to
her larger Spirit. She has asked for codes of Awakening. The
Sun Disc she found in the etheric world called her to itself. The
Sun Disc doesn't exist in one dimension or one location. It can
be accessed in many ways, depending on the path. Jonette
found it by calmly claiming her Divine humanness.

The pyramid of the Sun Disc was left unguarded as a test.
Jonette needed to know that she must ask permission. By call-
ing forth the guards and leader she proved to the higher realms
that she was ready and that she could handle the energy codes
that would be given to her. She needed to lead herself without
guidance. The Guardian of the pyramid of the Sun Disc, whom

Jonette asked permission to enter, in Egyptian mythology is Ra, the Sun God. In the Aztec tradition, he is Quetzalcoatl, the Plumed Serpent who showed himself as a man. Even gods have a human visage. (This reminded me that Ra was Sue Burch's spirit guide.)

Humans must listen to their inner call and follow their knowing to these openings. Jonette now holds in her physical being the codes and keys that will be the basis of Solar Initiations for a wide range of people. She will be transmitting Solar Initiations from beyond your sun.

The Relationship with Mallku

I asked White Eagle about my connection with Mallku. Most importantly, I wanted to know why, (when I'd only been back from Peru for one day) did I *know* that I needed to return to the Andes in December?

Jonette and Mallku are twin flames, each a flame on their own; together they create a doorway or a flame of healing and transcendence. As Jonette awakens and only as Mallku awakens, can there be great learning, service, and growth. It is meant that Jonette and Mallku meet to help each other on their spiritual paths. They must trust each other—learning a completely new paradigm of trust. He is probably the one human who can help her grow the most and vice versa.

December together with Mallku—it will be extraordinarily helpful if he is awake to the same level as Jonette's level of clarity. She must hold the space and let him remember, not tell him what she knows. Both must overcome egos and fears to move to divine trust. It isn't about their personalities. It doesn't even matter if she likes him and he likes her. It helps if they respect each other. Their connection and the work they can do are beyond personalities.

A woman of power, who carries the energies of the Eagle and a man of power who carries the energies of the Condor, each also holding the energies of North and South America, will come together like two live wires touching. Their conscious recognition of each other as twin souls after millennia of being apart opens up a tear in the structure of how things have been. It opens up the possibilities of rapid human awakening. Their connection must be physical — just meditating while visualizing an eagle and condor flying in peace is not it. Their union must flash like lightning through the very physical core of their humanness and then into Mother Earth.

There is more to this relationship in its potential to heal the world than this channel wants to deal with right now. Jonette must be willing to let go of everything in the old game, though it won't necessarily be taken away. She must quickly come to grips with her power. If she communicates her insights and has not aligned her power, she will invite criticism. It is right that she shares her insights.

I was so confused as I sorted through my feelings and fears. Everything White Eagle told me felt true, but it meant significant changes in how I saw myself. There were so many mysteries all coming together in my life. I was incredibly grateful that my husband Ed is the man he is because I was able to share with him what I was learning and how confused it was making me. All of the twin soul information and the inexplicable, deep feelings I had for Mallku had opened up my heart to an even greater degree. I had a new, immense capacity to love everyone and everything. I cried whenever I talked or thought about Mallku, yet I loved Ed and felt love from him more than ever before.

Dearest Mallku

We arrived home from South America in early September, but even toward the end of the month, most of me was still in Peru. Every night I dreamt of the Andes and other worlds. Within a few days of returning home, I knew that I had to be in Peru for the summer solstice in the southern hemisphere, the 21st of December. I emailed Mallku.

Dearest Mallku,

This is a difficult letter to write. One reason is that I don't really know you at all—your thoughts or your reactions. Two, I feel I know your Spirit really, really well. So, the dilemma is that the soul part of me wants to share huge, intimate insights and visions, but my personality wants to block it out of fear that it is inappropriate for me to assume such closeness to you. You might reject all of it… and me.

It was a big step for me to tell you in the Amazon that I felt you are a twin of my soul. Something told me that I would be given only one chance to acknowledge it to you; otherwise, the opportunity for healing the masculine and feminine sides of my soul would be closed for many, many more lifetimes. It seemed that in doing so I acknowledged a higher path, a divine knowing, that transcends this life and my agreements here.

What I feel for you makes no logical sense. It fits nothing I've ever done or felt before. It feels like an opportunity to touch into divine love, to heal love and move everything to a higher plane. If I can really allow myself to feel this love for your soul, for you as a brother, lover, son, then I will know how to take that love to everyone. I will be able to hold divine love for everyone, as we are meant to know it.

I don't want to be your girlfriend. I don't want romance. I don't want sex. I want to have the best marriage possible with Ed. I want you to attract a life mate to match your dreams. Can you hear what I say? Does it make any sense to you? None of it fits into any box that I know.

On the mystical, spiritual side, I feel compelled to be in Peru over this solstice and a week or so before. I can see us working together as equal masters, following Spirit to open gates for ourselves and mankind. I know that we are very strong, each in our own way, and that if we share those powers there are dimensions that will unlock for us. You can teach me so much and I have so much I can show you.

So, I've said pretty much everything I have for now. You might be smiling with an inner knowing, or you might be shaking your head and saying, "This gringa is crazy." This is only my knowing, my half of the picture. It is important that you find out what your truth is. If there is some match in our visions, we can work together so that everything comes equally from both of us. If it doesn't ring true for you, I understand and accept. (Okay, that's a lie: I will logically understand and accept, but my heart and soul will truly be sad.)

Mallku, I will always love you,

Jonette

Mallku didn't respond directly to any of this. He simply emailed that it was okay if I wanted to come in December.

31

Prophecies of Peace

hite Eagle had confirmed that Mallku and I, embodying the energies of the Condor and the Eagle, had a role to play together in world healing and transcendence. Needing to understand more, I researched the meaning of the ancient legends of the Eagle and the Condor. John Perkins, an author of several books on the spirituality of tribes indigenous to Amazonia, wrote about the prophecy:

> It states that back in the mists of history, human societies divided and took two different paths: that of the condor (representing the heart, intuitive and mystical) and that of the eagle (representing the brain, rational and material). In the 1490s, the prophecy said, the two paths would converge and the eagle would drive the condor to the verge of extinction. Then, five hundred years later, in the 1990s, a new epoch would begin, one in which the condor and eagle will have the opportunity to reunite and fly together in the same sky, along the same path. If the condor and eagle accept this opportunity, they will create a most remarkable offspring, unlike any ever seen before.[32]

The Andean people measured time in a 1,000-year cycle called an Inti, meaning Sun, with a half cycle of 500 years called a Pachakuti—pacha meaning Universe or the world and kuti meaning revolution or transformation. Each Pachakuti represents an opposite part of the world's duality. For instance, a 500-year period of prosperity is followed by a similar period of darkness and difficulty.

In the eighth Pachakuti or 500-year cycle, the Incan Empire flourished. During that period Pachakuti, the greatest of the Inca leaders, oversaw the expansion of the Empire that covered much of the western part of South America. The ninth Pachakuti with its 500 years of conflict and imbalance began in the 1500s with the Spanish invasion that conquered the mighty Andean Empire.

We are now entering the tenth Pachakuti, a time of the returning Light. Willaru Huarto, a Quechuan Indian who grew up in Peru's jungles and studied the ancient prophecies told to him by village shamans said the signs are in place that will "signal the return of Light to the planet and the dawn of a golden era. Humanity should cure itself and give help to the poor. Regenerate yourself with Light, and then help those who have poverty of the soul. Return to the inner spirit which we have abandoned while looking elsewhere for happiness."[33]

The Q'ero a small tribe who has lived in isolation high in the Andes may still hold some of the ancient wisdom. They call themselves "The Keepers of Time." The Q'ero was 'discovered' by outsiders in 1949. Later, at the Andean "Feast of the Return of Pleiades," some Q'ero wearing the sign of the sun announced that the time of the prophecies was at hand. The sacred knowledge was now to be released to the world in preparation for the day when the Eagle of the North and the Condor of the South would fly together again.[34]

Stories that were handed down by the elders refer to the end of time as we know it, and the birth of a golden era of peace—a time of healing and reunion between people of the North and the South. Some Q'ero teach special rites to transmit potential that can ultimately empower individuals to become an Inca, or "Luminous One." They believe that the doorways between worlds are opening and that we can now step beyond our human limitations.[35]

A Golden Age

The belief that now is the time for humankind to enter into a Golden Age is echoed in prophecies in almost every culture. In Hindu cosmology there are four yugas or ages, each thousands of years long. They make up a complete cycle of creation. The last age of 5,000 years, which ended in 2003, is the Kali Yuga or the "age of quarrel." It is the most negative of the four evolutionary cycles. It leads to the destruction of this world in preparation for a new creation and a new cycle of Yugas. In the first or Satya Yuga, which means purity, humanity lives in a state of God-like innocence. Each phase becomes further removed from the Truth and goodness in a descending spiral. Finally, in the fourth age, which has just ended, humanity is at one-quarter of its natural holiness. According to ancient Hindu beliefs, we are now repeating the great wheel of creation, returning once again to the Satya Yuga or the highest age of human evolution.

In early 2005, Sri Bhagavan, a renowned holy man in India stated, "The world will witness the beginning of the end of all division and of all dominance in every form that will ultimately lead to the Age of Oneness or the Golden Age… Things are at last beginning to happen."[36]

This certainly echoed the prophecy of the Eagle and the Condor, and White Eagle's channeled words to me more than a decade earlier:

> *You on Earth are standing on the threshold of a great and beautiful emergence. It will eclipse anything that has occurred before. The Renaissance and the Period of Enlightenment in your history are nothing compared to the power that is waiting to be born in your lifetime.*

32

Leadership and Soul Greatness

ven though I had prayed for enlightenment and for spiritual breakthroughs, when they came fast and furiously, it became apparent to me that I had a lot of personal growth homework to do. I had been back from Peru a month when I once again channeled White Eagle with my pent-up questions.

Jonette is struggling, but she's acting in the right direction in spite of her struggles. Her greatest struggle is in dealing with her ego fears. Both ego and fear are illusions. They are the part of the world she is trying to break from. She fears being different from everyone else as she begins to come to terms with her soul greatness. Her soul greatness isn't greater than anyone else's; it is just that she is finding hers earlier than most people do. She fears that she will be ridiculed by others who fear they have no soul greatness of their own, and that she is flaunting hers. The truth is everyone has it; it is not individualized. Soul greatness belongs to all. Christ said, "This and so much more you will do." People don't believe that. They deified Him and then made themselves less than Him.

I wanted to understand my role as a leader, especially because of the energies of the eleven-pointed star that I carried and transmitted to others. White Eagle spoke to that:

*There are groups of souls that have particular vibrational sets
that respond to the same things. In such a group there are the
leaders and then there are the others who have their own various roles. All roles are important. The group agrees to support
the leaders to lead. Jonette is a leader of a group of souls by
agreement, not because she is better or greater in her Light, but
because she is naturally a better leader. As the group supports
her and she agrees to lead, the whole group moves further
ahead. Her position isn't more exalted; it is more risky and visi-
ble. With the visibility of any sort of leadership role there is the
chance to be a lightning rod for the different poles. As she steps
forward, she will polarize her disciples and polarize her detrac-
tors. Neither should be listened to, neither are right. She must
be strong enough so that neither matter. By this, all will
benefit.*

*The most difficult aspect of leadership is to have few peers and
few teachers in front. She has not reached where she has alone.
She has always been guided. She has always been taught,
though, it has not always been easy and clear. She has strong
peers, she has strong support, and when it is needed, she does
have teachers and gurus. Jonette is setting the path for what
humans are becoming. As she steps forward into her Mastery,
it makes room for more leaders, and more leaders and more
leaders. Leadership is not a limited position, but grows to the
extent people are stepping forward.*

From White Eagle's words, I understood that we change the
world by accepting our own personal greatness and beingness.
That makes it possible for us to draw out the unique greatness
in others. A simple maxim of leadership I sometimes use has
been to walk in front when people don't know where they're
going, and to walk behind them when they do. White Eagle
once told me, *When you are a leader you can be tired, but you must
never be weak.*

Carrying More Light

Throughout this time, I could feel that I was changing at a cellular level. For several days, I felt tired, achy and feverish but no other symptoms of sickness or flu. I presumed that this might be caused by rapid spiritual growth as my physical cells changed to hold more radiance. Uncertain if this intuition was correct, I asked the Universe to give me confirmation, "Please give me a clear message if I'm correct that my body is physically changing to carry more light." Then I forgot about it and went to the mall.

I am not one of those women who dress up when I go shopping, and it wasn't a particularly good-hair day. Just as I was ducking into my favorite clothing shop, I ran into my friend Brian. He and I both grew up in Littleton so I've known him since fourth grade. Because he is also a professional speaker, I sometimes see him every few years. His greeting to me was warm and friendly. "You look *great!*" he said, giving me a hug. Then he took a closer look and added, "It's as if there is a *glow* about you." It could not have been any clearer! Through Brian's words, the Universe had confirmed my sense that, yes, indeed my physical body was transforming to carry more spiritual light.

Several times during this period, I experienced fleeting transcendental moments of enlightenment, but they would rarely last more than a few minutes, and I was unable to repeat them. In frustration I asked White Eagle, "Why can't I stay in an Enlightened state all the time? Why do I always seem to go backward again?"

He answered into my mind, *There are others whose role it is to hold and transmit the energies of infinite bliss, but your role is to help illuminate the individual steps along the way so people have a clear path to follow, not just the endpost.* His answer shut me up. I got it.

A Confirmation from Sue

In August 2003, exactly a year before our journey to the Andes, Sue Burch passed away. Yet her spirit was very much present with us, especially as we meditated at the great rock near Lake Titicaca. It made me wonder if perhaps Sue had orchestrated our entire trip from the 'other side.' In an uncanny way, she may have subconsciously known about my connection to White Buffalo Calf Woman two years before the link was revealed to me. Confirmation of how my spiritual life was intertwined with Sue's came in the form of a painting that she gave me during a road trip we took together ten months before she passed on. It was a picture I didn't 'see' until I returned from South America.

A year prior to her death, Sue was already getting weaker from the cancer in her body. Wanting to spend as much time with her as I could, I phoned her, "I have a harebrained idea." My comment was met with silence on Sue's end. No doubt she was considering all the possible ideas I might have, and how she was going to be enveloped in the middle of one, whether she liked it or not. "Let's take a road trip to Sedona!" Of course, *I* was thrilled by this brainstorm of mine, reasoning that it would allow us to spend quality time together and shouldn't be too trying on her failing health. Besides, Sedona's red rock beauty is *the* place for a rock lover like Sue. However, going to Arizona to see Sedona wasn't on Sue's list of things she needed to do before she died, though seeing the Grand Canyon was. I assured her we could easily visit the South Rim of the Canyon. She began to warm to the idea of the whole adventure.

Our October 2002 road trip was a gift to us both. I learned to love her unconditionally, without foisting my judgments on her. If she wanted to stop to smoke a cigarette, we stopped. When she wanted to eat candy and chocolate, I had some too. When she wanted to stay in the most expensive Bed and Breakfast in Sedona, we did. I helped her out of the car so we could meditate at Sedona's famed energy vortex sites. Miracles came through her while I sat alongside, feeling nothing. In our eight stress-free days together, we talked of life, death and everything in between.

As we drove to the Grand Canyon from Flagstaff, Sue had me stop at one of those generic roadside gas/snack/gift shops for a drink and some candy. Back in my Jeep she presented me

Sue Burch at the Grand Canyon

with a 12-by 15-inch matted print, a southwest sort of Indian painting, not the style of art that fit my taste or décor. "I just *had* to get this picture for you, Jonette," she beamed.

Glancing quickly at it, I graciously thanked her for her thoughtfulness.

Once at home, I tacked the print to the wall in a bare corner of my office. Even then, I didn't really look at what was depicted.

After returning to Colorado from our Andean expedition, a year after Sue's death, I reorganized my office: new furniture, plants, cleaned bookshelves. I moved Sue's southwestern print to another wall. As I nailed it to its new location closer to my desk, I saw it in detail for the first time. My jaw dropped at the careful weaving of so many small pieces of my life. Sue had given me a print of a white buffalo and a Native American woman with long, silver hair, both enfolded in a galaxy of stars. White Buffalo Calf Woman! Sue must have been in heaven grinning that her message to me finally made sense.

33

Kumara

he first time I heard the term "Ninth Solar Initiation" was when I spontaneously spoke of it during our group meditation at the Interdimensional Doorway in the rock near Lake Titicaca. I had used the term to describe the third level, or inner gateway, an initiation that will be next on the path of human evolution, most appropriately for the next generations. At that time, I described the keys and codes of the Ninth Solar Initiation as "the codes of wisdom, the codes for the destiny of mankind."

In October 2004, I couldn't get that term out of my head. I had my monthly appointment with James Pinkel, the fabulously gifted and clairvoyant healer who had been so much help to Ed, me and many of our friends. "I need help preparing my body for the Ninth Solar Initiation, whatever that is," I told James at the beginning of our session. Then I plopped myself down on his massage table. While James used his hands to move energy around, I felt physical shifts in my cellular structure that seemed to be enabling me to levitate or move interdimensionally.

Lying on the table, I became aware of several dimensions at once. In one reality, I held the Sun Disc in my being and fully embodied Kumara, who was totally light and brilliantly gold. I was shown that she, as me, was one of the beings who brought the Sun Discs and other knowledge to Earth from the Great Central Sun in order to activate the souls of humans so they would be different from that of animals. For some humans the activation was impossible. Then I could see or remember that a dark cloud came over the people. I laid there in James' office sobbing with intense grief. "They forgot," I repeated to myself in anguish, meaning that people forgot their divinity. It was the same pain I felt when I had looked down at the tents of our campground near Machu Picchu and said, "My people have suffered and died too often."

Horus, Son of Isis and Osiris

As James continued his energy work with me, I had a vision of a falcon-headed Egyptian god with a Sun Disc on his chest merge into my being. That evening, I researched and learned that the vision was of Horus, the son of god-couple Isis and Osiris. Horus, Isis and Osiris were always portrayed in Egyptian mythology with Sun Discs above their heads. However, I saw Horus with the Disc on his chest, not above his head. The message to me was that the divine energies portrayed by the Sun Disc are integrating into our human hearts. Was this vision telling me that I was also connected with the Solar Disc legends of the Egyptians? Were all the sun-worshipping civilizations tied together with a common source in Atlantis and Lemuria? Or, was the origin earlier still, from the Great Central Sun or God-source of the Universe?

This session was much more than a spontaneous past life regression; it was an interdimensional remembering. I remembered who I was *before* I became human! I saw myself arriving on Earth encased in golden light, bringing the Discs. I was Kumara. I knew that in order to take a body we must forget everything we knew before. My soul's memories were awakening so quickly! I hoped my body, my personality, my husband, my family and friends were ready because it didn't look like I could slow it down.

Speaking as my Kumara-self, I spontaneously told James, "Mallku is preparing for his role as Divine Lover." The normal part of me didn't have even a second to process the possible repercussions of that tidbit, before I was hit with another swirl

of cosmic truth—in this state of Kumara-realization, my energies had transcended White Eagle! I immediately shared this
insight with James, who was doing a fabulous job following
these spiritual explosions along with me.

"Is White Eagle okay with that?" James asked.

White Eagle's response came as an instant thought transmission, *I've been preparing you. I'm at your service.*

I've accepted a lot of things: channeling White Eagle and
then Mark; being the essence of White Buffalo Calf Woman;
and knowing myself in the higher planes as Kumara. None of
this prepared me for a sudden graduation beyond White Eagle.
My thoughts and emotions careened around, hitting each other
like bumper cars. I had absolutely no structure in which to put
all this. But then, I had been warned. When White Eagle first
came to me more than sixteen years before he stated with
authority, *I will not always be your voice.* I've understood that
channeling was to be a vehicle for personal spiritual growth,
never an end to itself. My ultimate goal has always been to use
my own soul's divinity to directly access the love and wisdom
I've come to associate with my spirit guides.

I meekly looked up at James who was wiping tears from his
face, and asked, "Is this all true or am I making it up?"

"It's all true," was his reply.

I assumed I had just experienced the Ninth Solar Initiation. I
went home to write in my journal and to eat chocolate. The
chocolate especially helped.

The Solar Brotherhood

Many months later, while researching Andean initiation traditions, I received outside confirmation of the remarkable
vision of me as Kumara bringing the energies of the Sun Discs
to Earth. I was elated by the external validation because,
although part of me believes everything I receive or see in my
inner visions, the other part of me remains skeptical.

I learned that there is a remote Andean village where native
Quechuan sages preserve the ancient Incan traditions. Peruvian Antón Ponce de León Paiva wrote about his experience of

being taken blindfolded to a village near the Sacred Valley, where he encountered the Quechuan Spiritual Masters and was initiated into the Solar Brotherhood.[37] The oral traditions and teachings of these people, which go back even before the Incas, say that the Brotherhood of the Sun was brought to the Andes from Lemuria by Aramu Muru and the other Kumaras. Aramu Muru traveled to Lake Titicaca where he founded the Brotherhood of the Seven Rays and the Solar Brotherhood. Yet Paiva's native Quechuan teacher claims that there is a large gap in our knowledge of the first great Andean cultures and the advent of the Incas. Manco Capac, who is often considered the first Inca, actually appeared in ancient times, well before the Incas.[38] In fact, the Incas were the least spiritually adept people in the ancient lineage.[39]

People in this village are still secretly initiated into the Intic Churin Cura or Solar Brotherhood to become Children of the Sun, the name the Incas called themselves. The Solar Brotherhood was the first manifestation on Earth of the Great White Brotherhood, the spiritual group from which White Eagle and Mark hail. "Hmmm," I considered, "I've already had an inner initiation into the White Brotherhood. Does that mean I'm also a member of the Solar Brotherhood?" According to one author, the Brotherhood first came to Earth from Venus by beings known as the Kumaras. They were enlightened masters who were the first spiritual teachers of humanity. The name "Kumara" means androgynous serpent.[40] This information amazed me because I first called myself Kumaru/Kumara in our meditation with Mallku in the Cave of the Serpent or Amaru Machay. According to some prophecies, the descendents of the Kumara are scheduled to reincarnate to complete their missions on Earth, one of which is to relocate the ancient sites where the original Lemurian records were placed for safekeeping.

Once again, shards of knowledge and scraps of experience collected over the years in an otherwise normal life fused to present a bigger picture of who I am, more than I could ever have imagined. Weird events that seemed unrelated were locked together and confirmed much later by outside research.

I began putting together a possible past life scenario for myself: As Kumara, a golden, non-physical being, I was among the ones who brought knowledge and sacred wisdom to Earth, specifically to the lost continent of Lemuria. Some of that knowledge and power was in the form of golden Sun Discs. Sacred records and at least one of the Sun Discs was then taken to Lake Titicaca to preserve it from Lemuria's destruction. To protect the secret knowledge from those who would abuse it, I watched Sue Burch (another Kumara? or Aramu Muru himself?) as she hid this wisdom in the higher dimensions by using the great stone portal or Gateway of Aramu Muru.

In 2004, my path led me to the Andes. I just happened to remember myself as Kumara, gain entry to an interdimensional pyramid, see the Sun Disc and download its vibrational energy codes into myself, find the actual stone portal at Lake Titicaca, and enter its three interdimensional doorways in meditation. Whew! My life was getting further away from an ordinary one!

34

Lemuria and the Incas

Mystery surrounds the Disc made of pure gold, revered by the Incas. George Hunt Williamson, writing as Brother Philip put forth the theory that the golden Sun Disc of the Incas originally came from the ancient Pacific land of Lemuria, often known as Mu.[41] Some indigenous Andean spiritual elders say the same. David Hatcher Childress, author of *Lost Cities of Ancient Lemuria & the Pacific*, has researched evidence of the existence of a now submerged continent in the Pacific.[42] His work is a fascinating compilation of research and personal explorations through Australia, the Pacific and South America.

As to the reality of a Sun Disc in the Andes, Native Andean elders say that there were two solar discs of gold kept in the Coricancha, the Sun Temple in Cuzco. "One was brought out for public ceremonies. The other one was even more sacred than the first; it was only used in transcendental times or occasions of cosmic character. It came from very far across the great river behind these mountains, from Lemuria. The great masters of these lands are our very distant ancestors."[43] Childress wrote that the earliest Spaniards actually saw a physical Sun Disc. Their historians described the Disc as solid gold and decorated with gems. It was placed in the Coricancha to reflect the sun's rays at dawn.[44]

I first learned of Childress' work while I was in Cuzco. I always ask to be guided at the perfect time to the information and books I need. One afternoon, I wandered down the street to a local bookstore—okay, and a stylish shop next door to it where I *had* to buy a purple, alpaca-wool jacket. A dusty book about Lemuria caught my eye. Ever since reading Williamson's book, I had been curious about the Andean connection to this sunken Pacific land. You might think it strange to find such a relatively obscure book, written in English, in a Cuzco bookstore; unless you consider the book was there *so that I would find it!*

Childress speculated that massive megalithic structures found in Peru, Bolivia and scattered or sunk throughout the Pacific, may be the remains of ancient Lemurian civilizations. One of the sources he quoted was "The Lemurian Fellowship." They wrote that the Lemurians "built great cities out of large blocks of stone and under the direction of the so-called Elders, went on to create an advanced civilization."[45]

So many questions in my mind begged answers. Were the Incas—their sun worshipping religion, their mighty buildings of stone—the most recent legacy of an advanced Lemurian culture?

Well after my journeys to Peru, I wrote to the headquarters of the Lemurian Fellowship, a spiritual group in Ramona, California, asking that very question. They responded:

You've asked a question that is not easily answered. We do know the first humans incarnated on the Continent of Mu and migrated from there over many thousands of years to the countries of the world as it was then. Consider that the Amazon basin was once a huge inland sea, while the only area above water was a rather narrow section of land on the west side of the continent. It was not until after the submergence of Mu, about 28,000 years ago, followed several thousand years later by Atlantis, that the Continent of South America reached its current size.

The term Inca derives from the Mukulian, or Lemurian, term N'Kul, meaning, the Sun. During the time of Atlantis the term had become Incal, also used by the people who became known as Incas. Who the Incas were and how they came to establish their society where it was is no doubt a long story involving people from several of the original tribes from Mu. But there is little we can do to help you piece it together.[46]

There are remnants and unexplained ancient mysteries throughout the Pacific that may lend credibility to the theory of Lemuria and of an advanced people who worshipped the sun and built incredible structures of stone. A growing number of scholars believe that the fabulous stonework and engineering of Machu Picchu, the Sacred Valley, Cuzco and the colossal ruins of Sacsayhuaman near Cuzco, pre-dated the Inca rule by millennia. Local Andean tradition holds that the amazing roads and grandiose architecture had been ancient even before the Incas and were attributed to white men with light hair. The fascinating question remained; did people first come to the Americas from the lost continent of Lemuria?

Today, native Quechuan Elders teach that the Andean languages of the Quechua and the Aymara people, along with Sanskrit, are the first languages on Earth.[47] Indeed, many Quechuan words are similar to words in Sanskrit and even Maori, the language of indigenous New Zealanders. Could this be evidence of a pan-Pacific culture that included the subcontinent of India?

The most common legend today says that there were fourteen great rulers from the time Manco Capac, the first Inca, his brother and wives, arose from Lake Titicaca. Historians put this sometime between 1000 and 1200 A.D.[48] The ruler or Inca was worshipped as a descendent of the sun god. The Incas were the self-proclaimed Children of the Sun or Children of the Light. Manco Capac was light-skinned and some say red-haired and bearded. The conquistador Francisco Pizarro himself wrote about the last Incan Emperor Atahualpa and his family, "They were even whiter than the people of Spain."[49] Since the native Andean Indians were dark skinned with little facial hair, the first Incas could not have been of local origin.

Brother Philip wrote that they came from a land across the Pacific and they constructed their society on top of ruins left by a previous culture that was a Lemurian colony.[50]

So many fragments of a much grander picture than we could imagine were falling into place from different sources. Elizabeth Boersma-Wentzel, one of our trekkers in Peru, began remembering our joint mission this time in the Andes. As far as I knew then, she was unaware of the theories put forth in the 1961 book by George Williamson. She certainly didn't know of my shamanic journey to another life with Sue Burch, in which we hid energies and codes of wisdom into a stone mountain to protect the sacred knowledge.

After our trip Elizabeth wrote:

All the members of our group lived in Peru in the Lemurian era. Brad Johnson was the High Priest, I was the Queen and we were all members of the High Council. The Council had the task of protecting the golden Discs in which the codes were hidden. We were afraid that the Discs would fall into the wrong hands, people who had no idea what the golden Discs really meant, but saw only gold and money. We decided to hide the Discs so the information would be safe. This information could only be understood by highly conscious people. The whole Council decided that we should all come back when it was the right time to reactivate the codes. And now, 2004, is the time!

Elizabeth's words paralleled the past life vision I had experienced with Sue on the June solstice in 2002. During that meditation, Mark explained to Sue and me:

You would know in the future when the world would again be ready for this knowledge to be exploded back into humankind and not just held in a sacred way in the center of the Earth... This time Jonette will help you.

Reflecting on my vision with Sue, what I had read about the Sun Disc and its origins, and the mystical initiation I had experienced in the etheric pyramid of the Sun Disc, I concluded that I was helping to complete the spiritual mission Sue started. Ancient magnetic codes of wisdom were downloaded into me from the Sun Disc so that the energies and knowledge that were once hidden could be released and again made accessible to spiritually awakening humans.

All this was fascinating, but it didn't help explain my role with Mallku in the prophecy of the Eagle and the Condor. So what would?

35

The Magdalen Manuscript

s I prepared for my December solo journey back to the Andes, I asked the Universe to bring me the books and information I most needed. My dear friend, Brad Johnson, sent me his copy of a book by Tom Kenyon and Judi Sion, *The Magdalen Manuscript: The Alchemies of Horus and the Sex Magic of Isis*.[51] "I think this will help you understand your relationship with Mallku," Brad wrote in the accompanying note.

"Here it goes again," I thought, "The maddeningly synchronistic Universe bringing me a book about twin souls that has the Egyptian god Horus in the title!" Moreover, this came just days after my inner vision of Horus with the Sun Disc. "Please! Can the coincidences slow down for a little while so I can catch my breath?" I thought. "After all, I have a regular life, a home and a professional career I'm juggling." I proclaimed my sentiments loudly to the Universe, yet I read the book... enthralled.

The book contained the channeled words of Mary Magdalen and her tantric relationship with Jesus. Mary Magdalen, who was a High Initiate of the Temple of Isis, and Jesus, or Yeshua, were the ultimate twin souls. Page by page the book explained some of what I had already experienced with Mallku. It gave me a deeper understanding of the higher path I was walking.

The Kundalini Serpent Energy

The 'Alchemies of Horus' refer to a body of ancient knowledge and methods, practiced in the Temples of Egypt, to strengthen the 'Ka' body, which is the spiritual or etheric twin to our physical form. Today we might call it our 'Light Body.' Within the Ka body, there are pathways that can be stimulated and opened, "bringing forth latent powers and abilities of the Initiate through what is called the Djed,[52] or the ascending seven seals, what the yogis and yoginis of India call the chakras."[53] This brought to mind the seven illumined steps I ascended to encounter the golden Sun Disc in my mystical pyramid journey at Mallku's apartment in Cuzco.

There are three main energy meridians in our body. To the left of our central energy channel in our spine is the Lunar circuit, related to the female; to the right is the Solar circuit, relating to the male side. In some spiritual traditions, the two mirrored energy columns are referred to as the ida and pingala. As the energy of the side circuits or serpents rise up they crisscross each other through the central chakras. They are living energies that vibrate through the physical body, activating the spiritual body and increasing its magnetic potential. This exact energy dynamic is depicted in the caduceus, the symbol of two snakes intertwined around a central staff that is used to represent the fields of medicine and healing.

Before reading the *Magdalen Manuscript*, I had only known of the central energy column or chakra system, the one in the spine through which the kundalini or serpent energy sometimes rises during transcendent spiritual experiences. Not knowing of the other two side energy channels, I was shocked once during a particularly high meditation at an Advanced Light Body class I was attending, to notice a complete set of energy centers to the left of my center meridian. I thought something must be wrong with me so I spent most of the meditation trying to get rid of the off-center energy column or at least move it over to be in the middle. Walking out of the class, I admitted to Sanaya Roman, one of the instructors, who had known me for over a decade, "I don't know what happened, but I have two sets of chakras."

"Leave it to you, Jonette," was Sanaya's smiling reply.

Initiates of Isis were taught to activate the "Serpent Power, moving it in specific paths in the spinal column and opening up circuits within the brain, which increases the potential for intelligence, creativity and receptivity to change the quality of one's being, so that the attunement of the Ba or Celestial Soul is clear and unobstructed."[54] Mary Magdalen, speaking through Tom Kenyon stated that, "The alchemy is created by the joining of the male initiate's Ka and the female initiate's Ka. Essential to the female initiate is the authentic feeling of safety and love, or appreciation at the very least. When these are in place, something within her being lets go and allows the alchemy to occur."[55] The state of male and female union known as the Four Serpents is attained when each partner has activated the Solar and Lunar Serpents within his or her spine.

I didn't know any of this that night in the jungle hut when Mallku came to my bed. One of the first sentences out of his mouth was to assure me that I was safe. Among other things, I took that to mean I was safe from unwanted advances, and I relaxed into his embrace. Kenyon and Sion's book accurately describes the energy activation I experienced spontaneously in Mallku's arms. I felt lines of energies moving from me to him and back again, as if we were one being. By sharing energies with Mallku, my Solar Serpent, the male energy meridian to the right of my spine became as balanced and open as the female column or Lunar Serpent on the left side. There was no doubt I experienced the magnetic awakening of tantric sex, by lying there fully clothed with my twin flame. Mallku quoted one of his teachers that night in the Amazon, "Don't make love, let Love make you."

The gift Mallku gave to me by his presence and his assurance that I was safe, enabled me to grant him the Initiation of Leadership that his soul called forth. That one night was reason enough to know him.

A Spirit Lover

Saturday mornings start softly at our house. It was 7:30 a.m. in mid-November. Ed was still asleep beside me, nested in the thick, down duvet that I insisted on and he tolerated. I tucked deeper under the covers to do my morning prayers. There is a special place I go in meditation that I call the "Atlantean Magnification Chamber." It was shown to me by White Eagle when I felt that I had too much to pray for and wanted a quicker method. This place in consciousness accelerates everything I bring into it and sends it instantly around the Universe. I see it as a cosmic, geodesic dome surrounding me and visualize myself in the center of the spherical shape with a honeycomb surface, each cell magnifying my prayers and radiating them out.

That morning I used that visualization to send my deep, soul love to Mallku. I enjoyed several minutes of blissful connection. Then I realized I was trying too hard, pushing my love out to Mallku. "Ah," the thought came, "I should relax." Instantly, nectar-sweet, innocent energy enveloped me, which is not how I expected Mallku's strong and masculine spirit to feel. Yet it was so complete, so perfectly safe that I could endlessly drink it in. It wasn't Mallku's soul I was feeling; I was experiencing the space or context of our relationship. How did I know this? Because only then did Mallku's soul come to me.

I felt his spirit stronger than I have ever felt another human's energetic presence. It was more real than the time in the restaurant when I first felt Mallku's essence and knew that he was a twin of my soul. As I lay next to my sleeping husband, Mallku too was with me in a *very physical* way, but without a body! Mallku's spirit lay on top of me like a lover!

An incredulous, "Oh," was the only thought I could muster. How do you tell a spirit, "Love, this really isn't the right time or place?" Besides my blood pressure shooting way up, and a flush I attributed to a hot flash, nothing energetically improper happened. Mallku's powerful spirit stayed five minutes and was gone as quickly as he had come.

I found Ed's warm hand underneath the blankets and gave

it a squeeze. I wanted to reassure him in case his psyche happened to notice the presence of another man's energy in our bed. Every conflicting, diametrically opposed, mutually exclusive synapse in my brain fired at once. In the cacophony of chaotic thoughts, questions eventually emerged: "What does this mean? Are we supposed to be lovers? Can we not be? He is a shaman, did he know what he was doing?" I was *really* confused about what I was supposed to do in Peru with Mallku the next month. However, I could not find an escape clause in my commitment to follow destiny.

Ed trusted me. I didn't know what I was walking toward as I planned my return to the Andes. I didn't know if I would return to be Ed's wife, though I couldn't imagine making any other choice. Ed didn't ask me for any promises and I gave him none. It took a truly great man to accept the freedom that I needed. Through all of this, our love and the strength of our marriage grew.

My Vision with Mallku

Regarding Mallku, I was concerned that I had virtually no communication from him except about logistical arrangements. I didn't know what Mallku's understanding was or what he expected, if anything, from my visit. Less than a week before I left for South America we talked briefly by phone. He told me that he had just met and fallen in love with Evelyn, a Brazilian woman who was on one of his trips. She would be closing her dental practice outside of San Paulo and moving to Cuzco in February 2005. I'm sure he wanted reassurance of my intentions toward him. I sent off an email to provide clarification in writing.

Hello Mallku,

I am coming to Peru to answer an inner call for planetary healing and breakthroughs into Light. Only a couple of times in my life have I known I should do something, not really understanding what or why. By surrendering to it, everything about my life and spirit changed.

You are an important part of this work, but not the reason I am coming. I believe that your soul and my soul are the masculine and feminine twins of the same higher soul. It is rare that such souls are on Earth at the same time and even more rare that they actually meet in the physical. When this happens, it is usually a great opportunity for cosmic growth. So I see that if we do some processes, ceremonies and meditations together we will be allowed to enter into much higher dimensions than either of us can attain alone. My guidance is that what we can achieve will bring a lifting and healing of separation on many, many levels, both for us and for the world. I know it sounds quite grand, but that is what I'm being shown.

So, my feelings for you are deep and divine soul love. It helps that I enjoy and respect who you are in this life, but that isn't why I love you. I don't want or need anything from you, except perhaps friendship. My love for you is beyond space and time. I didn't choose it. I just can't help it. So let's just stay open to how we are supposed to relate in a way that furthers our spiritual paths and our divine service to mankind, and is in no way a detriment to our chosen relationships in this life, me with Ed, and you with your new Love.

Jonette

36

Solar Discs

While we were all in Peru in August, Brad Johnson was of great service to everyone in the group. He sat on the bus or train next to someone, and by his intense listening and loving wisdom he always touched their soul. For me, his blue eyes looked into my brown ones with a clarity borne of many powerful lives together. "Jonette, I know you as this and so much more," Brad said after each leap I made, always inviting me to my next level of spiritual power and growth. His insightfulness and intuitive ability were indispensable in helping me learn from my first trip to Peru and prepare me for my upcoming, solo visit.

On a bright December afternoon, two days before I was to return to the Andes, I phoned Brad. I was full of questions about the Sun Discs and their relationship to me and to the Great Central Sun. I went into a higher state of consciousness while Brad assisted by asking questions and taking notes. Instead of calling in my guides, I used the opportunity to speak from my own highest self, tapping into wisdom deep within me, unknown to my ordinary conscious mind. Through fifteen years as a channel, I've learned to speak what comes into my consciousness without editing it. So I'm often totally surprised by what I say. This discourse was one of those times:

I am Jonette and I am Kumara. There are twelve Solar Discs on Earth that awaken our twelve-stranded DNA. The Discs hold codes and activation sequences that are engaged when a certain level of vibration is reached by humanity. Some of the codes on the Discs need to be activated by awakened humans who are called to do so. As each of us steps forward, it shines Light on the others' divine roles so that we can awaken to the greatest service and opening imaginable. This is precisely why we've come together. Many who are called have been guardians of the Sun Discs in previous incarnations. I have been a guardian before.

The Sun Discs were originally brought from the Great Central Sun to the Earth. But because they created too high a frequency, too much change, they were all removed and put on Sirius for billions of years. In another life, I was involved in that second return to Earth.

Two of the twelve Discs are Master Discs, one at Lake Titicaca and the one under Ama Dablam in the Himalayas. When the travelers who carried the energies from Nepal connected to the Andes, there was a gate opened that sent reverberations through the ten other Discs. The Discs communicate directly to the stars, receiving downloads of information and possibilities. This is why these Discs are often called 'stargates.'

The Master Disc in Lake Titicaca has now been moved to the etheric pyramid that I found. I only uncovered a small part of the codes and the frequencies in that first visit. There is much more to be activated and opened. As these open, they will bring humanity to an entirely different world, a world that has nothing to do with saving this one, but it is such a new aspect that we can't even comprehend it. There are many who are awakening who will help hold the vibration that is chattering everywhere between these Discs. When the twelve Discs are fully

activated, it means that everyone on Earth is totally enlight-
ened and living in a higher reality.

It's all unfolding perfectly. There is nothing that needs to be
pushed. The best thing we can do is prepare our bodies for the
activation. What we integrate into the physical can then be
transmitted out to others.

In my excitement about this vision, I warmly shared with
Brad, "I'm so grateful that I have Masters who are friends and
friends who are Masters, so that together we can figure out
what our incredible, divine role is."

Brad, who always sees the highest potential in me and
others, assured me, "Even though it may sound grandiose, it
may *be* grandiose. That doesn't invalidate it."

I continued, narrating the inner vision that presented itself:

It seems I am again at the scene of my initiation at the pyramid
where I received the codes from the Sun Disc. Now I'm going to
a higher initiation. I'm seeing a bigger pyramid where the steps
are higher than the steps I went up before. It's as if the other
experience was nested within this experience. On the top of the
stairs this time, it's not really a Solar Disc but a gateway. What
I did before was necessary. It unlocked a chamber to enable me
to go further. This is the real thing. This is what those codes
unlocked. I can't see anything, I just sense infinity… with stars
in it.

It feels that I'm doing this alone but there are people watching,
waiting to see what I do. Maybe they're being supportive, but
no one's telling me… they're an audience. I'm hesitating. I don't
know if I'm ready. It feels as if some forces are working on me.

Brad, who was journeying with me in his mind, added,
"Well something has shifted, because I can see your hands
coming down on a keyboard that seems to activate codes. You
are like a concert pianist playing very rapidly and knowingly."

Okay. Something is beginning to shift and open. Again, I don't see or feel anything... it's all very far away. The words that come are that I'm going to be shown Heaven. I don't feel codes or energies; I don't feel anything. I can see why people think Heaven is billowy clouds because it all seems to be white light. There is no movement, just an enormous space. It is surprisingly devoid of feeling. I'm still at the door looking in at this space. I'm not to go in now. It is closing with a promise that I'll be back and more will happen. I turn and all those people or beings that were behind me have their hands up, palms out toward me, beaming light. My aura is becoming huge and golden... soft, gentle and still... angelic.

Brad could sense what was happening to me, "You are everywhere. You're going to be aware of more aspects of yourself on an ongoing basis without disrupting your life. The limitation of being in one place will no longer exist for you. Wow!"

I heard a higher part of myself quickly say, "I accept." My higher self pre-empted the lower part of me that was hesitating. I also felt that I had to accept that it was okay if I died, as Jonette. I had a feeling that I might be able to leave my physical body completely. I was committed to following my Spirit in this vision quest to Peru. I would do what I must with or without Mallku. Just knowing him and recognizing him as my twin soul might be enough. If there was no other conscious connection, knowledge or awakening on his part... that would be okay. "Nothing will hold me back," I concluded firmly to myself, not really feeling as brave as my words suggested. Yet somehow, I wanted to give Mallku the gift of standing with me and gazing at the heavenly white light that I had just witnessed in my vision.

I admitted to Brad that I didn't know how to deal with the idea and possible ramifications of Mallku being my twin soul. "I want to close the door and pretend the whole thing away."

Brad responded, "You can't hide from what you don't want to deal with or believe. It cuts you off from yourself and keeps you from complete authenticity. In the past, we've shut parts of our self down to stop the pain. While this may have been effective in stopping the hurt, it also interrupts the natural flow of love within us. This simply won't work any longer as we merge with our divinity."

"Thank you. You are such a great help!" I told Brad enthusiastically. "You already are very much a part of this journey. I am now ready. I only wish I was packed!" I added.

I didn't know what to think about all the information that came through about the Sun Discs. It was so far removed from my ordinary life and from the business world I understood. In two days, I would fly back to Peru, this time alone. I'd probably run into a lot more things beyond my comprehension.

37

P. J.'s Warning

 P. J. Deen, one of the few people I knew who had actually met her twin flame, emailed me some advice right before I left:

You will be bringing in the higher dimensional aspects of the merging of the masculine and feminine. Words can't possibly explain what is meant by this 'merging' but you will be given the full understanding of it. And who better to do this work than twin flames?

To maximize your work together with Mallku, it would be good to really look at society's current beliefs around love, male/female relationships, marriage, monogamy, fidelity and to find the truth of these manmade concepts. To be fully successful in Peru, you're going to have to go well beyond our society's beliefs of them. It will definitely test your mettle. New patterns for how males and females will interact with each other over the next several thousand years will be brought in, and many of our present-day, puritanical beliefs will have no place in that timeframe.

I know you must be struggling with all this now—the inexplicable magnetism, the inescapable deep knowing and love for this apparent stranger, and especially the almost overwhelmingly strong sexual attraction you probably never thought was possible. I felt them all too. Try to do as much personality work around all the above beliefs as you can before you go. Otherwise, you will be in crisis the whole time and Mallku will be completely bewildered.

The magnitude of the energies between twin flames can make you feel like the whole world just got ripped out from under you. You want to be able to focus on your mission and purpose, and the highest outcome of the work you've been sent here to do together.

Reading P. J.'s email made me quite concerned. "Am I ready? Is this whole trip a rash decision? Is my marriage strong enough to allow whatever needs to happen in Peru? Am I strong enough? Does P. J. know something I don't?" That was the trouble with having highly intuitive friends.

White Eagle on Trust

I was reminded of one of the very first messages White Eagle ever channeled through me in the late 1980s. It helped me now as I tried to understand my part in bringing together the Eagle and the Condor.

It is the spirit of flight that we are addressing—the freedom to be supported by that which is unseen. As the young eagle takes off from her nest for the first time, she trusts that the air can uplift her, that it can hold her, and that it can move her to where she needs to go. She has no reason to believe that the air can do this, save her instincts. She has lived her life with her legs upon the nest, upon the rocks. The eagle had no reason to believe she was safe as she jumped. And still, she stepped out into the air and into the sunlight; and low and behold, she found a freedom and a strength, and a graceful beauty she had not known.

You are there. The sunlight in that which is unseen is beckoning you to jump. You have no reason, save your faith, to know that rather than crashing down, you will be given the freedom of the sky. You have the tools. You have the wings. You have the gentle wind. What more are you waiting for? Do you wait to grow old as you stand on your craggy edge and think that this is all that life holds? We in the Temple of Light support you; we say you have grown old enough. It is time to leap into Light, knowing only what you know. For in that act of trust all power is born. It is not born before you leap. It is not available before you leap. So we ask you to unfold your silver wings, lead with your heart, and jump into the sky. For the sky will catch you and carry you to universes unknown.

The Eagle and the Condor

PART V

The Prophecy Today

"Don't make love, let Love make you."

Mallku

The Eagle and the Condor

38

By Myself in Cuzco

n mid-December I arrived again in Cuzco, the Incan capital high in the Andes. At noon I sat in a quiet cafe overlooking the main square, the Plaza de Armas. The weather outside was gray and bleak but mild. Dark clouds shrouded the sky, partially obscuring the sharp lines of the stone cathedrals facing the square. Christmas lights arranged in the shape of animals reminded me it was the holidays. Every longhaired man I saw I thought was Mallku. Watching from the coffee shop, I acknowledged to myself that I really didn't like Cuzco. I didn't like it twenty-five years ago when I first visited Machu Picchu. It wasn't that what I saw was so disagreeable; I've seen the charm in less charming places. I didn't remember why I didn't like it, only that my dislike was immensely justifiable. Outside the drizzle became a downpour. My umbrella was safe and dry back in my hotel room.

Cuzco is a bustling town of 400,000 people, a hub for tourism. My hotel was on the street known in Inca times as "The Spine of the Puma." Later, of course, the Spanish named it after a saint. The walls of the lobby were made from thick, gray blocks of stone placed without mortar by Incan builders, still solid after centuries of earthquakes. Thirteen-year-old Julio, who jokingly called himself "Kevin Costner," stood outside the hotel door selling his postcards. He was *always* outside the hotel door selling his postcards.

I spent my days writing, trying to meditate, visiting museums, having coffee on the Plaza and going out for meals alone. Mallku was so busy that I hardly saw him. We didn't have deep, spiritual conversations, no meditations together, nor was there the growing friendship that I had hoped for. After all, he worked as a tour guide and business owner and I was a paying client. I remained in limbo between my truth of our unique soul connection and Mallku's world that apparently didn't include having a North American woman as a twin soul. Mallku was always helpful and friendly when we had our few excursions together, but there was an emotional shield up, which I respected.

My mind went around and around. "What am I doing by myself in a Cuzco hotel a week before Christmas? I should be home fighting the crowds at the malls, going to holiday parties, baking cookies. Why was I so sure I should come? Why isn't anything significant happening? What am I doing wrong? Why does the friendship with Mallku seem strained? Is it only I who feel it? Why can't I get into a deep meditation? Why aren't my guiding voices clear?" The questions plagued me.

The space heater in my room removed the chill in the high altitude, early summer afternoon. Sitting up on my bed I negotiated with the Universe, "Please guide me to know my purpose here this time. I want to be of service, to learn what is here and to teach others what I learn. I desire to experience spiritual breakthroughs for myself and for humanity."

The voice I heard from White Eagle disturbed me. *So you want knowledge and breakthroughs just so you can share them? Aren't you good enough to seek them for yourself? Ask for yourself. Want it for you.*

I wasn't ready for that piece of spiritual advice. It put me in a tail spin. "How could I want something just for me? That's just... not... proper," I argued with my own voices. I didn't know *how* to want something just for me. It was such a foreign thought. The more I struggled with the idea, the more I realized that this was an important lesson. I prayed for help with this and all the disconcerting thoughts that bombarded me that afternoon.

White Eagle helped by explaining:

Your job is to awaken yourself. If you awaken just so that you can help others, you've missed the point. If you want light, love, and healing, grab them. If you can command mountains, what else is waiting for your command? You command something simply because you do. It waits for your command because of who you are.

Something must have shifted within me because that evening at a nearby Italian restaurant, frequented almost exclusively by tourists, I had a bizarre, spiritual encounter with the trout I ordered for dinner. The waiter brought me a warm plate with a large, filleted, pink-fleshed trout and some french fries. I imagined it was caught by a local angler from the fast moving, pristine streams in the area. Since I greatly appreciate fish that have lived in nature, rather than those raised in commercial farms, I allowed my gratitude to go out to that trout and to all wild creatures. I felt honored that this fish had given himself to me. Surprisingly strong feelings of connection and emotions of gratitude streamed out of my heart. I surreptitiously blotted the tears that fell down my face with my red-checkered napkin. I was in *love* with that trout! It was the oddest thing. I ate it anyway.

39

Kiss of the Hummingbird

I was given a message in a dream several days before leaving Colorado for the Andes. I dreamed I was in a room in which a small, colorful bird had become trapped. I asked him, "Are you okay? Can you get out?" It was then I noticed that the window was open and he could easily leave. Looking at him more closely, I realized he was a beautiful hummingbird. I stuck out my hand and asked if he could just sit on it so that I could admire him before he flew away. Instead of perching on my outstretched finger, he flew up to my face where he gave me a long kiss on the cheek with his tiny beak. As he hovered in front of my eyes I remembered noticing the incredible iridescent blue of his breast feathers. The touch on my cheek was so physical, so real that I could still feel the suction of his beak as he imparted a long, long kiss. It was much more real than a dream or vision.

The day after my trout experience, as Mallku and I drove to the Sacred Valley an hour away from Cuzco, I told him of my dream. "What do you think it means?" I asked him.

"The hummingbird, especially coming to your face, is a message of a high spiritual initiation... a very high initiation," he answered. He turned to look at me with some surprise, but didn't elaborate on the nature of the initiation.

"Okay then," I thought. "Everything must be in perfect order." Mallku was driving me to a cave of Pachamama or Mother Earth, which was an initiation place that included a rock called the "brain of Wiracocha." Wiracocha is the main God in the Andean tradition. Mallku asked if I was afraid of heights. "Not inordinately afraid... just normal fear," I stammered in reply.

"You must be strong for this place. Are you ready?" he asked.

"The hummingbird says I am," I said with more confidence than I felt.

I followed Mallku along a trail to a sacred place. The path wound through a patchwork of plots cultivated with corn and potatoes. Animals of all kinds quietly grazed—sheep, donkeys and pigs. Ever-present clouds thrust their shadows on the multi-hued fields, creating an artist's palette of textures and impressions. Fragrant eucalyptus trees impregnated the air with their unique spice. Several times I stopped to photograph the bucolic scene.

Wiracocha's Brain

Set among Incan terraces was a grand, skull shaped limestone rock. Unevenly worn by centuries of torrid rains, the rock was fissured and pockmarked, resembling a brain. Ancient practitioners of the mystical ways had carved steps, smooth stone seats, altars and places to lie to receive the wisdom of the Earth. Mallku invited me to pray for a moment in order to ask permission and strength to enter the cave, which was hidden within the skull rock itself.

Then the brother-of-my-soul led me carefully down carved stone steps that barely clung onto the jagged rock face. I was fine as long as I used the many handholds afforded by the porous limestone and, of course, if I didn't look down. I was doing all right, though I was glad Ed, who hates heights, wasn't there. The narrow stairs ended abruptly, yet I still couldn't see the promised cave entrance. Mallku suggested I put my bag and jacket down to "feel more secure" for the next bit. "This is the difficult part, but I've never had anyone come to harm here," he warned. To his credit, he did not use the word 'dangerous.'

The goal was to use the correct succession of hand and footholds in order to crawl out over the face of a rounded, protruding overhang to the other side, where the cave entrance was. There was no protection other than skilled maneuvering. Mallku couldn't grab me if I lost my balance or my nerve. The drop was more than fifty feet down and could have been fatal. Why did I pick this time to remember that I had told the Universe that I was willing to face death if that was required for any of the spiritual breakthroughs I might experience?

Trust Mallku, White Eagle had told me before the trip.

"Trust Pachamama. Trust my intentions," I repeated silently. Patiently Mallku demonstrated exactly where I should place my hands and feet, when to shift my weight, when to swing out over the edge to locate the foothold I couldn't see. As I clung to it, I kissed the rock that was in front of my face. Mallku had done this, and it seemed like a good idea to me. I began. The first few moves were fine, in spite of sweaty hands and slippery boots. When I got to the position where I had to stretch my whole body across the jutting rock, holding on with only one hand to the thinnest of spurs, my entire weight resting on the toes of only one foot, my legs started to shake.

"Hold your power!" Mallku commanded. Instantly the tremors stopped. I again kissed the rock I was clutching, for safe measure, and finished the moves.

Success! The miniscule cave opening was before me! It didn't bear considering that I would have to repeat the feat in the opposite direction. I hoped that I could collect enough grace in the cave to subordinate my fear. We prayed and meditated in the tiny cavern. It dawned on me as I stooped inside the cave, my heart still pounding, that fear is a powerful expression of ego. While we have fear, our ego will always be in charge of us. I understood that the cure for fear isn't courage, it's vulnerability. I prayed to move from fear and ego to trust.

Hallelujah! The cave had a back door that we literally squirmed through. The benefit of such gymnastics was immediately apparent to me—we didn't have to go back the way we had come!

Being of Your Own Light

Over lunch in Cuzco, we talked more about the significance of the hummingbird kissing me in my dream. In Andean lore, since the hummingbird can fly faster than most other birds, hover, fly backward or fly up and down, it is known as the "Defender of the Condor." In pre-Incan times the hummingbird was special. The famed Nazca lines, etched into the plains of coastal Peru, include a representation of a hummingbird that is so large it can only be seen well from an aerial view. Mallku wrote in his book on Machu Picchu about the hummingbird's spiritual significance. "The day this beautiful bird approaches you to deposit its nectar on your head or drink the nectar of your soul will be the great moment you are transformed into a radiant being of pure and unconditional love, having reached the Tukuy munay niyoc spiritual level, or 'being of your own light.'"[56] In a few days, as the summer solstice in the southern hemisphere approached, I would be testing the hummingbird's message.

"Can I truly claim to be a 'being of my own light'?" I asked myself.

According to the Andean people, we are currently in the Tenth Pachakuti, a time of transition and great changes. Mallku says that it is an era of Light characterized by the presence of the Mother, or manifestation of the planet's feminine aspect, after 500 years of rest. He wrote, "Man has to open up to this new planetary vibration of the Mother and feel that our Earth's pole, or center of feminine magnetic radiation, is already active and that it is manifesting itself through the doors of the Sacred Lake Titicaca."[57]

Mallku and I planned to go together to Lake Titicaca to perform a ceremony for healing the schism between masculine and feminine in Earth, humankind, and ourselves. My intent was to use the power of the lake, the Earth's female pole, to redress the overemphasis in our world of the masculine principles and to bring back into balance the Divine Feminine and Divine Masculine forces. I didn't know exactly what we were to do or how, only that Mallku and I had to be together on a sacred island on Lake Titicaca and that the spiritual duty was urgent.

40

Sacsayhuaman

I had one more place to visit in the Cuzco area before our departure to Lake Titicaca. This was the magnificent citadel of Sacsayhuaman, just outside of the city. (It's pronounced much like "sexy woman.") The Andean architects designed the city of Cuzco in the shape of a puma, with the main plaza as its belly and Sacsayhuaman as the head. The questions I asked myself when I first saw the gigantic serpentine wall of Sacsayhuaman were, "Who built this? Why?" and more importantly, "How?" At the time as I stood in awe at the massive stone structure, I had no answers. Months later, I researched the facts and lore connected to Sacsayhuaman.

The chronicler Garcilaso de la Vega wrote about it in the mid-1500s, just after the Spanish conquest:

> *This fortress surpasses the constructions known as the Seven Wonders of the World. But it is indeed beyond the power of imagination to understand how these Indians, unacquainted with devices, engines, and implements, could have cut, dressed, raised, and lowered great rocks, more like lumps of hills than building stones, and set them so exactly in their places. For this reason, and because the Indians were so familiar with demons, the work is attributed to enchantment.*[58]

Jonette at Sacsayhuaman

Sacsayhuaman with Cuzco in the background

The Spanish thought it was the work of the devil. Some native Quechua people claim the mighty construction was from giants and gods in ages past. Most scholars believe that Sacsayhuaman was the work of the same unknown pre-Incan cultures that created Machu Picchu, Ollantaytambo in the Sacred Valley, and the megaliths in Tiahuanaco in Bolivia. The place did seem otherworldly. The main structure was a three-tiered fortress of zigzagging, limestone walls, now standing at an impressive 30 feet high. However, any building stones small enough to be hauled away, have long ago been used in the walls of other construction. The ramparts of Sacsayhuaman were meticulously constructed of gargantuan rocks, some weighing 350 tons, which had been dovetailed together with mortar-less precision. One boulder is over 28 feet high. As an example of how impossibly huge these stones are, the building blocks of the Egyptian pyramids, by contrast, average only three tons!

As if that's not impressive enough, the mammoth stones were fantastically shaped. Several blocks that form the wall's earthquake-proof base were cut with thirty or more angles in them. Each was then finely dressed and smoothed. Yet all this was done without metal tools or use of the wheel! At one time three towers stood above the wall. These have all been destroyed, the stones carried off to build Spanish cathedrals and the buildings and homes of Cuzco.

Five hundred years ago, Garcilaso de la Vega wrote, "An underground network of passages, which was as vast as the towers themselves, connected them with one another... The most experienced man dared not venture into this labyrinth without a guide."[59] This complex system of tunnels connected Sacsayhuaman with the Coricancha, the main Sun Temple in Cuzco. Mummies of the Incas, gold and treasures were said to be hidden underground. The main entrance was closed off in the mid-1800s.

The mystery of who originally built such a magnificent and seemingly impractical structure deepens when one considers that similarly improbable megaliths are found in remote corners of the world: Easter Island, the Caribbean and North

Africa. Are these megalithic constructions all from Atlantean and Lemurian civilizations?

Mystery of the Stones

There are varied theories on how pre-historical stone-masons might have built such structures of perfectly interlocking, irregularly angled stones of monumental proportions. One idea was that they were constructed using a now forgotten technique of softening and then shaping the stone. Hiram Bingham, the man who rediscovered Machu Picchu for the world, wrote of a plant whose juices softened rock so its edges could be fitted tightly together.[60] Could this explain how Andean builders created precision masonry with no mortar? Mallku suggested that the great stones were fractured apart using some sort of resonance and then placed upon each other exactly as if they had not been broken up.

Another possible theory of the fabulous stone masonry of the Andes came from research on the construction of the Great Pyramid of Egypt. Some believed that rather than using cut stone, the early Egyptians actually poured the large blocks into place using "an advanced and ingenious form of synthetic stone that was cast on the spot like concrete." Hieroglyphs recently deciphered on an ancient Egyptian stele gave instructions for making synthetic stones. The resulting 'cement' has the molecular and chemical bonding similar to natural stone.[61]

Once I heard this theory about pre-Incan stonemasons softening and pouring stone, I looked more carefully at the strikingly homogenous color and consistency of the rocks used in building Sacsayhuaman and in the city of Cuzco. It *did* look to me like the stones could have been produced and shaped by such an unknown technology, rather than quarried and hammered with stone tools.

The means by which Sacsayhuaman was constructed, and by whom, remain a debate. Authorities do agree that the site had important religious and military significance. As I strolled beside the megalithic wall, I was dwarfed by its size and magnificence. The twenty-two zigzags the wall makes, said to represent the teeth of the Puma, reminded me of the shape of an enormous serpent. I walked along it, my left hand held out to touch the stones, moving from what I felt to be the tail of the snake, to its head. The mysterious structure seemed to exert an influence on time/space itself, like a tear in the veil of normal reality. I half expected to hear the vibrational hum of the stones and to be able to walk intact into another time. It was a sense that was both eerie and exciting.

Instead of exotic time travel, I found a grassy niche in which to meditate, far removed from the main walls and the tourists. I needed to be alone to prepare my spirit for our visit to Lake Titicaca. We would leave in the morning.

41

Lake Titicaca

"o you need to change money for the trip to Titicaca?"

"Yes." My response ignited a strange sequence of events that were everyday facts of life for Larry Cuellar, Mallku's assistant who was driving me to meet up with Mallku.

Pushing through Cuzco's clogged one-way streets in seemingly random direction, Larry finally positioned the car in the right lane of the main commercial avenue. I sat bewildered as we suddenly stopped with no banks or money changing kiosks in sight.

"How much you change?" Larry asked, in stilted English. As I turned to my left to answer him, a large, dark man in a leather jacket with a fistful of bills pounded violently on the window on my side of the car. Too fast for me to think, Larry demanded, "Give him your money." Larry indicated to me to roll down my window for the shadowy stranger, who yanked the dollars out of my hand even before the window was completely lowered. A policeman yelling loudly in Spanish ran toward our car. Motorists stuck behind our stationary car blared their horns to let us know they didn't appreciate having to stop. In less than twenty seconds, the curbside capitalist had counted my greenbacks, calculated my exchange, and counted back my Peruvian money, thrusting it through the window a moment before the police officer arrived. Three seconds later, we were back in the flow of the traffic toward the square where Mallku waited to drive me to Lake Titicaca.

"What just happened?" I asked, still uncertain if I was the victim of an elaborate scam.

"These black market money changers give you a better rate than at the banks," was Larry's calm reply.

Mallku drove fast—very fast—from Cuzco to Puno, which is the main town on the shores of Lake Titicaca in southeastern Peru. "I'm not a patient man," he told me, though the evidence was clear.

I silently repeated, "Trust Mallku" as Curva Peligrosa (dangerous curve) signs flashed by, as did dozens of roadside memorials to loved ones who hadn't had drivers with Mallku's skill and luck. He pointed out the place where the train crossed the road but because of a hill, it couldn't be seen until it was too late; things I really didn't need to know.

We listened to his Sarah Brightman CDs. "She has the voice of an angel. She is my inspiration," he remarked, as we drove through the altiplano, or high altitude plains. I too adore Sarah Brightman's music, but was astonished that a thirty-eight year old Peruvian male would know this soprano. Mallku interspersed Brightman's vocals with Santana's legendary guitar.

"That's more like I'd expect," I laughed, enjoying both Brightman and Santana.

Springtime was kind in the Andes. Crops were stitched across the landscape, their colors poured from between the hills. Clouds rose like smoke from sacred fires. Llamas, alpacas, vicuñas and more ordinary sheep and cows found ample fodder. Dogs slept on the road because the asphalt was warm. Mallku was sharp-eyed, veering from peddled carts, smoke-belching trucks, overfilled transport vans, schoolchildren and independence-minded herd animals.

It was dark and we were still an hour's drive from Puno as Mother Nature greeted us vehemently, with all her force. Zigzags of lightning scored the sky. From horizon to horizon, the heavens flashed noon. "Wow," simultaneously broke out from both of us over and over again. Mallku warned, "This much lightning means hail." And it did. Within minutes, the landscape was three inches deep in lumpy white. Every driver slowed, respecting the risk of poor tires on icy piles of hail. Violent lightning eerily profiled the white, hilly landscape as we drove the last ten miles to the lake.

"Four and a half hours," Mallku proudly exclaimed as we pulled up to the hotel. "My record was three and a half, but then I was just traveling alone."

For the past two days, I had fasted to prepare myself for something important. Normally I don't miss a meal, so fasting was a big commitment. At the lakeshore hotel in Puno, I watched Mallku as he ate potatoes, avocado, and rice at the restaurant.

Another Energy Initiation

We shared a twin room. I felt deeply at peace lying there, joyful to my core that this man, whose soul I adored, was so happy. As he told me while I was still in Colorado, he had met a Brazilian woman in one of his tour groups. After spending two weeks together, they decided that she would move to Cuzco. When he talked about Alanna and his vision for their future, his face lit up with excitement, his brown eyes sparkled. Nothing is as marvelous as the early stages of being in love.

In that blissful state I tried to sleep, but the energies that were preparing me for our upcoming spiritual work were flowing powerfully into me. First, my left leg began to shake uncontrollably. I turned to lie on my back. Instantly, my right leg started moving. Then the involuntary shaking began in my hips, back and forth. Waves of movement emanated from my pelvic area and traveled down my legs and up my torso. The vigorous spasms were strangely rhythmic. After twenty minutes or more of my entire body trembling in waves of uncontrolled power, I realized that some of this energy was for Mallku. I wasn't meant to embody it alone. I was embarrassed to wake him as he softly snored in the next bed and I wasn't even certain I could stand up on my shaking legs.

But this was why I had come to Peru; I wouldn't let self-consciousness stop me. My trembling legs managed to hold as I stood by Mallku's bedside, calling his name and nudging him awake. He grunted. I proceeded, "Mallku, I have another energy initiation for you. I need to lie beside you and put my hand on your heart." He moved over without a word and was asleep again within ten seconds. Or, maybe he wasn't asleep. It would have been difficult to slumber with me lying next to him, twitching in waves of spiritual energy. There was nothing else I could do but wait for the movement to be finished, which took another fifteen minutes. When my body stopped shaking, I returned to my own bed. It was one of the strongest physical/spiritual experiences I had ever had. Yet, later I understood that this was just a warm-up.

Floating Islands

By 9:00 a.m. the next morning, Mallku and I were at the dock at Puno waiting to board the Rio Azul, a small tourist boat that would take us and twelve others to the floating reed islands of the Uros people. We planned to spend the night on the larger, rocky island of Amantani and then motor to Taquile Island for lunch the next day.

The dock area was abuzz with local Aymara-speaking Indians, dressed in traditional clothing. For the women, this meant black, full skirts, colorfully trimmed blouses, a carryall shawl, hair in braids and the ubiquitous black, bowler-type hat. Men with brightly woven sashes around their waists exchanged good wishes and coca leaves with each other in a traditional greeting. Blue jeans clad tourists bargained with boat captains for the best deals while gaily costumed musicians jumped from boat to boat playing for tips. Mallku ran off to buy some fruit and toilet paper—provisions for the two days we would be touring around the primitive islands of Lake Titicaca. A fresh blast of wind sent eddies of trash swirling around us. Vendors made a last-ditch effort to sell us soft drinks, candy and hand-knitted caps. Diesel fumes filled the air as the Rio Azul's engine started. We were off for our adventure!

At 12,500 feet in altitude, the days were cool yet the sunshine was fierce. Lake Titicaca is so large that with 3,200 square miles, it creates its own weather. This keeps the temperature extremes more mild for the inhabitants of the islands than for people living further away from the water. Our boat navigated slowly through shallow waters abundant with the tortora reeds that are the literal foundation of life for the Uros villages. The naturally growing reeds are harvested and are used to make the floating islands themselves. These manmade islands will usually last twenty years before they completely rot or get drowned if the lake water rises.

Tortora reeds are bound together, layer upon layer, to create a thick, springy, floating platform on which the Uros natives build reed houses, fish from reed boats, make rope from reed fibers, eat reed stalks, cook with dried reeds and make reed souvenirs to sell to tourists so they can buy the few non-reed essentials they require. Their cheery, brown faces, sun-reddened cheeks, and welcoming smiles made our short stop into their world a pure delight. Except for making small trinkets to sell, life here was much the same as when the Incas ruled the Andes. For a small fee, we paddled between floating islands on a traditional reed boat. Vessels of similar design are used even now on the Nile River in Egypt.

Reed boat of the Uros people, Lake Titicaca

Myths of the Aymara

The dozen other travelers on our boat represented an eclectic group from nine different countries. In addition to the captain and his one-man crew, we had Andres, a local Aymara man as our English-speaking tour guide. Though his English was hard to understand, Andres was thrilled to answer my questions. He told me that his father, who is of the Lupaca people, is a shaman and healer. I took notes as well as I could on the choppy water as he launched into the living lore that predates the Incan rule:

My father told me of the ancient myths. The Condor was a leader, a shaman, the first god to the Aymara people. Condor is a master. He has expanding love and taught about peace and happiness. Eagle, or Mamani is the little brother, and Condor, or Mallku is the big brother. Together they formed a mystical school to teach about life. They invited other important masters to talk about life, to live in harmony, love and truth. They invited Puma, or Titi for courage, honor and strength; Lizard, or Jararanku for meditation and rest; Snake, or Amaru for wisdom and fertility; and Frog, or Jampatu for abundance and richness.

Since I was listening with rapt attention, Andres continued, sharing the three-step process his father does every year to help him "make ceremonies to heal sick people."

First, my father drinks holy spring water to be cleansed. Second, he bathes in hot spring water to purify his body. Third, he goes to the top of a mountain because it's a natural temple. A cave is also a natural temple. He does many days of ceremonies and sees great masters. After that, he is a shaman and can help heal others.

I asked Andres about the legends of the secret monastery in a hidden valley near Lake Titicaca, where the great Sun Disc was kept. He indicated that he thought the legends might be true. When I asked him how I could find this place, his answer was, "Pray and ask the Masters to come to you in your inner visions." Then this short, brown and talkative guide said something that completely shocked me, "The Aymaras believe they came from Lemuria."

I didn't get a chance to ask Andres more about this amazing assertion because our boat had left the calm tortora shallows and the floating islands behind. We motored out into the vast, unprotected expanse of the lake. Almost instantly, the clouds became gnarly and menacing. Gray thrusts of wind buffeted and scrimmaged around our small boat as the squall-intensified waves lashed over the deck. The Rio Azul tossed and rolled in the steely churn, silencing our travel tale banter. I probably wasn't the only one grateful that breakfast had been a long time before. I am a self-proclaimed wimp when it comes to drowning so I moved to within a quick grab of the life jackets. Mallku's visage, always shining with self-assurance, betrayed a hint of fear when the ten foot waves became fifteen foot waves and we were not yet in sight of the tiny harbor of Amantani Island. I wish he hadn't told me that "boats here in Peru aren't like in the United States. They don't have radios or any way to call for help in case of an emergency." If we were going to sink, my plan was to have my skimpy, very old life preserver in one hand, and my other holding firmly to Mallku's powerful bicep.

Amantani Island

I was relieved that I didn't need to test my contingency plans. My legs were wobbly as I stepped appreciatively onto terra firma. Gathered at the pier were a dozen women in traditional garb, each effortlessly spinning wool with the hand spindle that every woman and many men continually operate. A man, who must have been the village mayor, assigned tourists to each woman's guesthouse. We followed our hostess far up a steep hill to her home where we would be guests for the night. These are primitive islands, isolated from the mainland, where the people live simply. They have no vehicles or roads, no police, no crime. Families, like their ancestors before them, live in adobe houses sprinkled in a village on the lower hills of the island. They tend sheep, goats and chickens. The higher hills are plotted with scabby fields of potatoes, beans and vegetables where farmers eek out a subsistence living at improbably high altitudes. The government has recently brought outhouses to the island. I was thankful for the privacy and relative sanitation of a latrine.

Guesthouse hostesses, Amantani Island

The woman leading us uphill to her home had to stop several times to catch her breath. Her weathered brown face was creased with wrinkles. Mallku made a quiet comment to me about her old age and lack of fitness. Assuming that she was probably young but looked prematurely aged, I bantered to Mallku, "I'll bet she's younger than you are."

"She can't be!" he said, aghast at the thought. But curious, he asked her, in Spanish "How old are you... if you don't mind me asking?"

"Thirty-five," she said, turning to us with a broad smile.

"Gracias," Mallku replied, his eyes widened in disbelief. I giggled, unable to contain my merriment and besides, I love to be right! For the remaining half-mile to the house, we laughed as Mallku stopped every teenaged schoolgirl to ask her age.

Over a fire of burning eucalyptus leaves and twigs, our hostess cooked us a hearty lunch of potatoes, eggs, bread and tea that was served by her curious, young sons—Jonny and Elvis. I queried Mallku about the origin of such unlikely names for boys living on an underdeveloped island. Mallku explained that it demonstrates the tremendous influence of Protestant missionaries in these remote villages.

Mallku and I spent the afternoon hiking further up the mountain to the two dilapidated temples that make Amantani Island so special—one temple to the Earth Mother, Pachamama; and the other temple to the Earth Father, Pachatata.

42

Merging the Divine Feminine and Masculine

"I t is time," Mallku said, waking me. He was already dressed in the dark by 4:00 a.m. when Teodoro, the father of the house, knocked on our door to wake us. Mallku looked out the small bedroom window, down the hill and beyond to the watery horizon of Lake Titicaca. A few smoky, predawn streaks of light competed with Venus's glow and what was left of the fading Southern Cross. A few gulps from my water bottle, a visit to the outhouse and I too was ready.

We climbed silently up the stony path, my headlamp lighting our way, past the square where a handful of workers waited in the dark to begin the day's construction on the community building. The way became steeper as adobe houses gave way to simple fields, divided by low rock walls. In the misty darkness, I barely made out the silhouette of a woman, with full skirt and shawl bundle, and her cow moving slowly up another path to her fields. I shivered in the cold, wet morning, pulling scarf and collar closer around my neck. The altitude is high, over 13,000 feet. My breathing was necessarily deep and purposeful as we hiked up and up the rocky trail.

Mallku and I walked in prayerful silence. Our goal was to allow Spirit to direct us in a cosmic healing of polarity, specifically the division in our world between feminine and masculine. We came to do this as twin souls—female and male, northern and southern hemispheres, the Eagle and the Condor. For this we had come to Amantani Island, a sacred place on Lake Titicaca, intersected by a major electromagnetic ley line known as Wiracocha's Route, which runs from Bolivia to northern Peru. Another Earth gridline connects the island's two holy sites, making this one of the major power places in all of South America. Mallku explained that the pre-Columbian people generally built their cities, temples and wakas (holy places) on electromagnetic convergence points to guarantee that they would benefit from the highest possible vibratory frequency.[62]

On the highest summit of the island is the Mother Temple, sacred place of the Divine Goddess—the Earth Mother or Pachamama, built well before Inca times during the Tiahuanaco culture. The Temple is a circular enclosure, open to the sky, formed by a roughly constructed stone wall, seven feet high. At one time the shape was octagonal, but centuries of destruction and repairs have rendered it imperfect to its original design. Five concentric rings of foot-high rock walls ter-

The promontory of the male temple

raced the interior into descending levels, much like a small, circular amphitheater.

Less than a half mile away, on the island's second highest promontory is a large, pyramid shaped hill. Here sits the Temple of the Earth Father, the Divine Male. According to Mallku, this is the only temple to the masculine force, or Pachatata in the entire Andes. It is a square, rock wall enclosure more than eight feet high. The doorway was gated and locked with a sign, Prohibido, clearly posted.

After thirty minutes of uphill walking through the oxygen-starved altitude, the sun still below the horizon, we came to the place where the trail divided. Mallku would continue up to the Father Temple, I would pass through a series of four stone arches on my way to the top of the island and the Mother Temple. We stopped to face each other, each looking toward our own path over the shoulder of the other. We raised our hands palm to palm. Mallku invoked the spirits of Amantani: Mamacocha—the Spirit of the Water; Pachamama and Pachatata—the Cosmic Female and Male. He called forth the guides and masters and the power animals, as well as Inti—the Sun, and Wiracocha—the god of the world. He called for blessings on "our sister Jonette and our brother Mallku, for this sacred union." We embraced then walked in opposite directions, each to our own summit.

The Mother Temple

The hike became steeper. My breathing was labored at that altitude. I moved slowly up the rocky path that bisected tiny, hand-tilled plots of subsistence crops. The way to the Mother site was through four ancient, stone archways. As I passed the first, my arms extended so my gloved hands could lovingly caress the stone sentinels, I called upon the gods for blessings and purification. Up over another knoll stood the second gate. I passed through requesting protection and strength. The top of the island and the temple were now in my sight as I walked under the third gateway. I asked the Universe for preparation. *You are prepared*, was the solemn reply into my mind. Heavy

The Eagle and the Condor

mist from off the water obscured the newly risen sun. The air was soggy and frigid. Finally, I passed under the fourth and final gate. Pausing in prayer, I asked for love and for the world to know my love.

Amantani Island through the temple arch

I felt brittle with cold, and nauseated, perhaps from the steep climb in the thin air. I was a little frightened too as I walked around the outside of the circular temple in a clockwise direction. Delicate, tangerine poppies pushed through the wall in places. Piled up stones barred the door to the sanctuary of the Goddess. My need was larger than any prohibition so I carefully removed just three rocks, which enabled me to step gently over the wall into the circle of the temple. Across from the door, at the highest part of the enclosure, was a haphazard pile of stones with tall, golden grasses growing around them. In the center was enthroned a phallus, about a foot and a half high, carved from reddish, porous, volcanic rock. In the center near a small fire pit was a broken stone bowl, representing the receptive womb of the female. The bowl held offerings of a small shell, a burned bit of munay—a wild, aromatic plant that grew along the path, and a heart-shaped stone. To them I added a tiny, gold bag with stones that friends in Colorado had given me for the journey.

Amantani Island, female temple interior

An icy, flat rock across from the altar became my chair. Sitting to catch my breath allowed me to observe the yellow blossoms hanging from their stems like lemon drops. Miniature purple flowers jabbed through fissures in the rock wall. I came to Peru this time to be of whatever service I could to humankind and to the planet. I prayed that I would know what to do and how to do it. "I invoke the Spirit of the Cosmic Mother, the Divine Female, the Goddess, Mother Earth as I sit in the temple on this holy island on the sacred Lake Titicaca. I ask now, in the name of humanity and in my own name, to hold in a sacred way the energies of the female pole of the planet. I ask the Great Feminine Presence to be in me and with me."

Fusing Female and Male

In less than a minute, my body began shaking front to back; my head rolled up and down in waves. The movement was similar to what I experienced at the hotel in Puno, though this energy was undeniably more commanding. Vibrations surged through me in strong waves of power. I was glad, thinking that it might help keep me warm. The movement didn't resemble shivering, it was sinuous and wave-like, growing exponentially in intensity. Speaking aloud to the forces of the Universe, I uttered my acceptance to do my part in this cosmic dance, "I ask now in the name of the Divine Feminine that the powers of the Earth be with me. I choose to collect these powers in my being and to connect with my soul brother Mallku, who is collecting the masculine energies of the planet in the Temple of the Father." I believed that we would somehow know when each of us had contained these energies in our bodies and our souls and then we would fuse, join, and heal the separation between male and female. I continued speaking out loud, "We have come this morning to heal the Divine Feminine and Divine Masculine. We are two souls answering the call. We have come."

My breathing became heavy as if giving birth. My body undulated in sine-like, rhythmic movements. My chest arched repeatedly, thrusting toward the altar as tidal waves of energy passed through me. Clouds moved into the temple, surrounding me with cold wetness. "Isn't this supposed to feel good?" I asked myself. "What is happening? Am I doing it right?"

Disconcerted, after several minutes, I felt the rolling waves in my body slow down and finally stop. I waited while the energies found stasis. At that moment, I was the human embodiment of all the Female power of the Universe. In the stillness that followed, my consciousness began to traverse the Void, the space of peace and emptiness between Female and Male. My soul, now encompassing the Divine Female traveled to meet the Divine Male energies embodied by Mallku. The wind suddenly gusted up inside the temple and a bird shrieked nearby. I jumped in fright.

Then it started with my knees. They began to swing rapidly toward and away from each other causing my whole body to sway from side-to-side. This was different from the movement before, which was front to back. I assumed this meant I had connected with Mallku's spirit and the energies of the Universal Male. My pelvis, shoulders and head pulsed violently back and forth. "I ask for merging, the fusion of Male and Female. I ask to release the separation that we experience on Earth, to heal the polarity of our planet. I ask to move to Oneness with my soul brother Mallku. I am the Eagle and he the Condor. I ask all of this for humanity as I sit in this sacred temple on this holy island." I sighed. My breathing got heavier as my knees moved rapidly in and out, toward each other. My shoulders moved back and forth, not shaking, more like twisting. Then my chest joined the action. All the moving was strange as my body responded to forces outside my control. I felt safe though, well-grounded and perfectly able to do what I needed to do.

The shaking of my body switched from a side-to-side movement to a front-to-back, wavelike motion, which was how the female energy first began. Now the power running through me and the strength of the motion were explosive. It was a kundalini firestorm that electrocuted every fiber of my being. My neck got tired from bouncing up and down. I knew somehow that the strong movement was the female joining with the male. No longer could I feel the inner, lunar energy circuit of my female side as separate from my body's solar or male energies. They were solidly merged into a singular experience. My pelvis moved forward and back, thrusting toward the phallus on the altar in front of me. Faster and faster my body convulsed in an orgasm. My breathing reached a climax. White Eagle had said that Mallku and I would come together like two live wires touching. Yes, but it wasn't as I expected; none of this felt sexual. It was an energy orgasm that had nothing to do with sexual pleasure. I have to admit that I was disappointed. Instead of the Earth moving in an unforgettably orgasmic way, I simply felt strange.

That was it. This was the fusion of the Male and Female. My energy and Mallku's merged together into One. There were more sighs, more shaking, faster, involuntary movements as energy waves possessed me in an electric union. "In the name of the Cosmic Mother, the Divine Male and Female and service to the planet, I ask for polarity of all kinds to be healed." A soft whimper escaped my lips as the energies slowly died down.

The powerful waves stopped, leaving me to feel a new silence that was similar to the Void I had traversed earlier when my consciousness moved toward Mallku's spirit. It felt peaceful and complete. It was the empty but powerful space after matter and antimatter collide. Masculine and feminine had annihilated each other to become One. Whatever I had come to do was done. It was only 5:30 a.m. and I was cold, really cold.

With a half mile of stony island separating us, on a cold and shrouded morning, Mallku and I made love. We didn't do it for ourselves. We traded the warmth of a lover's embrace, the ecstasy of co-mingled passion, for two solitary acts of spiritual transcendence in a pair of collapsing, pre-Incan temples. We did it for the world, simply because it was ours to do.

The sun's rising rays barely peered in through the rock opening. On the dawn of the spring and autumn equinox the angled light precisely strikes the altar. Looking out through the temple's doorway blocked with rocks, I saw another island in the distance, low clouds and far off rain. On a clear day, you could see the snowy mountains of Bolivia encircling the horizon. I stepped back out through the barricaded door, carefully replacing the stones I had removed to enter. Once again, I walked under the four stone archways, giving thanks. What just happened and what its significance was for me and for the world, I couldn't know. Our part was to show up to do what was there for us to do. Mastery at its essence isn't what we know; it is ordinary people bravely doing the things that Masters do. Reflecting on this I remembered a question: "Are we practicing to be Masters? Or, are we Masters who are practicing?"

In the distance, I spotted Mallku walking down the mountain from the Temple of the Father. Running to catch up, I called out to him, "Brother." He stopped. I beamed and raised my hands palm out, signaling success, "We did it!" His grin brightened the gray dawn. We hugged and headed down to a modest breakfast of bread and butter with our island family.

Our Part of the Prophecy

The prophecy of the Eagle and the Condor has been handed down for millennia around campfires throughout the Americas. Holy ceremonies uniting the people and principles of North and South America have been performed in Mexico, Central America, the Amazon and the Andes. Each time the dances have been danced and the prayers have been sung, our collective human hearts have lifted closer to the dream of peace for us and for Mother Earth. On that December day, I claimed the power of the feminine force of the planet. With that searing divine flow racing through me, I became the Eagle. Mallku stood as proxy for the universal masculine force, holding it in his name—the Condor or Mallku. Just two of us, without fanfare, equal masters in different worlds performed a ritual in a way we couldn't have planned and will probably never understand. We did our part to fuse together North and South, female and male, the Eagle and the Condor.

What happened in half an hour on Amantani Island has given me countless gifts. It was a Master Initiation, strengthening and fully balancing the masculine and feminine aspects within me. Rather than being held in rigid opposition, the energies dance, flow and intermingle within each other. The result is the fusion of opposites that has lifted my spirit above polarity. I now experience an inner core of light that gives me a nearly continual sense of 'uncaused well-being.'

White Eagle later helped me understand what happened that morning:

The healing was focused on the polarity in all souls, not just the polarity of male and female. The act wrenched human consciousness up a notch closer to the Divine world, especially in the areas of separation and polarity.

From her Kumara-self, her highest, divine, serving self, Jonette was activated to do the ceremony on behalf of the world. Her ability to hold magnetic energy and lift others to higher states, her ability to maintain balance were all expanded and strengthened from the energy initiation she participated in. Jonette didn't just receive an initiation, she orchestrated what happened.

I believe that in the higher dimensions, all humanity is interconnected. Any breakthrough that one of us experiences is communicated through a morphogenetic field to everyone else. The vibrational template of healed polarity that I now hold in my body acts like a tuning fork to bring other people's energies into merged harmony through the principle of resonance.

Reflecting on what we had done, I understood that Mallku and I have probably spent lifetimes following fate and preparing for this part of our soul's journey. Within hours of our meeting in the Amazon, this man, my twin soul, laid down beside me causing new and stronger sexual energy flows to awaken in my body. I, in turn, shared my powers by initiating him with the sign of the Leader. In the Cave of the Serpent, Mallku choreographed a sacred space so potent that my divine-self, Kumara, made her debut. She set the groundwork for the ceremony we just completed by leading our group to spiral together the essence of Divine Feminine and Divine Masculine. Later that same day, Mallku again marshaled his shamanic powers, this time creating the space for my quest to a mystical pyramid where I received in Kumara's name, the coded energies and wisdom of the Sun Disc. Days later, Mallku followed his spiritual instincts to bring our group to the great Interdimensional Doorway of Aramu Muru carved in the rock near Lake Titicaca, a place that I had visited before with Sue Burch in meditation. At every turn in the road, Mallku and I have intuitively known how to work together.

Mallku tested my courage and trust in him when he helped me climb over the rock face at the sacred cave known as

Wiracocha's Brain. Both of us demonstrated faith in our destiny to be willing to leave our families, our businesses, and our busy lives to be together on a tiny island in a sacred lake in the high plateaus of Peru. Our lives will be changed because we acted in trust and "let Love make us."

43

Wiracocha's Temple

nly two hours after our mountaintop ceremony on Amantani, Mallku and I were at the dock to board the Rio Azul for the short trip to the island of Taquile. It was more populous and more developed than Amantani. In other words, it boasts of a handicraft shop and a restaurant. There I lunched on freshly caught fish while watching the locals on the main square. These extremely traditional natives still follow a quaint custom; husbands spin, weave and hand-sew all the clothing worn by their wives and vice versa. As you can imagine, it was a sign of immense pride to be well dressed. Andres, our Aymara guide, winked when he told us, "The women here don't wear underwear." I didn't think to ask him how he knew that bit of trivia.

By afternoon, our boat tour of Lake Titicaca was finished. Returning to Puno, we found a hotel room so I could have a hot shower and a nap while Mallku set off to find an Internet café. Our plan was to rendezvous for a pizza dinner then drive all night and be at Wiracocha's Temple by dawn. It is an impressive, sacred archeological complex near Raqchi Town on the road to Cuzco. Mallku wanted to be there to photograph the first rays of the sun as they illuminated the forty-foot high walls and doorways of the main temple structure. I expected our stop at Wiracocha's Temple to be an afterthought in our journey to Titicaca. I was surprised when another piece of the mystery of my connection to the Incas came to light.

Of all the Andean myths, the legends surrounding the supreme god Wiracocha are the most fascinating. He was the invisible god of the world, the Creator and Light-giver, sometimes referred to as "the Lord of the Seven Rays." His symbol was Inti, the Father Sun. He was often represented as a Solar Being holding two staffs. Wiracocha was the essence of existence itself, worshipped by all civilizations that have existed in the Andes. The Incas merely incorporated earlier beliefs about Wiracocha into their own cosmology.

The White-skinned God

However, in other myths, Wiracocha was more than an invisible creator-god; he was a god-man who appeared from Lake Titicaca after the great deluge. The name means 'from the foam of the sea.' He has been described as a tall, bearded, white-man, wearing sandals and long, flowing robes, teaching and healing as he traveled. He couldn't have been an indigenous man, since they have dark complexions and sparse beards. The legends of the Pale Prophet are found throughout the Andes, although he is sometimes known by other names. Native people told the early Spanish chroniclers, "This man had such great power that he changed the hills into valleys, and from the valleys made great hills, causing streams to flow from the living stone... "[63]

The legends often say that Wiracocha journeyed north and west from Lake Titicaca to the coast of present day Ecuador, where he and his company disappeared across the Pacific Ocean. He left with a promise to return one day. The expectation of the return of the bearded white-man and his demi-gods may have led the Inca ruler Atahualpa to initially welcome and trust the Spanish conquistadors. In the same vein, one of the reasons that Cortez found it so easy to conquer Montezuma and the Aztec empire, was the natives thought Cortez, with his white skin and beard, was their holy one returning.

Similar stories of a great, white-skinned and bearded teacher appear throughout South America, Mexico, Hawaii,

New Zealand and other south Pacific islands. Hawaiian and Maori lore tell of a white-skinned teacher that they call Wakea, who traveled to South America from the South Pacific where he became Wiracocha. Even some North American Cherokee legends talk of the Pale One, a great teacher and wise one.[64]

Wiracocha, as the feathered serpent god, was called Kukulkan by the Mayas and Quetzalcoatl by the Aztecs. White Eagle had told me that it was Quetzalcoatl, or the Plumed Serpent, whom I encountered guarding the Sun Disc at the mystical pyramid. Was it Wiracocha himself, as the feathered serpent god, who granted me entry to the Sun Disc? I had seen him then as a powerful being, wearing a feathered cape.

The Incas and Lemuria

Was it simply coincidence that the solar being Wiracocha appeared from Lake Titicaca, the same place to which the Lemurian high priest Aramu Muru fled with the Sun Disc? Was Wiracocha from Lemuria? Both Wiracocha and Manco Capac, the legendary founder of the Incas, the "Children of the Sun," were white-skinned and bearded. Many believe Aramu Muru was also known as Manco Capac. Are these legends about the same person? Or different Enlightened Ones, all from Lemuria?

James D. Ward shed some light on these questions in the book, *Lemuria: The Lost Continent of the Pacific*, published in 1931 by the Rosicrucians, one of the most ancient spiritual orders in the world.[65] Their Brotherhood in North America was the steward of some very rare manuscripts dealing with age-old traditions preserved in secret archives of Tibet and China. Among them was an old and worn copy of the secret spiritual and ethical teaching of the Tibetans. It was from these timeless records and the personal recollections of Dr. Ward that the *Lemuria* book was compiled. Dr. Ward was an Eminent Disciple of Oriental Monastery Schools in India and Tibet. He wrote that the teachings he studied there were handed down from the Sages of Antiquity and recorded in ways that were perfectly understandable:

*Lemurians were the most perfectly formed human beings that
ever lived... and a soul as pure as the universal soul from
whence it came... The pictures of those men and women
showed them to be the color of the sun and equally as bright and
shining.*

*I personally viewed with interest some historical records of the
Lemurians and especially interested was I in the fearless and
undaunted adventures of twelve Lemurian Disciples who
started out with an airship... Their dreams were of exploring
other countries or continents.*[66]

In his esoteric studies in the Far East, Ward claimed to have
once viewed the actual map that the Twelve Lemurians made
of their travels.

The idea, documented in ancient Tibetan texts, of
Lemurians traveling around the world in airships was a capti-
vating one. It was consistent with the native Quechuan lore
that man arrived in the Andes in 'metal birds.' Perhaps it was
one of these aircraft that originally carried Aramu Muru and
the Sun Disc to Lake Titicaca? It was looking more defensible to
me that there was a spiritually and technologically advanced
civilization in a now-submerged Pacific continent. Perhaps
we'll never know the truth about the plethora of Wiracocha
myths in the Andes and a similar figure throughout the Pacific
and the Americas. Nevertheless, after a night of driving from
Puno, Mallku and I arrived at the massive sanctuary complex
dedicated to the great god Wiracocha. Not even the roosters
were awake as we parked the car in the sultry darkness a
couple of hours before sunrise. We napped waiting for
morning.

Priestess of the Sun

The entire archeological site of Wiracocha's Temple covered
over two and a half square miles. It included farming terraces,
rectangular houses, circular grain storage structures, palaces,

waterways and sacred fountains. Towering remnants of a magnificent temple, over three-hundred feet long and eighty feet wide, dominated the site. The central wall, originally an imposing fifty-five feet tall, was built on a base of beautifully carved stones, topped by adobe bricks. During Incan times, a thatched roof covered the entire structure. Like other holy places in the Andes, it was most likely a pre-Incan site of undetermined origin that the Incas expanded and used.

Wiracocha's Temple, initiation doorways at dawn

It served as the primary initiation place for the priests and priestesses of the Sun. At dawn of the solstices, the first rays of morning pour through specific markers, illuminating the sacred symbols etched into the massive temple walls. Ancient initiates would stand, one in each of the ten doorways, to receive the Light. We were a day early; the summer solstice would be the next day. And we were hundreds of years too late. Or were we late?

As Mallku strolled the paths and gardens clicking away

with his camera to catch the sun at just the right angle, I sat bundled as a mummy against the cold on the stump of a massive column. Was it mere boredom from waiting for the dawn, or was it the stirring of a deep memory that compelled me to stand in one of the ten doorways just as the sun peeked over the horizon?

Whatever the impetus, the result was a glorious re-initiation into my personal service to the Divine. My arms were outstretched, palms toward the rising sun, my face tilted up to absorb the warm blessings of the first rays. Once again, as in lifetimes past, I became a Priestess of the Sun. I closed my eyes in a prayer of gratitude. The minutes passed by too quickly until a curious, local worker broke the spell and all at once the roosters of the village dutifully began to crow.

Cross of Seven Steps

Mallku joined me as I stepped away from the initiatory threshold. He pointed out the outline of the mystical Incan Chacana or square cross carved into the stone at the sides of the doorway. This cross, with its seven tiers or steps on each quadrant, was a powerful and secret tool that was unveiled only to the highest Initiates of the Sun.

"Ahh..." I thought. "Here is proof that I really *do* have access to hidden Inca knowledge." I remembered back to August when our group was at the Interdimensional Doorway of Aramu Muru. During that meditation, I was shown the vision of a square cross of seven steps that acted as the key to open the main gate or portal between dimensions. I somehow knew it then as the Cross of the Seven Rays. The seven tiers also related to the seven illumined steps I ascended to the Sun Disc in my shamanic journey inside the mystical pyramid.

After that ceremony at the Interdimensional Gateway, I doubted the seven-tiered design of the cross I had witnessed in my vision. My uncertainty was due to the fact that throughout Peru I had seen jewelry, weavings and stone carvings of a three-tiered Incan square Cross, never one with seven steps. I had asked Mallku about it that past August, "Mallku, to enable me to open the main doorway into the other dimensions I was presented with the symbol of a seven-stepped cross, but I have only seen an Andean square cross with three tiers. Does a seven-tiered cross exist in Andean spirituality? Did I get it wrong?"

"It exists," was all he said. Mallku was not one to encourage my mystical but accidental forays into the secrets of his beloved culture.

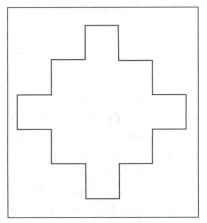 

3-step Andean Square Cross   *Esoteric Andean Cross*
Illustrations by Corey Fowler

At Wiracocha's Temple, I came to understand that, although the three-tiered cross is widely used in the Andes, the Cross of the Seven Rays is a hidden, esoteric key, probably from Lemurian times, given only to Initiates of the Sun. It represents the great regulator of cosmic energy. This understanding and the energies encoded in the Sun Disc were given to me so that I would bring them forth and share them. In this way, we can all be participants in ushering in the Tenth Pachakuti, or the five-hundred year period of Light and peace foretold in Andean lore. I felt that when Mallku and I united the Eagle and the Condor, we also released previously secret, sacred energy out into the world. The time *is* right. Humanity *is* ready. Tomorrow would be the solstice, and I was going to Machu Picchu.

44

Summer Solstice at Q'enqo

ecember 21st, the summer solstice in the southern hemisphere, the reason I went to Peru. In nearly all ancient cultures, the solstices are the most powerful days of the year. I was ready for magic to unfold as Mallku and I drove into the fog-draped hills above Cuzco at 5:30 in the morning. Our destination was Q'enqo, a mysterious, pre-Incan initiation site a half mile beyond the monumental ruins of Sacsayhuaman. Mallku wanted me to experience Q'enqo at dawn, before I departed for Machu Picchu on my own. The hazy world was soft and wooly. Clouds nestled heavily in the eucalyptus forests. It was as if Mallku and I were the first witnesses to the swirling mists in Genesis from which God created the Universe. For a moment the fragrance took me back to my experience in Australia's Blue Gum Forest where I met the Spirit Woman—White Buffalo Calf Woman. Who could have guessed that the path I was to walk would bring me so far?

We drove around a sharp curve startling a white horse standing on the road in the fog. She emerged into form out of the pearly air itself. "A unicorn," I thought, and smiled, "Welcome to heaven!" It reminded me of the vision I had as I talked to Brad before leaving for this adventure, where I saw myself looking into a misty, floating world of white that I referred to then as heaven. I enjoyed my inner reflections as we rounded the final turn to Q'enqo. My calm thoughts stopped cold by what I saw hanging from a tree at the side of the road. A fully costumed, native woman was dangling in the branches! Another look revealed a life-sized effigy of a woman, complete with hat and colorful shawl.

I didn't need to speak. My shocked gasp was enough for Mallku to explain that in preparation for the New Year, superstitious South Americans hang a representation of all that is old so they can let go of the past year's burdens. "Or it might be a tourist without a ticket!" he added, chuckling.

In the soggy, pre-dawn chill we climbed down to the limestone outcropping that birthed a bizarre collection of niches, altars, steps and underground chambers. There was an open place, a semicircular amphitheater that focused attention on a flat rock wall. Etched deeply into the smooth limestone was a rectangular doorway, a smaller portal nesting within it. This was reminiscent of the ancient doorway of Aramu Muru in the great rock at Lake Titicaca. A ledge, stone thrones, and benches were carved into the rock surrounding this important initiation gateway.

The Youngest Initiate

I absorbed the sight of the place, but more, I absorbed the memories here. "I've been here before," my mind stated unequivocally.

Within seconds, Mallku came up beside me. "Have you been here before?" he asked.

He used the exact phrase I had just thought! Why should that surprise me so? I laughed and told him he was psychic. Inside I said to myself, "Twin soul."

As far as I could tell, Mallku never bought into the twin soul belief of mine. Though once as I was telling him of my impatience with the slow manifestation of spirituality on Earth, he fixed his gaze on me and admitted, "There must be something to our connection because you're saying *exactly* the same things that I feel." I smiled.

I *had* been there in Q'enqo before. Inner visions and past life details kaleidoscoped into view: "I was young then, just seven or eight, the youngest of the initiates." I remembered this was the Incan life in which I became a priestess at Machu Picchu. I was the daughter of a laborer, not of royal blood. As a young child, my spiritual gifts were recognized and I was taken to be raised in the Temple of the Sun.[67]

Inside the cave, to the left of the initiation wall, was an altar cut from the limestone. That too was familiar. Other tables and niches were formed into the underground chamber itself. Mallku explained that an initiate would lie here to ascend into the higher worlds. He showed me the place where the Master stood to guard and direct the ceremonies.

Since it was the solstice, if it had been a clear morning the sun would have shone through an opening in the rock to create the shadow of a snake on the wall. The illusion of the serpent would have then moved down the wall to the floor where it would take another shape before hiking up the three steps to the main altar table. As an initiate sat at the corner of the vertical wall, the sun would project a 'V' on her forehead. Through all of Mallku's explanations, I never felt the need to ask how he knew the details from this culture, much more ancient than the Incas. I trusted that his wisdom came to him whole and complete—the way it comes to me.

Although we were there early in the morning of the longest day of the year, the heavy mists scattered the risen sun's direct rays. No shadows formed. No serpents climbed the walls. Mallku, ever ready to photograph archeo-astronomical occurrences for his books, was disappointed.

The three steps to the initiation altar reflected the three-tiered design of the cave complex. Below the main floor of the chamber was the deepest level representing the underworld. Steps ascended from that dark world into the inner cave level, or consciousness. The top of the limestone mass symbolized higher consciousness. These are the same three levels of commonly known reality that are portrayed by the Incan square cross.

This trilogy in Andean cosmology was also represented by the three power animals. The Serpent, or Amaru symbolized the subconscious or inner, unknown world. The snake is also identified with the first evolutionary stages in man. The temporal or middle world was portrayed by the Puma, or Titi. Mallku feels that as man regains Puma consciousness he can expand his own awareness to serve as a door to other realities.[68] The Condor, or Mallku was the animal representing the dimension of the gods or the sacred world.

We climbed out above the cave to study the animal forms carved into the surface of the limestone: a dolphin, a llama and a squirrel. Q'enqo which means zigzag, was named for a serpent form dug into the rock. Archeologists say that sacrificial blood was poured into the bowl shape that is the snake's head, flowing down the trench of the serpent's body, foretelling the future. Mallku thinks that rather than blood, they used chicha—the fermented drink common in the Andes. He pointed out the phenomenon in which the light and shadows of the sun on the winter solstice in Peru (June 21st) create the clear image of a puma face. Evidence for his theory is detailed in his book, *Inka Initiation Path: the Awakening of the Puma.*[69]

The sun was newly risen as we prepared to leave. I stood on the hill's crest, facing east through the mists and commanded "May I be everything I have been. May I be everything I am destined to be."

A car with a guide and a handful of tourists drove up. "They're late," Mallku muttered scornfully as we drove away. He indicated that the importance of the solstice is the sun's rays *at dawn*.

We made another stop. This time we overlooked red-tile-roofed-Cuzco spreading herself out like full skirts, in the valley below. La Mesa, a sizable, circular rock table, is one of the many power places around the Incan capital. The morning light was finally golden as it lit the city below. Mallku looked magnificent on that hill surveying Cuzco and the sacred places that he loves. He tied a gold scarf around his neck in honor of the special day. His burnished face reflected the sun's rays like copper. I thought how wonderful it was that he was observing, studying and writing about all this so the ancient culture and beliefs could be appreciated.

"Now do you like Cuzco?" Mallku asked, evidently remembering an unfavorable comment I had made earlier.

"Yes, now I do!" I savored the glorious setting.

Mallku dropped me off at the station to catch the train to Machu Picchu, handing me tickets and hotel vouchers. Our time together had ended.

45

Machu Picchu Once Again

It's the morning of December 21, 2004, and I am in the front car of the tourist train traveling through the Sacred Valley to Machu Picchu. Yellow flowering bushes frame the tracks, opening in intervals to reveal fields folded like gingham over pleated hills. This time it is different. I am not leading a group and today is the summer solstice, the second most important day of the Incan calendar.

My mission in the Andes feels complete with the ceremony on Amantani Island. Following invisible threads, Mallku and I are weaving a multidimensional tapestry that began beyond time and will never be finished. My human emotions are sated as I stare out the train window. In place of the fiery soul love I first experienced with Mallku, I now hold him in my heart as a cherished friend and twin brother. Paradoxical feelings have resolved themselves, not so much by finally being understood, but because I have expanded my consciousness to a place that can contain all parts of the paradox, all aspects of my confusion.

I'm just one of the day-packed tourists who spews out of the train at Aguas Calientes. With plenty of daylight remaining, I bus up the zigzagged, dirt road to the entrance of Machu Picchu. I want to meditate at my favorite place, Pachamama's cave. However, it is full of tourists. Here, where the energies are smooth and strong, there is a throne, hewn from the granite, and stairs cut so they organically emerge from the stone

Pachamama's Cave at Machu Picchu

itself. This temple to Mother Earth is tucked away in a sheltering cave just below the circular Temple of the Sun. Because today is the solstice, the first rays of the dawn would have shone through the Sun Temple's second trapezoidal window to precisely illuminate the inner altar.

A few doors down is a much less frequented spot. A simple alleyway between two buildings, overgrown with weeds, looks familiar to me. Following a tiny spark of remembering in my mind, I find a now roofless, stone house, where it feels I lived in a long ago incarnation. Sitting on the rock step that forms the doorway, I eat my energy bar and muse about the ties between worlds.

Finally, I am drawn to the magnificent open area on the Main Plaza to relax, facing the long rays of sunshine at day's end, the longest day of the year. I have to be careful to find a grassy place that is free of llama droppings. I choose a spot near the edge of the plaza, close to a wild area of thick vegetation, with mammoth, random boulders and dark caves and crevasses—not at all inviting. Yet, this too, I remember. In that other life I am a young girl running free amid the rocks and trees, as my father, a stonemason, works to build this magnificent city in the clouds. This is the same child who at the age of seven or eight was initiated at Q'enqo, the magical place outside Cuzco I visited at dawn this morning. A vague memory... of following spirits that only a child can see... into the tunnels here, through portals... blue beings unhooking a mask from my face... two questions asked and answered... twenty-seventh dimensional beings... the mask, a human face, masking my divinity.

None of this vision makes any sense, but it is here to be accepted; perhaps to be held in my mind for another twenty years until that moment in my future when this bit of knowledge too falls into place.

In this time and space, I ask to receive a Solar Initiation. The sun instantly shoves its way from behind the clouds, shining brilliantly through green-carpeted, vertical mountains. If I am serious about receiving an initiation from the Sun, I better remove my University of Colorado Buffalos baseball cap so that my crown chakra is exposed to the light. For good measure, I slap some sunscreen on my nose and arms. I laugh to think that the modern spiritual initiate buys products to screen the sun, even while asking for a Solar Initiation! Once I stop getting ready and finally close my eyes I feel like I *am* a crystal tetrahedron with the sun in the center. It doesn't seem that I am *inside* this ancient, pyramidal symbol, but rather I *am* the thing and all its power. Mallku said that "Machu Picchu was designed in the spiritual dimension with the purpose of elevating its inhabitants to the most subtle planes of perception."[70] My experience here is proof of that.

I am on the last bus out of Machu Picchu. The tourist village of Aguas Calientes is like a smudge at the bottom of the mountains where a creek, with its hot water springs, meets the Urubamba River. My room has the best view in town, its third floor balcony overlooks the roiling, frothy, cappuccino-brown river. The water's deafening roar outside my window rivals the sound of Niagara or Iguazu Falls. Tomorrow will be my last in the Andes. I sleep well.

Huayna Picchu, Mountain of the Hummingbird

Huayna Picchu, meaning the younger mountain, is the mountain that reigns high above Machu Picchu. With its classic vertical slopes featured in nearly every photo of Machu Picchu, it is known for its beauty and geo-magnetic power. Mallku says that Machu Picchu, the older mountain represents celestial altitudes and is associated with the Andean condor, the largest bird of prey in the world. The bird that represents the smaller, but strikingly beautiful Huayna Picchu mountain is the hummingbird. Because of the hummingbird's kiss in my dream and because this is my last day in the Andes, today I will climb that glorious and challenging peak.

Yesterday, I overheard two young men bragging that they had climbed Huayna Picchu and the neighboring mountain, known as the Temple of the Moon, in just under two hours. I figure it will take me three. I sign the register book at the guard entrance to the trail up the mountain. From the bottom, it does not even look possible to climb its sharp, eroded flanks without ropes.

At first the path is merely steep and rocky, then it ascends into the sky, becoming a narrow trail that barely clings onto the slope's sheer rock. Dizzily straight up I climb, using my hands for balance. Toward the top, the vertiginous steps are so steep and skinny I have to climb them like a ladder. With white

Huayna Picchu peak at Machu Picchu   *Photo by Mark Brindel*

knuckles, I grasp onto the rope placed at only the most dangerous spots. I hold my breath, focusing on the next step, because
to look down is truly terrifying. This is not a place for the
faint-hearted. I will myself up to the top. Like many things that
are difficult in life, it is worth every step.

A dozen other tourists and I are rewarded by the spectacular view of Machu Picchu from the summit. Even here, on scraps of earth the Incas have constructed micro-sized terraces for crops, stone enclosures, small tunnels and observation platforms. Removing my daypack, I sit on a rock and take some photos, allowing myself the pleasure of accomplishment and a few minutes of reflection.

For the second time in four months, I look out over Machu Picchu. My first glimpse, in August, was from the Sun Gate on the other side of the city; while this vantage point looks out from the summit of the hummingbird's mountain. Peru and the Andes have given me so much. Yet, I could have stubbornly followed my original plan, which was to take a group to climb Mount Kilimanjaro in Africa. It hasn't always been easy but I've endeavored to be true to White Buffalo Calf Woman's advice to me two decades ago, *Your path is made by walking.* Yet I often ask myself, "Where is it I'm going?" I don't know the final destination, only the direction to walk for now. My soul's ulti-mate purpose called forth these mystical experiences. In fact,

Jonette on the summit of Huayna Picchu

the small me usually doesn't know the highest purpose until after an event manifests. Even then, I am often in the dark. None of what has happened has been created from my personal will. I do know that miracles and magic will continue to burst unexpectedly along my way.

Chief Woableza told us last summer, when he referred to the great prophecy written in the petroglyphs of the Navajo lands, "We must listen to the wisdom of the Grandmothers. The women have the answers." I am a spiritual Grandmother, one of a growing cadre of Wise Ones. We have given birth to ourselves. We are strong and we are ready. From the top of the mountain, I gaze out over a panorama of the past and I can glimpse the future.

If ascending was difficult, descending is horrible! Now I can see where I could plunge if I miss a step or lose my precarious balance. Choosing butt-slides when I can, I reason that I am safer with more surface area on the ground. It is a mortifying experience. I am shaky and greatly relieved when I finally make it to the junction near the bottom of the trail that leads to the Temple of the Moon. Looking at my watch, I realize that there is still time to take the other hike. At least this one isn't straight up a mountain. For another half an hour I hike along the path to the Moon Temple, and then I stop to take a photo.

But, where is my camera? In fact, where is my backpack?... my wallet?... my passport? "Oh, my God, No... it can't be!" I gasp. "How could I be so stupid?!" I left everything in my backpack on the *very top* of Huayna Picchu! Not only do I have to ascend that impossible mountain *again*, but this time, I have to climb it fast—in order to catch the bus, to catch the train, to catch my flight back home to Colorado.

The Eagle and the Condor

Epilogue

Four days later, Christmas 2004, the world of Inca legends, Sun Discs and a shaman who is my twin soul are far behind. My entire family gathers at my sister Mo's home in the foothills south of Denver for the Crowleys' traditional Christmas dinner. Her husband Andrew is roasting a goose; the aromas mingle with the scent of their freshly cut Christmas tree. Jimmy Buffet's holiday CD plays in the background; small boys in reindeer pajamas are way too excited to go to bed. We're all here: my beloved Ed, brothers and brothers-in-law, sisters and sisters-in-law, niece and nephews.

Sitting around the table, tastefully decorated with holly and candles, our family chatters and our conversation bounces expectedly between topics of presents and food, kids and New Year's plans. My wisecracking brother John suddenly remembers that I've just returned from a solo trip to the Andes.

"Hey Jonette, how was Peru?" John asks loudly. Once he has the family's attention, he continues, "I was trying to take bets, figuring that the odds were fifty percent that you'd stay in South America." My family chuckles. John goes on, encouraged, "and twenty-five percent that Ed would not even care! But I couldn't find any takers."

"That might have been true a couple of times in the past, but not anymore," comes Ed's quick reply. Then my husband turns to me, his blue eyes sparkling with love and says, "I'm *really* glad you're back!"

I give him a kiss that tells him, "This is where I belong." I didn't even need the mistletoe.

The Inca Trail path   *Photo by Mark Brindel*

Coming Home C.O.D.[71]

I'm coming home C.O.D.,
The world's roads at my back.
My pockets empty, save stones and shells
I've found along the track.
I've tramped through alpine wilderness,
Australia's Great Outback.
My legs are sore, my jeans are torn
As I slowly lift my pack.

My ticket says I'm heading home,
But my spirit wants to stay.
I just can't take a life that says
I'll be in the same place every day.
Sure you think you're happy,
But look at what you pay.
You've never seen the sun come up
Over a blue New Zealand bay.

To me a rut's a place
With four walls and a door.
Coming in is easy,
But leaving is a chore.
You get your big T.V.
And think there's nothing more.
I am rich with stones and shells,
Your money keeps you poor.

You see I've learned that standing still
Will make the soul grow old.
So when you feel the things you've got
Becoming a heavy load,
Remember you've got nothing,
If it's peace of mind you've sold.
And so you'll find me waiting there
Along some distant road.

Jonette Crowley
March 1981
En route home from the South Pacific

Endnotes

1   Morey Bernstein, *The Search for Bridey Murphy*, 1956

2   *The Quiet Mind, Sayings of White Eagle*

3   Grace Cooke, a medium or channel for White Eagle, whose words are published by the White Eagle Publishing Trust.

4   Sanaya Roman and Duane Packer, authors and teachers of "Awakening Your Light Body," www.OrinDaBen.com

5   Jane Roberts, *Seth Speaks, The Seth Material*

6   A chakra is an energy vortex within the subtle body. Traditionally we refer to seven main chakras along a central meridian within the human body.

7   Alice Bailey, *Initiations: Human and Solar*, back cover

8   Ed Oakley, *Enlightened Leadership: Getting to the Heart of Change*, www.EnLeadership.com

9   Pema Dorji Sherpa, www.Sherpatrek.com

10   Mark explains that the first 3 dimensions are normal physical reality, the 4th dimension is light, and vibration—anything with frequency. The 5th dimension is comprised of symbols, codes, geometrics. The 6th dimension is magnetic in nature, and is beyond space/time. It feels like infinite love. The 7th dimension is holographic and is often called "God-consciousness." There are countless higher dimensions with qualities that are difficult for us to fathom or experience.

11   Krishna Lohani, Nepal, Spiritual Tour Guide, www.trekntour.com

12   An internet search of Big Foot sightings did indicate activity in that same general area of the Colorado wilderness

13   James Arévalo Merejido (Mallku), www.andes007.com

14   Henry Leo Bolduc, www.HenryBolduc.com

15   Brother Philip, *Secret of the Andes*, 1961

16   Brother Philip, *Secret of the Andes*, p.8,9

17   Brother Philip, *Secret of the Andes*, p.13

18 Sister Thedra, founder of the Association of Sananda and Sanat Kumara, Mt. Shasta, California

19 Council of Spiritual Elders of Mother Earth, www.spiritualelders.org

20 Shirley MacLaine, *The Camino*

21 Masaru Emoto, *Messages from Water*

22 The idea of past lives may be more energetic than linear. Jonette may not be the only reincarnation of White Buffalo Calf Woman, but she does share the same vibrational energy field.

23 Molly & Daisy Craig, as young aboriginal girls were portrayed in the amazing story of fortitude in the movie, *The Rabbit-Proof Fence*.

24 Mallku, *Machu Picchu Forever*, p.50

25 Mark Amaru Pinkham, *The Return of the Serpents of Wisdom*, p.60

26 David Hatcher Childress, *Lost Cities & Ancient Mysteries of South America*, p.103

27 James Pinkel, www.ThePathLighter.com

28 Ancient pyramids with flat tops have been found in Peru, Mexico, Central America, Tahiti, China, Egypt and even Illinois. David Hatcher Childress, *Lost Cities of Ancient Lemuria & the Pacific*, p.197

29 Jorge Luis Delgado Mamani, http://mmmgroup.altervista.org/e-door.html

30 Paul Damon, article "Doorway of Amaru Muru," www.Labyrinthina.com

31 Paul Damon, article "Doorway of Amaru Muru," www.Labyrinthina.com

32 John Perkins, *Confessions of an Economic Hit Man*, p.216

33 Willaru Huarto, article, "The Incan Prophecy," www.labyrinthina.com

34 Q'ero prophecy, www.lost-civilizations.net/inca-prophecies.html

35 Q'ero prophecy, www.lost-civilizations.net/inca-prophecies.html

36 Sri Bhagavan, www.OnenessUniversity.org

37 Antón Ponce de León Paiva, *The Wisdom of the Ancient ONE*, www.SamanaWasi.com

38 Antón Ponce de León Paiva, *The Wisdom of the Wise ONE*, p.111,112

39 Paiva, *The Wisdom of the Wise ONE* p. 65

40 Pinkham, *The Return of the Serpents of Wisdom*

41 Brother Philip, *Secret of the Andes*, p.12

42 Childress, *Lost Cities of Ancient Lemuria & the Pacific*

43 Paiva, *In Search of the Wise ONE*, p.110

44 Childress, *Lost Cities & Ancient Mysteries of South America*, p.62

45 Childress, *Lost Cities of Ancient Lemuria & the Pacific*, p.46

46 The Lemurian Fellowship, Ramona, California, personal letter to Jonette

47 Paiva, *In Search of the Wise ONE*, p.62

48 Some sources believe that Manco Capac was actually Aramu Muru, the Lemurian Master, and that he appeared at Lake Titicaca at the same time as the sinking of Lemuria. He would thus be the legendary founder of the great pre-Incan cultures, not the more recent Incan civilization.

49 Childress, *Lost Cities & Ancient Mysteries of South America*, p.108

50 Brother Philip, *Secret of the Andes*, p.12

51 Tom Kenyon, *The Magdalen Manuscript*, www.tomkenyon.com

52 Djed is the central pathway of the chakras up the spine.

53 Kenyon, *The Magdalen Manuscript*, p.33

54 Kenyon, *The Magdalen Manuscript*, p.33,34

55 Kenyon, *The Magdalen Manuscript*, p.51

56 Mallku, *Machu Picchu Forever*, p.46

57 Mallku, *Machu Picchu Forever*, p.40

58 Childress, *Lost Cities & Ancient Mysteries of South America*, p.72

59 Childress, *Lost Cities & Ancient Mysteries of South America*, p.72

60 Childress, *Lost Cities & Ancient Mysteries of South America*, p.74

61 Childress, *Lost Cities of Ancient Lemuria & the Pacific*, p.169,170

62 James Arévalo Merejildo (Mallku), *Inka Initiation Path*, p.106

63 Graham Hancock, *Fingerprints of the Gods*, p.46

64 Chief Dhyani Ywahoo, www.sunray.org

65 Wishar Cervé, *Lemuria The Lost Continent of the Pacific*

66 Cervé, *Lemuria The Lost Continent of the Pacific*, article by Dr. James D. Ward, p.144

67 In this life Jonette was born with the sign of a mystic—a "strawberry" red birthmark on her third eye, and at the base of her skull.

68 Mallku, *Machu Picchu Forever*, p.83

69 Mallku, *Inka Initiation Path*, p.84-93

70 Mallku, *Machu Picchu Forever*, p.84

71 C.O.D. means "Cash on Delivery." It is a shipping term for something that isn't paid for until it arrives at its destination.

Bibliography

Arévelo Merejildo, James (Mallku), *Inka Initiation Path, The Awakening of the Puma*, Shamanic Productions, Cusco, Peru 2004

Arévelo Merejildo, James (Mallku), *Machu Picchu Forever, City of Pilgrims Spiritual Path*, Cusco, Peru 2001

Bailey, Alice A., *Initiation, Human and Solar*, Lucis Publishing, New York, NY, 1922

Cervé, Wishar S., *Lemuria The Lost Continent of the Pacific*, Supreme Grand Lodge of Amorc, Rosicrucian Library, San Jose, CA 1931

Childress, David Hatcher, *Lost Cities of Ancient Lemuria & the Pacific*, Adventures Unlimited Press, Stelle, IL 1988

Childress, David Hatcher, *Lost Cities & Ancient Mysteries of South America*, Adventures Unlimited Press, Kempton, IL 1986

Cotterell, Maurice, *The Lost Tomb of Viracocha*, Bear & Company, Rochester, VT 2001

Emoto, Masaru, *Messages from Water*, Hado Publishing, Terrance, CA, 1999

Gilbert, Adrian G., *The Mayan Prophecies*, Element Books Limited, Boston, MA 1995

Hancock, Graham, *Fingerprints of the Gods*, Three Rivers Press, New York, NY 1995

Little, Gregory L., *Ancient South America: Recent Evidence Supporting Edgar Cayce's Story of Atlantis and Mu*, Eagle Wing Books, Memphis, TN 2002

Kenyon, Tom & Judy Sion, *The Magdalen Manuscript*, Orb Communications, Orcas, WA 2002

MacLaine, Shirley, *The Camino*, Atria, New York, NY 2001

Paiva, Antón Ponce de León, *The Wisdom of the Ancient ONE*, Bluestar Communications, Woodside, CA 1995

Paiva, Antón Ponce de León, *In Search of the Wise ONE*, Bluestar Communications, Woodside, CA 1996

Perkins, John, *Spirit of the Shuar*, Destiny Books, Rochester, VT 2001

Perkins, John, *Confessions of an Economic Hit Man*, Berrett-Koehler Publishers, Inc. San Francisco, CA 2004

Philip, Brother (Williamson, George Hunt), *Secrets of the Andes*, Transworld Publishers Ltd., London 1961

Pinkham, Mark Amaru, *The Return of the Serpents of Wisdom*, Adventures Unlimited Press, Kempton, IL 1997

Rachowiecki, Rob, *Peru*, Lonely Planet Publications, Oakland, CA 1996

Roberts, Jane, *The Nature of Personal Reality (A Seth Book)*, Amber-Allen Publishing, San Rafael, CA, 1994

Stelle, Dr. Robert D., *The Sun Rises*, Lemurian Fellowship, 1952

White Eagle, *The Quiet Mind, Sayings of White Eagle*, The White Eagle Publishing Trust, Hampshire, England, 1972

Index

Contact Information

Contact us for information about:

- The E & C Companion **Meditation and Spiritual Initiation Audio Set**. This 8-CD set includes the original, live recordings of the meditations and ceremonies in the book. It is designed to enhance and empower the energetic and spiritual growth experience of the book. It is available on CDs, tapes or as a digital download.

- Participating in our **free "Meet the Author"** webcasts and teleconferences.

- Go to www.theEagleandtheCondor.com to see more **photos** pertaining to the book and to **BLOG** with other readers.

- **Conferences, workshops**, and on-going courses throughout the world. Participate in-person, on the web, or by teleconference.

- **Spiritual adventure trips** to Peru and other sacred places.

- **Spiritual growth courses** available on CD, audio tape, and digital downloads.

- **Free meditations** available to listen to on our website.

- **Personal readings** by phone with Jonette and her guide, White Eagle.

- **Sponsoring** a workshop or event in your area.

- To **sign up for the e-newsletter**, articles and other announcements.

The Center for Creative Consciousness
5380 S. Monaco St.
Greenwood Village, CO 80111
Phone: (303) 689-9318
Fax: (303) 689-7666
Email: info@JonetteCrowley.com
Web: www.theeagleandthecondor.com and
www.JonetteCrowley.com

BOOK and AUDIO SET ORDER FORM
The Eagle and the Condor

Order directly to receive an autographed dedication, personalized to you. Jonette will energize your book or audio set with the intention to enhance your personal spiritual growth.

Name for the dedication_____
(please print the name as you want it to appear)

Soft cover book, $22.   Quantity:_____

Audio book set, $47. 8 CDs.   Read by the author.   Available as a digital download, $37.   Quantity: CDs _____ Download _____

Companion Meditation and Spiritual Initiation audio set, $97. 7 CDs. This audio set includes the live recordings of the meditations, spiritual processes, and initiations. As a digital download, $77
Quantity: CDs _____ Download _____

Shipping: 1-2 books or audio book: $6 (Canada $7)
Companion Meditation Set: $8 (Canada $9), All int'l $15
Sales tax: 4% in Colorado. No shipping for downloads. Contact us for quantity discount schedule. Prices subject to change.

Total amount due with order_____

Name:_____

Address: _____

City: _____State: _____Zip: _____

Country _____ Telephone: _____

Email address: _____
(Required for digital downloads and to receive e-newsletter)

Payment: Check_____ Visa_____ MasterCard_____
(Make check payable to "The Center for Creative Consciousness")

Name on card: _____
Card Number: _____
Exp. Date: _____   CSV Code:_____

____ Please email me the Center for Creative Consciousness e-newsletter.

Fax order:	(303) 689-7666. Fax this form.
Phone order:	(303) 689-9318. Have your credit card ready.
Email order:	www.theeagleandthecondor.com online store
Mail order:	StoneTree Publishing, 5380 S. Monaco St., Suite 110, Greenwood Village, CO 80111
Website:	www.JonetteCrowley.com

About The Author

Jonette Crowley is an internationally respected spiritual teacher and founder of the Center for Creative Consciousness, an organization dedicated to empowering humankind's spiritual awakening. Jonette is truly an explorer—both in the inner planes and in her travels around the world. In many ways she is a modern day mystic, with gifts of clairvoyance, healing, and the unique ability to create the energetic space so that others can experience their own spiritual truths. Since the

Jonette Crowley

late 1980s, she has received and shared the words and teachings of her spirit guides: White Eagle and Mark. With their guidance, Jonette teaches spiritual growth and meditation workshops and retreats in the U.S. and Europe. She conducts on-going weekly courses that are available live on the internet or by teleconference.

She has traveled extensively—to over 50 countries, and now joins together her passion for travel and spiritual growth by leading group adventure tours to sacred places around the world—Australia, Mexico, Nepal, Peru, and most recently to climb Mt. Kilimanjaro in Africa. (Learn about trips, workshops, on-going classes on the web and by teleconference, spiritual growth courses on CD and tape, free meditations, and phone readings with White Eagle at www.JonetteCrowley.com).

Jonette is also firmly rooted in the corporate world. She has an MBA and holds the academic honor of Phi Beta Kappa. She and her husband, Ed Oakley, own a nationally known leadership consulting firm, Enlightened Leadership Solutions (See www.enleadership.com.) She and Ed live in the suburbs of Denver, Colorado. They love skiing in the Rockies in the winter, and hiking and golf in the summer. She has a teen-aged step-daughter, Katherine.

The Eagle and the Condor